The Board of Directors of Prince George's County Crime Solvers, Inc., is pleased to make available this limited edition copy of Journey Through Time: A Pictorial History of the Prince George's County Police Department. As the second-oldest crime solvers program in the Washington metropolitan area, we are proud to be associated with the Prince George's County Police Department. We are certain that this handsome book will be a treasure your family will enjoy for many generations. We dedicate this book to the men and women of the Prince George's County Police Department—past, present, and future.

PRINCE GEORGE'S COUNTY CRIME SOLVERS, INC.

With the mid 1920s approaching, the county's population had almost reached the 60,000 mark. In 1927, legislation was enacted to create a small, full-time, professional county police force. The new force was to function under the supervision of the county sheriff and his chief deputy. Pictured in this photograph, taken sometime between 1927 and 1931, are the original members of the 1927 county police force. County Sheriff Charles Early is seated in the right front seat, Sergeant of Police Hervey Machen, Sr., is driving. Chief Deputy Sheriff Arthur Hepburn is seated in the left middle seat, while County Policeman

Journey Through Time

by
Lt. Dennis Campbell

A PICTORIAL HISTORY OF THE PRINCE GEORGE'S COUNTY POLICE DEPARTMENT

THE DONNING COMPANY PUBLISHERS

Claude Reese is in the right middle seat. County Policemen Frank Prince (left) and Vinton Nichols (right) are located in the rear. According to a note found with this photograph, the "automobile is a Lincoln Touring Car and was not a Police Car, but belonged to Mr. Machen."
PGPD photo

DEDICATION

This book is dedicated to all those employees who have faithfully served the Prince George's County Police Department

It is not the critic who counts, not the man who points out how the strong stumbles, or where the doer of deeds could have done them better. The credit belongs to the man who is actually in the arena; whose face is marred by sweat and blood; who strives valiantly; who errs and comes short again and again; who knows great enthusiasm, the great devotion; who spends himself in a worthy cause; who, at best, knows in the end the triumphs of high achievement; and who, at the worst, if he fails, at least fails while daring greatly.

Theodore Roosevelt

The Donning Company/Publishers
184 Business Park Drive, Suite 106
Virginia Beach, VA 23462

Richard A. Horwege, Editor   B. L. Walton, Jr., Project Director
Mary Eliza Midgett, Designer   Elizabeth B. Bobbitt, Pictorial Coordinator

Library of Congress Cataloging in Publication Data:

Campbell, Dennis, 1938-
    Journey through time : a pictorial history of the Prince George's County
Police Department / by Dennis Campbell.
        p. cm.
    Includes index.
    ISBN 0-89865-817-9
    1. Prince George's County (Md.) Police Dept.—History—Pictorial works.
2. Police—Maryland—Prince George's County—History—20th century—
Pictorial works. I. Prince George's County (Md.) . Police Dept. II. Title.
HV8145.M3C36 1991   91-16749
363.2'09752'51—dc20   CIP

Printed in the United States of America

For any errors of fact or interpretation, if any, the sponsor is not responsible.

CONTENTS

FOREWORD

T he research and printing of our departmental history encompasses a ten-year period of time and three police chiefs. I feel privileged that this narrative history was completed and printed during my tenure as police chief.

Every police employee, active and retired—both sworn and civilian—should look upon the publication of this history as a tribute to their dedication and hard work. The history should stimulate many nostalgic memories. It is also my hope that the history will contribute to a better public understanding of the police department.

It is significant that the history will be published as the department prepares to observe its sixtieth anniversary; six decades of dedicated and innovative service to the people of Prince George's County. May the record of our past history, as contained within the pages of this book, provide guidance and direction for the future.

The police department wishes to express its gratitude to the financial sponsors of this book: Prince George's County Crime Solvers, Inc., and to the many people who assisted in the book's research and publication stages.

David B. Mitchell
Chief of Police
Prince George's County, Maryland

I take pleasure in congratulating the police department on the publication of its departmental history. This is a story of an especially dedicated group of public safety professionals, men and women who have struggled to provide this county with an effective law enforcement service. It is also a story of uncommon commitment, of excellence, and personal sacrifice. Each and every police department employee should take pride in the publication of this history.

Parris N. Glendening
County Executive
Prince George's County, Maryland

The County Council wishes to acknowledge the police department's sixtieth anniversary and to congratulate all police employees on the publication of their departmental history. Police procedures have changed radically in the past sixty years, but the dedication we attribute to our police employees has remained constant. It took an especially dedicated person to do the job of a police officer many years ago, and it takes an especially committed professional to effectively function within our modern-day criminal justice system.

Pictured from left to right are: F. Kirwan Wineland, Sue V. Mills, Hilda R. Pemberton, Jo Ann T. Bell, James C. Fletcher, Jr., Richard J. Castaldi, Anne MacKinnon, Stephen J. Del Giudice, and Frank P. Casula.

PREFACE

Prince George's County was named for Prince George of Denmark. Born in 1653, the second son of King Frederick III of Denmark, he married Princess Anne of England in 1683. Upon Anne's accession to the throne in 1702, George was named Generalissimo of the Queen's Forces and Lord High Admiral. Prince George died in 1708 without ever visiting the English colonies.

Photo of Prince George is from a portrait by Sir Godfrey Kneller, now in the National Portrait Gallery in London.

There were many reasons for gathering the information contained in the pages of this book. Primarily the book tells a story about the origins and growth of the Prince George's County Police Department by establishing its identity with the past. Although published as a history, the book's most important goal is that of recognizing and paying tribute to the human spirit of all those employees who have served the police department over the past sixty-three years.

The concept of a county police department is relatively new to Prince George's County, originating in 1927. The early 1900s ushered in a period of rapid change to a rural Southern county that had existed in a state of suspended animation for more than two hundred years. Newly constructed rail transportation lines into the city allowed many federal workers to move out into what was then called the "Streetcar Suburbs." The automobile, previously too expensive for the average citizen, was now being mass produced and its newfound affordability came within the price range of many Americans. Previously rural areas began to take on a suburban atmosphere. As the county's population increased so did the need for governmental services. The two-century-old law enforcement system, which called for a few volunteer sheriffs and constables to perform police services, provided inadequate for the expanding needs of a growing urbanized population. On April 5, 1927, a state law was enacted that authorized the Board of County Commissioners to create a full-time, four-man "County Police Force." The new police force, which initially functioned under the supervision of the county sheriff, consisted of four constables at large.

A political squabble quickly developed between the sheriff and county commissioners over control of the police. In 1931, a new law was enacted that separated the county police force from the sheriff's office. This law also granted the county commissioners authority to appoint their own chief of police, thus creating a police force that was independent of the county sheriff.

The problems caused by a continually increasing population would plague Prince George's County for the next fifty years. Between 1940 and 1980 the county's population increased from 89,490 to 665,000 residents. In the mid-1960s, new residents were moving into the burgeoning county at the rate of 600 per week. The ever-increasing numbers of homes, apartments, shopping centers, industrial parks, and roads had forever changed the country. Gone were the small homogeneous communities, family farms, and endless miles of timber forests that had once permeated rural Prince George's County. The growth, frequently uncontrolled, placed a tremendous burden on the county government. Especially affected was the police department, the one government agency required to provide continuous minute-to-minute, up-front, and personal public service.

During this period of spectacular growth the police department found itself in the unenviable position of having to provide increased services without the corresponding increases to its budget or personnel. The county government was in a precarious situation; county residents made no secret of their aversion to a tax increase, yet they also expected the county to upgrade its services to meet the public's ever increasing demand for governmental services. Additionally, there was a demand for good public schools, a modernized road network, and more localized public services.

The county's population began to level off about the same time that the police department celebrated its fiftieth anniversary as an independent police agency (1931–1981). As part of the department's anniversary, then Chief of Police John E. McHale initiated a project to publish a short departmental history. The history project encountered immediate difficulties when it was discovered that very few records had been maintained. Further inquiry revealed that all the department's original members were deceased, and only a handful of retired officers from the late 1930s and early 1940s were still available. Interviews with those retired officers and with the families of deceased officers proved beneficial in that a number of old photographs and newspaper clippings were collected. The end result of the department's initial historical research was the creation of a historical file and the publication of several short historical articles.

After the fiftieth anniversary celebration in 1981, information concerning the department's history continued to accumulate. Over the next several years the history file increased to the point that it filled three cardboard boxes. From an extremely vague and somewhat hazy past, a historical picture began to develop. It was not the clearest of pictures, but the idea of a pictorial history had been born. In 1986, Chief of Police Michael J. Flaherty initiated a project to examine the possibility of publishing a complete history of the Prince George's County Police Department. This pictorial history is the end result of that project.

As previously stated, a major goal in gathering a departmental history was that of acknowledging and preserving the individual police employees' longstanding tradition of providing the citizens of Prince George's County with a high-quality law enforcement service. This record of commitment, dedication, and sacrifice is a source of pride to every police department employee. It is also a legacy that should be preserved for future generations of Prince Georgians.

In researching this book, it was found that what little information was available was widely scattered in both the public and private sector. When information was located it was often sketchy and open to interpretation. As already noted, we were also handicapped because only a few "old timers" were available to give us first hand accounts of police activity. Due to the scarcity and vagueness of public documents, we had no other choice but to rely on old newspaper accounts of events. When possible, the account of one newspaper was matched with the account in another to effectively tell the most accurate story. Word-of-mouth descriptions of police activity that survived the passage of time were also matched with available newspaper accounts. In short, every reasonable effort was made to present a fair, accurate, and balanced account of the police department activity.

Historical information and photographs, once gathered, were placed in a decade file and later reviewed for inclusion within the history. Many of our decisions to include or exclude material were judgement calls on our behalf. Our goal in selecting material evolved out of a need to present a generalized nostalgic remembrance of life within the police department. If a photograph of a roll call or retirement was used within the history, that picture was intended to be symbolic of every roll call or retirement. If an account of some particular act of heroism is given, that account is intended to represent the uncountable number of similar acts of police bravery that have occurred over the years. Only a small portion of the photographs collected for this project were selected for publication. The criteria for selecting photographs was based on subject matter, uniqueness, and clarity.

In closing, we would ask our readers to remember that this history was researched and written by police department employees and not professional historians. Every reasonable attempt was made to present an accurate picture of events, the good along with the not so good. Limited space and in some cases a lack of detailed information restricted the amount of material that could be devoted to any one event. We also apologize for any omissions that might have been made in the collection of material for this book; in any endeavor of this magnitude such omissions are inevitable. During the early stages of writing this manuscript we assumed that our primary reader would be someone directly or indirectly connected with the police department. As the manuscript came together, we realized that the history might be of interest to people from outside the agency. Hopefully, those who fall outside our law enforcement family will find something of value in the pages of this history.

Dennis Campbell

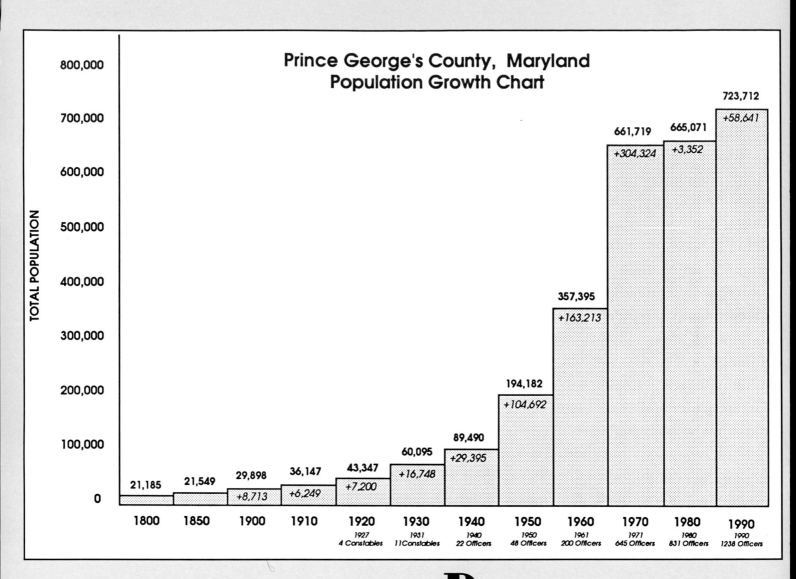

Prince George's County, Maryland
Population Growth Chart

TOTAL POPULATION

Year	Population	Growth	Police
1800	21,185		
1850	21,549		
1900	29,898	+8,713	
1910	36,147	+6,249	
1920	43,347	+7,200	1927 — 4 Constables
1930	60,095	+16,748	1931 — 11 Constables
1940	89,490	+29,395	1940 — 22 Officers
1950	194,182	+104,692	1950 — 48 Officers
1960	357,395	+163,213	1961 — 200 Officers
1970	661,719	+304,324	1971 — 645 Officers
1980	665,071	+3,352	1980 — 831 Officers
1990	723,712	+58,641	1990 — 1238 Officers

Population growth within Prince George's County remained almost static throughout the nineteenth century. The population began to increase in the early twentieth century with this increase leading to the creation of a full-time police force in 1927. An examination of the demographics displayed on the above chart reveals that local law enforcement services were frequently strained to their very limits because of a low officer/population ratio.

The 8,713 figure found in the 1900 shaded population column pertains to the number of new residents moving into the county during the 100-year period between 1800 and 1900. The figures in each subsequent shaded column relate to the county's population growth over the previous decade. With one exception, all demographic information contained on this chart was obtained from U.S. Census Bureau records. The 1990 total population estimate was supplied by the Maryland National Capital Park and Planning Commission. Police department strength figures were obtained from yearly report brochures.

ACKNOWLEDGMENTS

The gathering of this history would not have been possible without the help of many people, institutions, and organizations. Researching the police departments history was a long-term project, involving conversations with hundreds of people, both from within and outside the department. Space restrictions obviously prohibit my naming every person who contributed to this history, but the reader should be aware that the publication of this book could not have taken place without the help of many people, some of whom are no longer with us.

I feel a special obligation to express my deep appreciation to the hundreds of people who shared their experiences, photographs, news clippings, brochures, and other tidbits of information with me. Every item brought to my attention helped, in some way, to clarify the many ambiguities encountered while attempting to piece together this history. Because this is a photographic history, I want to acknowledge my special thanks to the hundreds of people who allowed us to duplicate their photographs. Space restrictions limited the number of pictures that could be included within this history, but each and every photograph contributed to our understanding of the past. It is my hope that the publication of this history, in some small way, repays the debt of gratitude I owe to everyone who helped with this project.

I am particularly indebted to the following people, all of who made substantial contributions to the publication of this history:

Maj. Howard Blake, Public Information Office
Tom Carter, Police Dispatcher
Mike Clover, Creative Typographers Inc.
Sgt. Chuck Cook, Public Information Office
Frederick S. DeMarr, Prince George's County Historical
 Society
Bob Donaldson, Pair Tree Photographic Studio
Francis X. Geary, Local Historian
Andy DeGagne, Photo Laboratory Supervisor
Brenda Duvall, Public Information Office
Michael J. Flaherty, Retired Police Chief
Cpl. Keith Evans, Training Services
Sarah Smith Gardner, Proofreading
Maj. Roy Gilmore, Management Services
Barbara Handley, Photo Laboratory Technician
Capt. Douglas Holland, Planning Division
Everett (Denny) Husk, Retired Captain
Cpl. Robert Jermyn, Vehicle Audit

Henry Jones, Department of Corrections
Cpl. Frank Kobilis, State's Attorney's Liaison
Pfc. Carol Landrum, Public Information Office
Maj. Allan MacDonald, Inspectional Services
John E. McHale, Retired Police Chief
Shirley Mangum, Police Records
Chief of Police David B. Mitchell
Capt. Clark Price, Fiscal Affairs Division
Joyce Rumburg, Public Information Office
Capt. Jack San Felice, Audits & Inspections Division
Edward Schauf, Retired Corporal
Maj. Larry Shanks, Commander District II
George Smith, Prince George's County Crime Solvers
Roland Sweitzer, Retired Police Chief
Rose Van Dyke, Proofreading
Cpl. Jan Veeder, Evidence Unit
Bernie Walton, The Donning Company/Publishers
Kathy Williams, *The Prince George's Journal*
Arden Woods, County Print Shop
Elizabeth Wyatt, Police Graphic Artist
Helen Young, Photo Laboratory Technician

The following organizations, associations, and governmental agencies made substantial contributions to the gathering of information for this history.

The Laurel Leader
The Prince George's Journal
The Prince George's Post
The South County Times
The Washington Post
The Washington Times
District of Columbia Public Library
Fraternal Order of Police Auxiliary, Lodge 89
Library of Congress
Maryland Hall of Records
Maryland Law Library
Maryland Police Training Commission
Prince George's County, Circuit Court Library
Prince George's County Historical Society Library
Prince George's County Retired Police Association

Dennis Campbell

INTRODUCTION

1696
A New County Is Formed

The first county seat for Prince George's County was located in Charles Town. Situated on the Patuxent River, time has eradicated all traces of this old colonial town. The only on-site reminder that modern society has to prove that this town existed is a historical marker found at the dead end of Mt. Calvert Road in Croom. Photo by author

Within is a country that may have the prerogative over most places known, for large and pleasant navigable rivers, heaven and earth never agreed better to frame a place for man's habitation. . . . here are mountaines, hils, plaines, valleys, rivers, and brookes, all running more pleasantly into a faire bay, compassed but for the mouth, with fruitful and delightful land.
—Capt. John Smith,
English Explorer,
June 1608

Prince George's County came into existence on Saint George's Day, April 23, 1696. Formed out of what had previously been parts of Calvert and Charles counties, the county was then Maryland's new western frontier with its boundaries encompassing all of what is now the District of Columbia, along with Montgomery, Frederick, Washington, Garrett, and northwestern Carroll counties.

The land was mostly uninhabited, but its rich fertile soil was ideally suited for farming. The first colonists settled in that portion of the county which bordered the Patuxent and Potomac rivers because the navigable rivers served as an accessible waterway for the transportation of their farm products to the European marketplace. Within a short period of time, tobacco had become the crop of choice, and it would reign supreme within Prince George's County for the next 250 years.

The county seat of government was originally located along the Patuxent River at a place called Charles Town. The government was administered by a county court which consisted of eight justices, or commissioners of the peace, as they were also called. The justices administered all those functions normally performed by a local government, along with the courtroom adjudication of all legal matters in accordance with provincial law.

In 1706, the province's General Assembly authorized the establishment of five new towns within Prince George's County: Mill Town, Nottingham, Queen Anne, Marlborough, and Aire. Over the next few years, Charles Town felt the loss of trade in that two of the new towns also offered port facilities on the Patuxent River. The loss of trade was further enhanced by the construction of new roads which tended to follow the northward movement of the county's growing population. On March 28, 1721, some twenty-five years after the county was established, the county seat was moved to Marlborough.

In 1748, the county's population reached 6,624 taxables and the General Assembly decided that it was time to realign the county's boundary lines. A small portion of land was returned to Charles County, and a huge tract of western land was used to create Frederick County. Except for land that would later be given to the federal government, Prince George's County had been reduced to its present size.

In 1763, the town of Marlborough became known as Upper Marlborough. In 1791, the General Assembly ceded land to the Congress of the United States for the formation of a federal city which was to be named the District of Columbia. The vast majority of the ceded land came from Prince George's County. Congress decreed that it would not take up immediate residence in the federal city and that Maryland law should prevail in that portion of the city ceded by the state of Maryland. For the next nine years, Prince George's County continued to maintain its authority over that portion of the District of Columbia formerly included within its boundary lines.

The 1776 enactment of a Maryland Declaration of Rights and Constitution brought a shift from provincial to state government. Independence from British rule and the birth of a new republic would eradicate many of the old English governmental terms. The English geographic designation of the "hundred" would now become an election district. The county would no longer be ruled by a County Court, but by Five Commissioners of the Tax who were also known as a Levy Court. This form of government continued up until 1851 when the State Constitution was amended to require the popular election of a Board of County Commissioners. A Board of County Commissioners would govern Prince George's County until the adoption of a charter form of government in 1971.

From its very conception, Prince George's County had been heavily dependent upon the farm as the basis for a strong economy. Because the soil remained rich in nutrients, successive family generations were able to work the same land. Although most Prince Georgians made their living by working a small family farm, others amassed a fortune from the operation of large farm and land investments. Tobacco, although labor intensive, was by far the most profitable of crops. Like other Southern States, Maryland had found it economically profitable to use slave labor for the purposes of planting, tending, and harvesting its crops. Accordingly, Prince George's County had a large slave population.

As time progressed Prince George's County stood firmly by what it knew best, farming, and little effort was made to diversify into the business of manufacturing. Content with anonymity the county remained in a state of suspended animation. The 1800 census listed the county's population at 21,185. One hundred years later, the population was listed at 29,898, a meager increase of some 8,713 residents in the 100-year period between 1800 and 1900. A special 1890 census report states that the state of Maryland had 3,083 manufacturing establishments employing a total of 28,703 people. A paltry twelve manufacturing establishments were located in Prince George's County, employing a grand total of 325 people.

Needless to say, the county entered the twentieth century as a sparsely populated, homogeneous farm community, with the vast majority of its citizens being native-born Prince Georgians, as were their parents and grandparents. The little growth that did take place occurred in the northern county communities around Bladensburg, Hyattsville, and Laurel.

The advent of the twentieth century brought a population explosion to Prince George's County. The federal government had remained relatively small up until the start of World War I. With the close of the war, government started to expand and take on additional responsibilities; accordingly, there arose a need for new employees and housing. Adequate housing soon became difficult to find in Washington, D.C., and many of the new federal employees were attracted to the Maryland and Virginia suburbs. Prince George's County proved particularly attractive because of its close proximity to Washington and the availability of streetcar transportation into the city. The communities of Mount Rainier, Hyattsville and Bladensburg became known as the "Street Car Suburbs."

A second event which seemed to spearhead and alter the growth of the entire Washington metropolitan area was the development and availability of the automobile. The automobile offered an expanded mobility to the average American. Rural areas, once almost inaccessible to the general public, were now only minutes away from the inner city. The quiet tranquility of living in the country was now being broken by the noise of automobiles speeding up and down the road. Longtime county residents, who had become accustomed to recognizing everyone who drove over their roads, began to see a steady stream of strange and unfamiliar people pass by their front doors. The theft of property, something almost unheard of in earlier years, began to increase. Doors previously left unlocked, now had to be secured. The flagrant disregard of traffic laws was also leading to an ever-increasing number of serious traffic-related personal injury accidents. Many native-born Prince Georgians felt uncomfortable with the increasing roadway traffic and the numerous strangers who were now moving into the county. Some old-time residents felt that the influx of new people into the county was a threat, and that these new residents would forever alter the uncomplicated rural lifestyle that had dominated the county for the past 200-plus years. Additional residents also meant that the tax rate would increase as the need for new schools, roads, and other governmental services surfaced. Up until this time, there had been no need for full-time police and fire services. The county sheriff and his chief deputy, assisted by volunteer deputies and election district constables, had provided a more than adequate law enforcement service to the sparsely populated county. Fire protection services had long been provided for through a number of community volunteer fire departments.

A popular and politically active movement during the early twentieth century was that of the anti-saloon movement. Many long-time county residents involved in this movement were fearful that the influx of new county residents would bring corruption in the form of additional gambling and liquor violations. Time would prove that many of these fears were unfounded, but the increasing numbers of people now moving into the county would soon end the county's 200-plus years of sheltered tranquility. The early twentieth century brought an end to that era in which the citizenry was capable of policing itself with volunteer part-time policemen. The influx of new county residents, the general public's accessibility to rapid transportation, and the public safety hazard caused by the automobile overwhelmed the 200-year-old sheriff/volunteer-constable law enforcement system. The time was approaching for old and new county residents to join together in a hue and cry for a professional full-time police service.

Note: Primary information pertaining to the county's early history was obtained from Louise Foyner Hienton's book, Prince George's Heritage. *Additional information was also obtained from Joseph L. Arnold's book,* Maryland: Old Line to New Prosperity.

CHAPTER I

Early County Law Enforcement

Montgomery County was the second of Maryland's twenty-three counties to form a professional county police force (Baltimore County being the first). Established in July 1922, the Montgomery County Police Force originally consisted of six constables at large, and one constable holding the title of chief. When Prince George's County reorganized its county police force in 1931, it copied the Montgomery County Police Law. Photo courtesy of Chief Donald Brooks, Montgomery County Police Department

During colonial times the office of county sheriff was considered to be extremely important. The office was almost always held by the power elite, or those with "sufficient estate." An appointment to office was also considered lucrative because the sheriff, as the county's primary tax collector, was allowed to keep ten percent of all taxes he collected. The early sheriff was described in Maryland Hall of Records Publication No. 16, *The Old Line State* as:

> . . . the county court's chief executive officer. All summonses, subpoenas, warrants, writs and other process issued by the county, and incidentally by the other courts of Providence as well, were served by the sheriff, and he also impanelled juries. He was the chief law-enforcement officer of the county. The county prison was in his charge and he was responsible for apprehending persons accused of crimes and for keeping them in custody if they were sentenced to jail. He also enforces other sentences of the court. He supervised the work of constables in preparing lists of taxables within their respective hundreds as well as their capacity as law enforcement officers. . . . In addition, he enforced the collection of officer's fees, fines, forfeitures and also the quit-rents, alienation fines and other revenues of the Lord Proprietary.

The sheriff was in fact so powerful that lawmakers placed numerous restrictions upon the office as a means of controlling the exercise of power. Many of these restrictions remained on the law books up until the recent past. One such restriction prohibited the sheriff from holding more than one consecutive two-year term in office, and that a newly appointed sheriff could not appoint his predecessor to the position of deputy sheriff. A rather unique restriction occurring during the early colonial period prohibited the sheriffs from serving court papers at church. Cyrus H. Karraker, in his book *The Seventeenth Century Sheriff*, states:

> The execution and return of writs and warrants comprised the bulk of his work in Maryland. . . . The sheriff . . . sought to avoid the hardships of travel to many homes and to those remotely situated in the county by waiting at the church doors to serve their warrants. But this seemed a desecration; besides, their presence frightened so many of those in danger of arrest away from the services that the colonial assemblies finally prohibited the practice altogether. The Maryland Assembly, for the same reason forbade the presence of the sheriff at the general muster.

As a court's chief executive officer, the sheriff was usually a busy individual who was required to spend much of his time tending to court business, operating the county jail, and dispensing court-ordered punishment. Cyrus Karraker states in his book:

> The colonial county courts made the sheriff responsible for building and repair of the stocks, pillory, whipping post, and ducking stool. . . . The

sheriff, or someone appointed by him, inflicted the punishment prescribed by the county court. The court records contain numerous orders to the sheriff like the following: to put Thomas Norcombe in the pillory for his second offense of hog-stealing "the full time & space of 4 hours; to give a certain Hamball and Elisabeth Slicer five lashes apiece for slandering John Court; and to nail John Goneere by both ears to the pillory, with three nails in each ear, and afterwards to whip him with twenty good lashes for perjuring himself."

The overburdened county sheriff usually found it difficult to provide the entire county with a law enforcement service. Colonial period county courts recognized the sheriff's limited ability to provide a law enforcement service and began to appoint constables as conveyors of the king's peace. Initially all adult males were responsible for temporarily serving a term as a constable within the hundred. The hundred being a geographic area used for the purpose of law, administering justice, and military defense. The constable was an ordinary citizen chosen to provide his community with a law enforcement service for a specific period of time. No allowances for pay were made; therefore, the constable was usually required to find a balance between his law enforcement duties and his regular employment. In communities located some distance from the county seat, access to the constable proved to be more readily available and many local residents chose to seek out his services over those of the more distant sheriff. Most citizens considered the constable's duties an unpleasant assignment and many well-to-do citizens began to pay others to perform this civic duty. Eventually, the constables' assignment became voluntary.

When the colonies asserted their independence from British rule, the old political subdivision known as a "hundred" became extinct. Henceforth, all geographic subdivisions within a county became known as election districts. The various counties courts (governing bodies) retained their authority to appoint law enforcement constables in each of their election districts. Prince George's County experienced very little change; the ancient sheriff/constable law enforcement system worked well within the framework of a rural county environment.

Between 1850 and 1860, Maryland's only full-time professional police department was to be found in densely populated Baltimore City. Closer to Prince George's County, the District of Columbia decided to form a Metropolitan Police Department in 1861. In 1874 expanding industrial growth in and around the Baltimore area led to the formation of the Baltimore County Police, which was Maryland's first county police department.

Although the United States grew in size, population, and economy during the nineteenth century, negligible growth occurred within Prince George's County. Residents had shown little interest in developing an industrial-based economy and rigidly stood by their agricultural past. As the county entered the twentieth century its population and basic form of government had remained basically unchanged for almost one-hundred years. But the new century would bring change—emigrants began pouring into the county, society was becoming more technically advanced, and the American people wanted desperately to improve their standard of living. The federal government

also began to grow and the possibility of federal employment attracted many people to the Washington, D.C. area.

The sheriff and the volunteer constables had provided rural Prince George's County with a more than adequate police service. But the twentieth century brought change to the sheriff's office. A recently enacted state law took away the sheriff's old responsibility for hanging condemned prisoners; henceforth, all executions were conducted at the State Penitentiary in Baltimore. Although diminishing in frequency, a few of the old traditions remained within the sheriff's domain. For example, the sheriff still retained the responsibility of administering a court-ordered flogging to those men convicted of wife beating. (The last Prince George's County flogging occurred in the early 1950s after a man was found guilty of beating his wife. The man received ten lashes at the County Jail in Upper Marlboro.)

With the close of World War I in 1918, the county's population started out on a fifty-year upward spiral. Most of the county's new residents chose to live in or around the older and now expanding northside towns of Bladensburg, Hyattsville, and Riverdale. Law enforcement within these towns was usually delivered by a town bailiff. The bailiff, a volunteer, received no salary for his services and functioned in a way that was quite similar to the county's volunteer constable. As the population of the county's municipalities increased, the volunteer bailiff system proved to be inefficient.

Most towns found it necessary to hire full-time policemen. The lot of an early town policeman was not an easy one. Inadequate funding and political interference in police affairs was almost always a problem. In 1929, the town of Hyattsville abolished its one-man police department for the supposed purpose of saving money. The town simply intended to revert back to the old method of using less-expensive volunteer bailiffs. One newspaper reported that a stormy town meeting had resulted in an accusation that the town fathers were doing away with the police department simply because the police chief was "doing his duty and stepping on someone's toes" and that the money issue was nothing more than a facade.

The county government initially insulated itself from the demands to improve police and fire services by claiming that most new residents lived within the confines of a municipality and that town government had primary responsibility for public service. With the approach of the mid-1920s, the county's population continued to grow and expand to those unincorporated areas immediately adjacent to the heavily populated municipalities. The old sheriff/constable system became strained to the breaking point with the burden of providing police services to a rapidly growing and mobile population. A 1920s Johns Hopkins University study on police services provided to rural and semi-rural Marylanders stated that police protection was "inadequate under modern conditions."

In 1913, motor vehicle registrations were approaching 18,000, and the need for standardized enforcement of the motor vehicle laws brought about the formation of a Maryland State Police in 1913. Known as "commissioner's deputies," the force functioned under the supervision of the Commissioner of Motor

Vehicles. Only authorized to enforce motor vehicle laws, the state police used motorcycles as their primary patrol vehicles. Powerless to make criminal arrests the commissioners deputies were frequently sworn in as deputy sheriffs by the various county sheriffs seeking law enforcement assistance. As motor vehicle registrations increased (105,000 by 1919) so did the need for traffic law enforcement.

In the 1920s, the state police patrolled out of five patrol districts, with one district office located in the town of Hyattsville. As the size and responsibility of the state police increased, so did the pressure to separate them from the Commissioner of Motor Vehicles Office. Legislation toward this goal was introduced in 1921, but failed. In 1931, Governor Ritchie reported that the state police were in a general state of mutiny because of their efforts to separate themselves from the Commissioner of Motor Vehicles Office. In June 1935, legislation was enacted removing control of the state police from the Commissioners Office and forming a separate Department of the State Police. The 54-member state police force was adminis-

tered the oath of office and immediately assumed their duties as a full-service police agency.

Old newspaper accounts of pre-1935 activity within Prince George's County seem to indicate that each individual county sheriff approached deputizing the state police officers from different perspectives. One newspaper from the 1920s reports that the state police could not be called in to assist with the crime problem because they had not been deputized. *The Evening Star* of June 26, 1923, printed that, because trouble was feared during a coroner's inquest hearing, "A dozen officers of the state police force were sworn in and were in attendance during the taking of testimony."

The old volunteer law enforcement system that had faithfully served Prince George's County for more than two-hundred years began to fail in the mid-1920s. Strained to the breaking point, the system became ineffective. People began to see the need for a full-time county-wide, law enforcement agency that was mobile, well equipped, and more knowledgeable in the complexities of modern life.

"Marietta," the home of U.S. Supreme Court Associate Justice Gabriel Duvall, was built in 1812 on Bell Station Road in Lanham. Recently restored and opened to the public, the house is a typical example of the many fine estate homes in Prince George's County. Gabriel Duvall was appointed to the Supreme Court by President James Madison and confirmed by the Senate on November 16, 1811. Justice Duvall remained on the bench for the next twenty-three years retiring in 1835 at the age of eighty-three. Gabriel Duvall spent the last ten years of his life at Marietta, tending to his 650-acre estate.
Photo by author

The law office of Reverdy Johnson (1796–1876), located at the corner of Main Street and Water Street, Upper Marlboro. This photograph was taken in 1906 (the County Fair poster on the building bears that date). Mr. Johnson, a well-known nineteenth-century lawyer, helped to defend Mary Surratt at her military trial for the assassination of President Abraham Lincoln. He also served in the U.S. Senate, as U.S. attorney general, and as ambassador to the Court of St. James.

This photograph is unique because it exemplifies that out-of-the-mainstream atmosphere that still prevails in modern-day Upper Marlboro.
Photo courtesy of the Prince George's County Historical Society

Upper Marlboro was also the scene of occasional patriotic ceremonies. This photograph of the County Courthouse was taken at the dedication of a memorial to those Prince Georgians killed in World War I. The memorial can still be found in the east front courthouse lawn. Photo courtesy of U.S. Capitol Police Sergeant Tom Finkle

This 1917 photograph of Harry Buck's General Store in Upper Marlboro is a good example of early twentieth-century mercantilism. Advertisements found in the Enquirer-Gazette *for the mid 1920s indicate that the county seat was a hub of business activity with the community being served by several banks, automobile companies, hotels, restaurants, and a host of other service-oriented businesses. Photo courtesy of Lewis Buck*

Growth within Prince George's County has always been directly connected to growth of the federal government in Washington, D.C. This 1904 photograph depicts an easterly view from the U.S. Treasury Building at Fifteenth Street and Pennsylvania Avenue. Some of the streetcars shown ran to the city of Laurel, thus providing county residents with transportation to the federal workplace. Photo courtesy of the District of Columbia Public Library

The District of Columbia's Metropolitan Police Department (MPDC) was formed in 1861. In the late 1920s, increased crime became an issue with many Prince George's County residents who looked upon the professional Washington, D.C. police with envy. Many old official and unofficial accounts reveal that county law enforcement authorities often sought advice and assistance from their more experienced neighbors in the District of Columbia.

Photo copied from a rare turn-of-the-century MPDC history book owned by retired MPDC Sgt. George Wilson

The Hyattsville Automobile Company was owned by Hervey G. Machen, Sr. Originally from Virginia, Mr. Machen came to Prince George's County as a young man and entered the contracting business. Later he became one of the county's first automobile dealers, opening a Ford dealership on what is now Baltimore Avenue. Actively involved in the affairs of the local Democratic party, Mr. Machen was once nominated for the office of sheriff. In the early 1920s, he volunteered to be a Hyattsville area deputy sheriff.

With the creation of a full-time county police force in 1927, Mr. Machen was offered and accepted an appointment as the sergeant of police. According to his son, Hervey Machen, Jr., the automobile dealership adequately supported the family, but his father accepted the police position because of his love for police work.

When the force was reorganized in 1931, The Suburban Citizen, a local Hyattsville newspaper, recommended in an editorial that Mr. Machen be appointed as the new chief of police. The paper wrote "We know of no other man, leader or otherwise, that has been as loyal, (was) promised as much and got so little as Hervey G. Machen. He is a Democrat, and in politics he plays a pat hand. He has sacrificed his time, his money, yea his business, believing in the men with whom he trains some day giving him recognition. . . . he is capable, he is loyal, he's a party man from his heart, and he's not afraid of hell itself."

Photo courtesy of Hervey Machen, Jr.

THE GREAT CLINTON BANK ROBBERY

As Prince George's County entered the 1920s, it became apparent that the old sheriff/constable law enforcement system was unable to provide the county an adequate police service. The following story vividly illustrates the inadequacies of the system and how a community pulled itself together when confronted with a crisis. The story was written by George Goode, a reporter for *The South County Times* of Clinton. Mr. Goode's account was based on information furnished by Thomas S. Gwynn, Jr., of Clinton.

"The new Clinton Bank was an impressive brick building for its time, the first brick commercial building in the area. The sturdy square structure looked like a mausoleum and must have seemed all the more imposing because of its location. It sat on a tiny dirt plot of ground carved from the pear orchard of the old Surratt farm on the corner across the dirt road from B. K. Miller's General Store.

With its barred windows and thick walls, the bank was meant to look imposing, to inspire trust in the country folk for miles around.

Shortly before noon on November 7, 1922, cashier J. Frank Dent was going about his daily routine in the two-year-old bank when several men entered and approached his window. One of the strangers (in those days a stranger was a stranger was a stranger) placed a five-dollar bill in the window and asked for change. Among the rural customers, five-dollar bills were sure enough. Bank robberies were unheard of. But when the strangers drew guns before he could produce the change, the situation was obvious to Dent.

To the bank robbers the bank, despite the brick facade, probably looked like easy game. They came from Baltimore and the bank must have seemed vulnerable, situated as it was at a lonely crossroads in the middle of nowhere. At the time, the county had no police force and Clinton's lone constable had not yet taken office.

But even in Dent's day, the Clinton bank was equipped with a new-fangled alarm system which could be touched off by a teller's foot. At the time alarm bells weren't wired to a police station, as is the case today. They were attached to the building itself and were designed to be heard for at least one-half mile in all directions.

So when Dent pushed the button that November day, it was an act of courage. He did the only sensible thing when the alarm sounded. He ducked.

At least one customer, the elderly George Simmons, had been trapped in the bank when the robbers pulled their guns. When the alarm sounded, the robbers panicked. They fired a warning shot over the head of old man Simmons and scrambled out to their car, leaving the unchanged five-dollar bill on the counter. The bullet landed harmlessly in a window sill above Simmons head. For years afterward the hole in the sill was an attraction for local curiosity seekers and a memorial, pointed out to any and all visitors, to the great Clinton Bank Robbery.

The robbers fled north on Old Branch Avenue (Rt. 381) but their car broke down a half-mile beyond Jenkins' Corner (Malfunction Junciton) and they took to the woods on foot.

Within minutes of the burglar alarm sounding, storekeepers, laborers, clerks, and farmers had gathered in front of the bank armed with shotguns, rifles, and revolvers.

Jack Davis, a local black whose wife Rosie had delivered most of the babies born in the Clinton area, toted his favorite hog-killing knife as well as his shotgun.

. . . Outside the hearing range of the alarm, word of the robbery spread quickly over the county party telephone line, on which listening-in was common. More and more armed citizens showed up to aid in the search. All fashions of dress from blue cover-alls to hand-pressed suits were in evidence. Excitement mounted as small groups peeled off to comb the woods and roads.

Of the four would-be robbers, three were brothers. When their car broke down, August, Frank and Henry Wood took off together in one direction, their compatriot William Coakley in another.

The Wood brothers were apprehended by members of the Clinton posse as they emerged from the woods onto Possum Pike, now Temple Hills Road. Coakley was eventually captured further north along Branch Avenue. All four were captured without a shot being fired. The robbers, far from getting away with any Clinton money, actually lost the five dollars left behind at Dent's window.

Today, bank robberies are all too common, but in 1922 they were rare and they posed a much greater threat to a bank and its depositors. The new local bank and its area clients had neither federal insurance nor a large, organized police force to protect their money. The posse which formed on that November day in 1922 was not just a bunch of thrill-seekers. They had turned out in numbers to protect Clinton's money and the officials of their bank. It was a day talked about with pride and excitement for years afterward."

Reprinted with permission from *The South County Times*.

The partially torn newspaper photo was furnished courtesy of Thomas S. Gwynn, Jr.

A Maryland State Police force was created in 1914 to enforce motor vehicle laws. Under the control of the Commissioner of Motor Vehicles, state policemen patrolled the state's highways on motorcycles. The law creating a state police force did not authorize its officers to make criminal arrests; accordingly, some county sheriffs deputized the state policemen and frequently called upon them for assistance. Numerous attempts were made to separate the state police from the Commissioner of Motor Vehicles Office, but all met with negative results. In 1931, the governor announced that the state police were in "a general state of mutiny" over the issue of separating themselves from the Commissioner of Motor Vehicles Office. Legislation enacted in 1935 finally resulted in the formation of a separate Department of State Police.

The state police assigned to patrol duty in northern Prince George's County initially worked from a Patrol District Office in Hyattsville, but later moved to a station located in Laurel. The Laurel Station remained in use until the new Waterloo Barrack was opened in 1938. State police patrolling the southern portion of Prince George's County initially worked from the Waldorf Barrack.
Photo obtained from a Maryland State Police History

The old election district constable had no uniform, his only symbol of authority being a silver-colored badge. This particular badge belonged to Constable Wiggins Boone of Forestville.
Courtesy of U.S. Capitol Police Sergeant Tom Finkle

W. Curtis Hopkins was one of the few Republicans to be elected sheriff in a predominantly Democratic Prince George's County. Sheriff Hopkins held office in the early 1930s.
Courtesy of Jean Hopkins

W. CURTIS HOPKINS

REPUBLICAN
CANDIDATE

FOR SHERIFF OF PRINCE GEORGE'S COUNTY

SOLICITS YOUR SUPPORT

As Prince George's County entered the twentieth century, its population reached a whopping 29,898. The largest concentration of residents lived in the area immediately surrounding the town of Hyattsville. This 1905 photograph of downtown Hyattsville shows a northerly view of what is now the 5100 block of Rhode Island Avenue. A portion of the Hyattsville Hardware Company building can be seen on the right. The building still stands today and the hardware company remains in business at the same site. The streetcar tracks in the foreground served commuters between Laurel and the Treasury Building at Fifteen Street and Pennsylvania Avenue in Washington, D.C.
Photo courtesy of the Prince George's County Historical Society

Capitol Heights was incorporated in 1910 and, for many years, remained on the southern fringe of the county's population explosion. Major development of those areas south of Capitol Heights did not occur until the 1950s.
Photo courtesy of Blanche Ennis

Although the first signs of urban growth occurred in the early 1900s, most Prince Georgians continued to derive a living through the operation of a family farm. Produce was usually transported by truck to one of several market places in Washington. In this 1916 photograph, Mr. Bean is shown with a truckload of milk. The Bean family operated a dairy farm at the southeastern corner of Marlboro Pike and Forestville Road.
Photo courtesy of Willard Entwisle

Thomas Garrison constable apprehend Geo W Whalley to attend coroner inquest at once

Aug 15 1905.

Wallace Raybold Foreman

Society's methods of maintaining law and order were much more direct and less complicated in the early 1900s. For example, in the case of an accidental death, the local justice of the peace would summon a jury of inquest to review the facts and circumstances of the death. The jury was composed of twelve citizens, one of whom would act as foreman. The jury was authorized to summon witnesses, to hear testimony, and then make a finding of fact regarding the death. The findings were then forwarded to the county state's attorney.

On August 15, 1905, Wallace Raybold, foreman of an inquest jury issued a handwritten summons ordering Constable Thomas Garrison to apprehend George W. Whalley "to attend a coroner('s) inquest at once."

An inquiry into the issuance of this summons revealed that an eight-year-old Riverdale boy had been struck and killed by a train on August 12, 1905. Justice of the Peace John F. Hickey ordered that the death be investigated by an inquest jury. Wallace Raybold was named as jury foreman and George Whalley as a jury member. According to The Sunday Star of August 13, 1905, the jury was scheduled to interview the train crew on the following Monday. It appears Mr. Whalley failed to appear at the inquest, and that the foreman issued a summons for his immediate appearance as a jury member. Summons and information from The Sunday Star courtesy of Francis Geary. News clipping from The Prince George's Post, August 27, 1937

Thomas H. "Tom" Garrison, of Hyattsville, whose name is synonymous with law enforcement, will be a candidate for sheriff of Prince Georges county on the Republican ticket, he announced this week. Election will be held next year.

The 65-year-old private detective will seek the sheriff's job as a climax to his 32-year fiction-like police career. Twenty-six of those years have been spent as a Prince Georges county officer in one capacity or another. He was chief deputy sheriff five different times, the first in 1912 and the last in 1934.

* * *

IS CHAMPION RAIDER

Reese is a picturesque Prince Georges County policeman, who has announced his candidacy for sheriff. Single-handed, Reese has raided 259 gambling houses and moonshine stills in the past eighteen months, and claims never to have lost a case in court.

CLAUDE A. ("TWO GUN") REESE

The forefather of today's county police officer was the old election district constable. Independent of the county sheriff, the constable received his appointment from the county commissioners, and served a two-year term of office. A volunteer who wore no uniform, the constable was an ordinary citizen who agreed to provide his community with a part-time law enforcement service. He received no salary for services rendered, and derived his only compensation from the service of court papers.

Constables maintained close-working relationships with other local citizens who had been sworn in as volunteer deputy sheriffs. These volunteer law officers were responsible for performing the vast majority of neighborhood law enforcement services. It is believed that the county sheriff and his chief deputy were primarily confined to the county seat tending to circuit court and county jail business.

Claude A. Reese's experience as a law enforcement officer began in the early 1920s, when he became an election district constable in the Berwyn area. When a full-time county police force was created in 1927, Reese accepted one of the four full-time positions as a constable at large. Claude Reese survived the 1931 reorganization and remained with the county force until 1936.

NOTE: The newspaper photo used on this page dates to the early to mid-1920s and was provided through the courtesy of Neva Reese. The meaning of the symbols on Constable Reese's holsters is not known; however, they probably relate to the American Indian.

CHAPTER II

1927–1931
A New Law Enforcement Concept
–A County Police Force

*ken sometime between 1927 and 1931,
is photograph shows the apparent result of
numbers raid conducted by the county
lice/sheriff's office. Pictured standing left
right are volunteer Deputy Sheriff Harry
binson, Chief Deputy Arthur Hepburn,
d County Policeman Frank Prince.
ting is Sheriff Charles Early.
oto courtesy of Mary Hepburn Robinson*

Law is a form of order, and good law must necessarily mean good order.
—Aristotle

In the mid-1920s, serious thought was given to forming a county police force. Sometime prior to the 1927 legislative session, the Board of Commissioners for Prince George's County asked the county delegation to the General Assembly to propose legislation authorizing the formation of a Prince George's County Police Force.

On April 5, 1927, Governor Albert C. Ritchie signed Chapter 518 of the Acts of the General Assembly, thus authorizing the formation of a Prince George's County Police Force. The new law designated that the county sheriff would assume the additional title of "Police Chief," and that the deputy sheriff would also hold the title of "Lieutenant of Police." The county police force was to be composed of at least three, but not more than six, constables at large. The constables were to serve a two-year term of office, after which they could be reappointed for successive two-year terms. One of the constables was to be appointed as a "Sergeant of Police" at a salary of $1,800 per year, while the remaining constables were to receive $1,500 salary. The law also stipulated that the sheriff and his deputy were to receive no additional pay for their duties of supervising the new county police.

The new force was to be funded through county taxes, the county commissioners being responsible for raising funds for the police budget. Although the sheriff recommended those appointed as constables, the final authority to hire or remove individuals from office was solely that of the commissioners. To ensure professional behavior, the law also prohibited the new constables from accepting any fee for the service of court papers, including arrest warrants. It was believed that accepting such fees might taint the quality of arrests that the officers made.

On April 27, 1927, the commissioners made the following appointments to the new county police force: Hervey G. Machen, sergeant of police; Vinton M. Nichols, constable at large; Frank P. Prince, constable at large; and Claude A. Reese, constable at large.

On April 26, 1927, the commissioners authorized the purchase of one Harley-Davidson motorcycle, a Ford 2-door sedan, and two Ford touring cars for use by the county police. It is doubtful that these vehicles were purchased because a subsequent record reveals that the commissioners later authorized the purchase of "Three Ford 2-door sedans for the use of the Prince George's County Police." The later record indicates that the automobiles were purchased from various county dealers at a cost of $581 each.

Further inquiry into police activity reveals very little information about actual operational procedures. Prohibition was in effect at the time, and newspaper accounts seem to infer that a great deal of time, effort, and money were expended on enforcing the so-called wet laws. Gambling was also a long-time problem within the county and the commissioners were continually bombarded with requests for stricter enforcement of gambling laws, especially those pertaining to slot machines.

Although the county's population was increasing, 43,347 residents according to the 1920 census, the vast majority of land was still used for agricultural purposes. An interesting police-related note found in the minutes of the commissioners meeting of November 13, 1928, stated:

Ordered, that the Sheriff be requested to designate a member of the County Police Force to personally notify Lee Thomas, Kendall Enslow, and Frank Baden, Brandywine, Maryland, each to kill his dog which destroyed fowls belonging to Lucy Henson, on September 6, 1928, and in the event of refusal of the owners to kill dogs in question the officer is to require the payment of $7.85 from each of the three persons above named and that if the owners refuse to either kill their dogs or pay the amount required the officer is directed to kill said dogs whenever and wherever they may be found, in accordance with the provisions of Chapter 387, Laws of Maryland 1927.

This cartoon, titled "HELPFUL HINTS TO MOTORISTS," was found in the October 10, 1928 issue of The Evening Star. *These simple words of advice to motorists, given some sixty years ago, still make a lot of sense.*
Washington Star *cartoon*

Shortly after the county police force was created, signs of political strife began to develop between the Board of County Commissioners and County Sheriff Charles Early. It appears that both the commissioners and sheriff felt uncomfortable with the law that had created the police force. As stipulated, the commissioners were responsible for hiring the new full-time constables and funding their operation, while the independently elected sheriff had supervisory control over the force's operation. Each found themselves in an awkward political situation: the commissioners had no control over the elected sheriff, while the sheriff had little input as to the selection of constables. Additionally, the sheriff had no disciplinary control over the constables he supervised.

On December 11, 1928, the commissioners asked the county's delegation to the General Assembly to submit new legislation repealing the 1927 police act, and enact a revised law "to separate the Prince George's County Police from the Sheriff's Office and to place said police under the direction and supervision of the County Commissioners of Prince George's County in a manner similar to that made and provided by the Montgomery County Police Law."

In August 1930, the dispute was further complicated when Sheriff Early attempted to suspend Sergeant Machen. The commissioners responded by having their attorney direct a formal letter to the sheriff stating that the law did not give him the authority to suspend any member of the force. As the squabbling between the commissioners and sheriff continued, a legislative bill to create a new and independent county police force received General Assembly approval. That bill was signed into law by Governor Ritchie on April 6, 1931. The new law, which took effect on June 1, 1931, separated the county police force from the sheriff's supervisory control and allowed the commissioners to appoint their own police chief. The law also increased the force's strength to eleven constables at large.

An unusual twist to the political dilemma between the commissioners and sheriff surfaced before the new police law became effective. It seems that the old police law, which remained in effect until June 1, 1931, required that the constables be reappointed every two years. The constables, then in office under the sheriff's supervision, were scheduled for reappointment in April 1931. Thus the legal question was posed: If the present constables were reappointed, would their term of office run until April 1933? If so, this technicality could possibly limit the commissioners' ability to have total control over the structure of the new force. To avoid this legal entanglement, emergency legislation was pushed through the General Assembly and signed into law by Governor Ritchie. This legislation allowed the county to temporarily abolish its police force on the expiration of the old constables' terms of office in April. Accordingly, the police force in Prince George's County ceased to exist between the months of April and May 1931. Beginning June 1, 1931, the new police law became effective and the Board of County Commissioners would then have total control over the appointments to the new and independent Prince George's County Police Force.

Located where the Northeast Branch now passes under Baltimore Avenue the old Blandensburg Jail served as a temporary county lockup between 1924 and 1931. Owned by the town of Blandensburg the jail was initially rented to the county for $100 per year. The county also furnished a jailer to care for the two-cell lockup. The jailer, who did not remain at the site twenty-four hours a day, would periodically check on the well-being of his charges. The jailer was also responsible for providing meals to those confined in the lockup. Because the lockup was located in a low-lying area, it frequently flooded during periods of moderate rain. In 1931, the county opened its new substation in Hyattsville and stopped using the Blandensburg Jail. The town of Bladensburg continued to operate the jail until April 1941.

On April 4, 1941, The Prince Georgean, a Hyattsville and Mount Rainier newspaper, published an editorial titled "Fall of the Bastille." A copy of that editorial, which describes the old Blandensburg Jail in rather bleak and humorous terms, is shown here.

Photo and newspaper editorial courtesy of the Prince George's County Historical Society

The old County Jail, in Upper Marlboro was built in 1927. It served as the county's main jail until 1987, when it was replaced with a modern forty-four-million-dollar detention center. The sheriff was specifically given the responsibility of maintaining a jail in 1696 and he retained sole control over the confinement of county prisoners until a County Department of Corrections was created in 1978. For a number of years, the Maryland State Police also occupied a small portion of the first floor as their south county barrack.

Photo from The Enquirer-Gazette of January 20, 1928

Fall of the Bastille

Ghosts of a thousand hapless prisoners must have chuckled with glee this week at the news that notorious Bladensburg jail has finally been demolished by the C. C. C. boys.

The site of the ancient bastille is being developed as a park area by the National Capital Park and Planning Commission and happy picnickers will now revel with the festive potato salad and hard-boiled egg where once the atmosphere was rent with the moans and shrieks of incarcerated drunks.

The wreckers found no trace on the walls of the traditional messages, scratched with finger nails or etched in blood, telling of the last anguished moments of poor wretches condemned to a living death within those two dank dungeons.

No tragic souvenirs, no records of social injustices to turn the blood cold. Lice, perhaps, and a distinctly foul odor, but little of tragedy. The record of this jail should be written, not in the blood and tears of a Dumas or Dickens, but in the raucous laughter of a Bugs Baer. The vast majority of those held here in durance vile were the wandering drunks, the boisterous singers in public, and an occasional sneak thief whose luck had run out.

For the most part, a maudlin humor pervades the history of this pokey or clink. To have its bolt closed on one was to lose the last vestige of human dignity to which all men are entitled. Regardless of what skirmish or head-thwacking was necessary to pop the victim within the walls, the real battle for the prisoner began after the door clanged, for then began the struggle against the vermin and the lice, the rats and the odor. The man who could long remain drunk under the physical effort required in scratching and swatting was indeed a rarity. Many an errant toss-pot signed the pledge immediately on his release rather than incur the rigors of another night within its confines.

In the rainy season, the luckless prisoner faced a double ordeal. The remorseless flood waters of the Eastern branch were wont to overflow and the inmates had to fight lice with their ears cocked for the first faint trickle which would warn them that Old Man River was coming in.

The story is told of two roisterers, taken suddenly drunk during the course of an evening, who were laid away for safekeeping one rainy night several years ago. The officer in charge, feeling the need of sleep, retired to his trundle bed, not caring much whether his charges escaped or not. When the jailer arrived in the morning, rubbing the last vestiges of sleep from his rheumy eyes, he was confronted with a spectacle that only the genius of Mark Twain could put into words. The prisoners were up to their necks, frantically trying to keep afloat with one arm, the while they fought the insects in their hair with the other. It seems that as the water rose, the lice rose likewise, until their only refuge was on top of the prisoners' heads. One of them later declared that he was on the verge of drowning himself sheerly for the pleasure of having the lice drown with him. The story also contains a fine note of human mercy. It seems the prisoners were released without being fined, on the theory that they had suffered entirely out of proportion to their crime. There is no record of their having been locked in the jail again.

It is a credit to the county that the jail had fallen into disuse. It is an argument commonly advanced that a law-breaker deserves little consideration after his arrest but many a respected pillar of society, who sneers at the drunks peering out of the jail windows, might well say "There, but for the grace of God, and a bit of artful dodging, go I." Prisoners are not necessarily worse than their jailers. They are there merely because they had the misfortune to be caught. Treat them well, Oh Jailer, you too may someday slip.

General Assembly legislation enacted in 1931 separated the county police from the sheriff's office. In this photograph, members of the reorganized police force line up beside their 1931 police cars. The Ford dealership pictured here, Suburban Motor Sales, formerly named the Hyattsville Automobile Company, was located in the present-day 4800 block of Baltimore Avenue in Hyattsville. The police cars were purchased from various Ford dealerships within the county at a

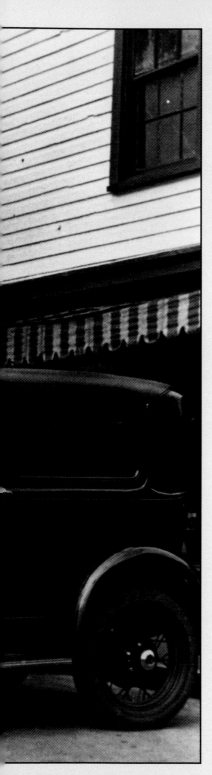

CHAPTER III

1931–1939
An Independent
County Police Force

Being poor is a matter of indifference to me, as long as my poor abilities are of any service to the public.

—Samuel Adams
American patriot

T he law creating a new County Police Force was signed and approved by Governor Albert C. Ritchie on April 6, 1931. However, the legislation did not take effect until the first Monday in June 1931. The legislation, entitled Chapter 231 of the Acts of the General Assembly, created a new eleven-member county police force which would function under the control and supervision of the Board of County Commissioners. The policemen still held the official title of constables at large and were to perform their duties under the immediate supervision of a chief and two sergeants of police. As with the old police law, the constables were to serve a two-year term of office, after which they could be reappointed for additional two-year terms. The police chief's salary was established at $2,100 per year, the sergeants received $1,800, a constable's pay was set at $1,500. Each member of the force also received an additional $300 yearly for uniforms and automobile maintenance. The commissioners still retained the power to remove a constable from office; however, the new law stated that the constable had to receive written notification of any charges against him at least five days prior to a hearing date.

The new law further provided that a headquarters must be maintained in Upper Marlboro, and that a substation be established at or near the town of Hyattsville. Both of these locations were to be staffed at all times, the first mandated 24-hour-per-day police service established by law in Prince George's County. The law further stated that the constables were to wear uniforms at all times, unless otherwise directed by the chief of police.

On June 1, 1931, the county commissioners appointed the following individuals as constables at large: Jeremiah J. Crowley, chief of police; Hyattsville Station - Hervey G. Machen, Sergeant; Arthur Brown; Ralph Brown; William E. Clifton; and Claude A. Reese; Upper Marlboro Station - Arthur W. Hepburn, Sergeant; Oscar Beall; George W. Gray; R. Arnold Naylor; and Elon Turner.

The selection of the eleven-member force reflected the political affiliation of the five-member Board of County Commissioners. An article in *The Laurel Leader*, dated May 23, 1931, explained that the Democratic constables were chosen by the Democratic commissioners, while the selection of the Republican members of the new department was left to the Republican commissioners. Most appointments were controlled by the Democrats because they held a majority of seats on the board. Chief of Police Jeremiah Crowley had formerly worked for the U.S. Marshal's Office and the Washington Suburban Sanitation Commission. He had also served one term in the Maryland House of Delegates and had been active in the Democratic party.

cost of $572 each. Chief of Police Jeremiah Crowley stands in the foreground beside Car 1. Next in line is Sgt. Hervey Machen, Sr., who also happened to own Suburban Motor Sales. County records reveal that two of the police cars were purchased from Machen's dealership. Possibly a conflict of interest by today's standards, but totally ethical and appropriate in 1931. Photo courtesy of Stanley Machen and Elsie Crowley Murrell

On June 1, 1931, the county commissioners arranged to rent the First National Bank Building in Hyattsville. Located at Gallatin Street and Rhode Island Avenue, this building would house the new county police substation and police court. The court, also newly created, would bring a judicial service to people residing in the more densely populated northern portion of Prince George's County.

Arrangements were also made to purchase eleven 1931 Ford 2-door sedans, which according to the commissioners' notes, were to be equipped with high-compression cylinder heads. The commissioners also noted that each automobile was to have "Prince George's County Police" painted on the side doors. The automobiles were purchased from various Ford dealerships within the county at a cost of $572 each. It was also specifically agreed that the new force would not use motorcycles. At the time, most police departments traditionally used motorcycles; however, the injury rate was high and for that reason the commissioners ruled out the use of such vehicles.

To ensure integrity and professionalize decorum, the county commissioners adopted a twelve-paragraph set of rules and regulations to govern the behavior of the county's new constables. *The Laurel Leader* commented that: "The new force is urged to be cautious at all times . . . not to loiter in poolrooms, garages, or bowling alleys." The new constables, dressed in olive drab–colored uniforms, assumed their duties as the county's new and expanded county police force. As with any new endeavor the county police force had more than its fair share of problems. Limited funding made the purchase of equipment difficult and the force's small size severely restricted the type of service that could be provided. Because the new constables received no training, they were forced to rely on their instincts and the shared knowledge of those members who had previous police experience. Due to an almost total lack of investigative expertise, the new force occasionally called on the District of Columbia Police Department in Washington for assistance when something out of the ordinary occurred. If a particularly complex crime was encountered, the county police also had the option of requesting specialized assistance from the Baltimore City Police Department.

One of the force's more experienced members, Sergeant Hervey Machen, Sr., died in June 1933. As a gesture of respect, the county commissioners cancelled their June 6 meeting to attend Sergeant Machen's funeral. The commissioners promoted Ralph Brown to the rank of sergeant, and placed him in charge of the Hyattsville Substation. Former Hyattsville town policeman Albert Anderson was selected to fill the vacant constable's position created by Sergeant Machen's death.

The county police force also celebrated its second anniversary in June 1933. An article in *The Enquirer-Gazette* of June 9, 1933, read, "Monday marked the completion of the second year of the county police force and Chief Crowley submitted statistics to show that 3,437 arrests have been made during that period by members of the police force besides thousands of civil papers."

Constables in the 1930s responded to a variety of calls for police service. It appears that an inordinate number of liquor and gambling complaints were received from a variety of highly vocal temperance organizations. Although federal Prohibition laws were repealed in 1933, the manufacture of illegal liquor remained popular. Gambling complaints remained a thorn in the force's side right up through the 1950s. In fact, the most serious and prolonged criticism of the early county police force stemmed from long-standing gambling operations, such as Jimmy LaFontaine's Place at Bladensburg Road and Eastern Avenue. In retrospect, it appears that the police failed to clamp down on LaFontaine with any degree of enthusiasm, but that his longevity was probably due to influences far beyond those normally found within a small police agency.

With the exception of the Hyattsville area, Prince George's County remained primarily rural with a 1930 population of 60,000 residents. County residents derived their income from a variety of occupations, with agriculture continuing to play an extremely important economic role. The well-entrenched homogeneous Southern culture of Prince George's County was not about to suddenly disappear, but the signs of change were inescapable. It was from within this down-home, close-knit environment that the constables provided their services. Most county residents were law-abiding citizens; accordingly, crime was not an overwhelming problem.

With Prince George's County encompassing a 386-square-mile jurisdiction, it was difficult for the eleven-man county police force to adequately serve all its citizens. One of the biggest hindrances in providing adequate service was the lack of police radios. Between 1927 and 1931, the force functioned without radios by establishing a procedure whereby the constables used gas station telephones to periodically call headquarters at Upper Marlboro in order to receive their calls for service. The constables would respond to the call and upon clearing it proceed to the next gas station and again call headquarters. This procedure was carried over to the new police force in 1931 and was used until August 1934.

Chief Crowley repeatedly asked the county commissioners to purchase police radios in the early 1930s, but the requests were always denied because of budgetary restrictions. In May 1934, the Young Men's Democratic Club of Hyattsville decided to raise money to purchase police radios by sponsoring two dances at the Beaver Dam Country Club. On August 10, 1934, the *Hyattsville Independent* announced that $846 had been raised and twelve radios would be purchased. Ten of the radios were placed in police cars, the remaining two were placed in the police stations.

The new radio system functioned on the Metropolitan Police Department's (MPDC) one-way radio frequency with calls being dispatched from the old Twelfth Precinct. County calls for service were received at the Upper Marlboro or Hyattsville stations. The information would then be telephoned to the MPDC dispatcher, who in turn would broadcast the call on three different occasions to ensure the likelihood of reception. The county scout car, as radio units were then called, responded to the scene, handled the call, and then telephoned a disposition to the station. The station then called the MPDC dispatcher and advised him of the car's status. Although awkward, this one-way radio system increased police efficiency, and was used until 1943 when the county police department received its own two-way radio network.

On December 4, 1934, Constable William E. Clifton resigned from the force to become the chief deputy sheriff for Prince George's County. A former election district constable by the name of Howard Slater was appointed to fill Constable Clifton's unexpired term. Mr. Clifton went on to become the county sheriff between 1939 and 1942. He also served in the Maryland House of Delegates and was once the county registrar of wills.

On May 23, 1935, Governor Harry W. Nice signed legislation permitting the county commissioners to hire a police desk clerk at a salary of $60 per month. Police strength was also increased from eleven to fifteen constables. The most unusual aspect of this legislation was that it reduced the constables' salaries by approximately ten percent. It is believed that this reduction occurred due to a taxpayers' revolt, which resulted in salary reductions for all county workers.

On June 3, 1935, the commissioners appointed Maurice J. Hampton, Edward D. Merson, Warren E. Peake, and John F. Dent, Jr., to fill the four new police positions. John Dent was assigned to the Upper Marlboro Station, the others were assigned to the more active Hyattsville Station.

According to the commissioners' records, $142 was spent to equip the new constables with "4 Colt Official Police Revolvers Caliber 38, 4 Folsum Tru-fit Holsters with Buck lacing and 4 pair of Peerless Handcuffs." Benjamin F. Beall was hired as the first civilian desk clerk and assigned to the Hyattsville Station. He was also given the duties of guard at the Hyattsville lockup with an additional salary of $28.50 per month.

Police agencies have been traditionally quasi-military organizations with strict rules and regulations governing appropriate police behavior. An interesting notation found in the county commissioners' meeting of July 16, 1935, reads as follows:

Ordered, that by unanimous action of this board the disciplinary action recommended in the report of the Chief of Police, dated July 15, 1935, for the admission by Officers Arthur Brown and Edward D. Merson, that they had an unauthorized person in their car during the pursuit of a robbery suspect on the night of July 9, 1935 at Cedar Heights, be amplified as follows:

The forfeiture of one month's pay each and the loss of their annual leave for one year; and That all members of the Force be informed of the disciplinary action taken; and That said Officers Brown and Merson be given the privilege of accepting the disciplinary action set forth herein, or stand trial before this Board; and that the said Officers signify their acceptance of this action taken in lieu of standing trial before this Board by signing their names in acceptance hereof on a copy of this order.

As of 1935, the investigative capabilities of the county police remained very limited. Because the force was still understaffed, no effort had been made to assign a policeman to plain clothes investigative duties. Uniformed officers continued to handle all criminal investigations resulting in an on-scene arrest. They also conducted follow-up investigations of obvious leads that might point to a particular suspect. Although only vague documentation exists, it is believed that detectives from the District of Columbia Police Department would informally assist the county police in some of their more routine follow-up investigations. The statewide practice of requesting that the governor assign specialized Baltimore City detectives to assist local jurisdictions in the investigation of unusually severe cases continued. The following are three well-known Prince George's County incidents that required the assistance of Baltimore City homicide detectives:

(1) 1930 — Brady Bombing. Occurring in the Seat Pleasant area, several people were killed by a bomb hidden in a Christmas package.

(2) 1931 — Colonial Tea House Murder. Several out-of-town gangsters entered a road-house in Bladensburg and shot up the place in a fusillade of gunfire. One man was killed and five people were wounded.

(3) 1935 — Loring Murder. A young woman who disappeared from her Mount Rainier home was found murdered in a nearby wooded area.

In late 1936, a scandal wracked the county police force. Six constables from the Hyattsville Station, a station clerk, justice of the peace, and a bondsman were indicted for an alleged "Bail Bond Racket." The scandal brought about radical changes within the county government and its police force. Almost half the names on police roster disappeared, and political influence on internal police operations was reduced. Stringent guidelines over police behavior were created and formal training was supposedly made mandatory. Manpower was about to be increased and a few police officers were about to be assigned certain specialized duties. The slow, agonizing birth of a modern police department was about to take place in Prince George's County.

Chief of Police Jeremiah Crowley formulated a twelve-paragraph set of departmental rules and regulations to govern the new police force. The regulations were approved by the Board of County Commissioners on June 9, 1931.

Upper Marlboro
June 9, 1931

Ordered, that the following rules and regulations, submitted by the Chief of Prince George's County Police, be approved by this Board:

---

1. The drinking of intoxicating liquors while on duty or in uniform is forbidden. Violations of this rule will subject the offender to suspension by the Chief, pending a hearing by the Board of County Commissioners.

2. Every member of the Police Force shall be subject to call at any hour, day or night, by the Chief, or in his absence by the Sergeant on duty at either the Marlboro or Hyattsville Station.

3. The Sergeant on duty at Headquarters, either in Marlboro or Hyattsville, shall have authority to act in the absence of the Chief in all cases, when the call is urgent and immediate service is necessary.

4. All Officers shall be assigned by the Chief to cover the several sections of the County, and shall be subject to change of location without notice.

5. Co-operation is absolutely necessary to the success of our efforts. Any member of the force refusing to cooperate with his fellow officers shall be subject to suspension by the Chief, pending a hearing by the Board of County Commissioners.

6. Insubordination will not be tolerated in any case. A violation of this rule will subject the offender to suspension by the Chief, and dismissal at the discretion of the Board of County Commissioners.

7. Should any member of the Police Force be accused of collusion, he shall have an opportunity to defend himself before the Board of County Commissioners, and if in their judgment he is guilty, dismissal shall follow.

8. Officers must not withhold information that may lead to the detection or prevention of a crime, or the apprehension of a criminal from his or their fellow officers. A violation of this rule, if proven, will result in suspension, and a repetition in dismissal.

9. All Officers shall be courteous as far as it is possible for them to be so, and shall use methods of force and intimidation only when in their judgment it is absolutely necessary in the interest of law and order.

10. Your revolver is furnished for your protection. You should be very careful in the use of it; it is your defense; you will not be justified in using it except when it is necessary to apprehend a criminal or fugitive from justice, or when you are reasonably certain that your life is in danger.

11. Officers, in making arrests, will take their prisoner to the Justice of the Peace nearest to the place of arrest, if he is not available, then the next nearest. Whenever it is possible for them to do so, Officers should take their prisoners to the Justice of the Peace for the District in which the arrest is made.

12. During the hours in which Officers are assigned to duty they must not loiter in public places, such as garages, pool rooms, bowling alleys or any other place of business except when it is necessary in the discharge of their duty.

Courtesy of the Maryland Hall of Records

The legislation separating the county police force from the sheriff's office also increased the force's strength to eleven constables at large. Shown in this 1931 photograph, taken on the Court House lawn in Upper Marlboro, are the eleven members of the new county police force. Pictured in the front row, left to right, are Claude Reese, Sgt. Arthur Hepburn, Chief of Police Jeremiah Crowley, Sgt. Hervey Machen, Sr. and Oscar Beall. Standing in the rear row, left to right, are Elon Turner, Willie Gray, Arthur Brown, Arnold Naylor, Ralph Brown, and Willie Clifton.
Photo courtesy of Hervey Machen, Jr., and Shirley Brown Teffeau

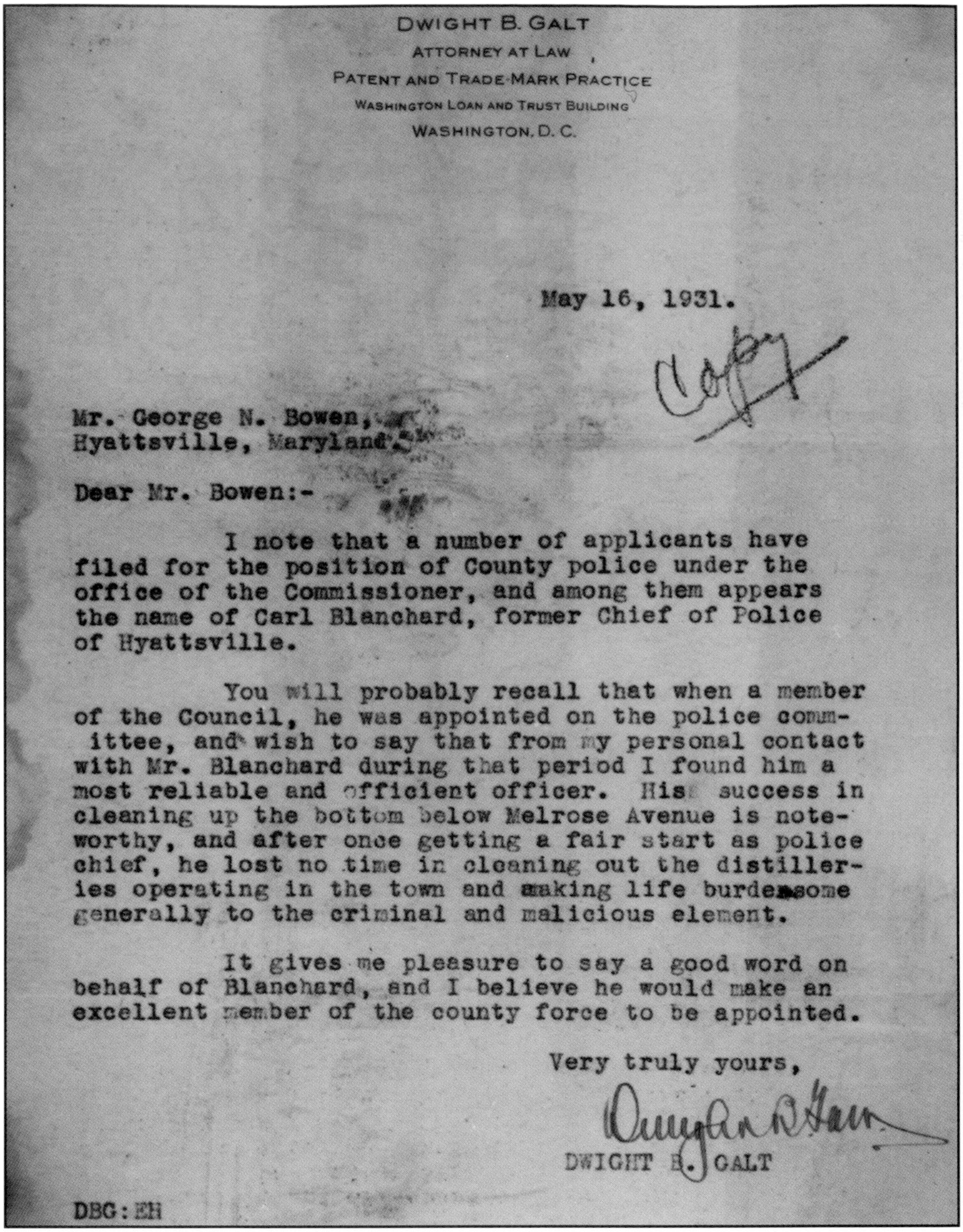

DWIGHT B. GALT
ATTORNEY AT LAW
PATENT AND TRADE-MARK PRACTICE
WASHINGTON LOAN AND TRUST BUILDING
WASHINGTON, D. C.

May 16, 1931.

Mr. George N. Bowen,
Hyattsville, Maryland.

Dear Mr. Bowen:-

I note that a number of applicants have filed for the position of County police under the office of the Commissioner, and among them appears the name of Carl Blanchard, former Chief of Police of Hyattsville.

You will probably recall that when a member of the Council, he was appointed on the police committee, and wish to say that from my personal contact with Mr. Blanchard during that period I found him a most reliable and efficient officer. His success in cleaning up the bottom below Melrose Avenue is noteworthy, and after once getting a fair start as police chief, he lost no time in cleaning out the distilleries operating in the town and making life burdensome generally to the criminal and malicious element.

It gives me pleasure to say a good word on behalf of Blanchard, and I believe he would make an excellent member of the county force to be appointed.

Very truly yours,

DWIGHT B. GALT

DBG:EH

Written criteria for the selection of policemen were nonexistent until 1937. Before the force's 1937 reorganization, policemen were selected based on their contacts and political affiliation. Since the Democratic party held a majority of seats on the Board of County Commissioners, most appointments came as a result of actions taken by the Democratic commissioners. An article in the May 23, 1931, edition of The Laurel Leader *explained that Democratic constables were chosen by the Democratic commissioners while the Republican members of the force were selected by the Republican commissioners.*

The practice of forwarding letters of recommendation to the county commissioners was also commonplace. A review of the minutes of the commissioners' meetings for the early 1930s reveals that hundreds of such recommendations were received for the few police openings that were available. Not only were these letters received from individual citizens, but many community, social, and fraternal organizations advocated the appointment of particular individuals. The letter of recommendation shown here was written on behalf of Carl Blanchard, and directed to County Commissioner George Bowen by Dwight Galt, an attorney and former Hyattsville town councilman. Mr. Blanchard did not receive an appointment to the county police force, but was appointed as a volunteer election district constable in Hyattsville.
Letter courtesy of Ms. Sandy Hall

No Disguise Here

UNIFORM ESTABLISHES CON-STABLE'S IDENTITY.

CARL M. BLANCHARD.

Tired of hearing persons whom he arrested complain that they thought he was a hold-up man because of his civilian clothes, Constable Blanchard of Hyattsville has outfitted himself with this uniform. He claims to have been the first Prince Georges County constable to discard civilian dress.

—Star Staff Photo.

Even with the formation of a professional county police force, the more-than-two-century-old tradition of appointing volunteer election district constables continued. However, the importance of the volunteer constables' role diminished with the employment of full-time county policemen.

After an unsuccessful bid to receive an appointment to the new county police force, Carl M. Blanchard accepted an appointment as a volunteer constable from the Hyattsville area. Constable Blanchard, who had previously served as a full-time chief of police in Hyattsville, was unique because he wore a uniform to distinguish himself as a law enforcement officer. Undoubtedly, the uniform was a carry over from his employment in Hyattsville.

Washington Star *photo courtesy of Ms. Sandy Hall*

Note: This newspaper photo was almost lost to posterity in a house fire. The dark areas on the top portion of the clipping are scorch marks from the fire.

On July 7, 1931, the county commissioners, with the permission of Circuit Court Judge Joseph Mattingly, authorized the establishment of a temporary headquarters for the police force in the witness room of the old courthouse in Upper Marlboro. It is believed that the police remained in this temporary location until July 1933. The following notation was found in the minutes for the county commissioners' meeting of June 13, 1933:

Ordered, that the Chief of Police be authorized to transfer the Headquarters of the Police Force from the Court House to the Pumphrey Building, adjoining the Court House Grounds, and that not to exceed $30.00 per month be paid for the rent of the two rooms beginning July 1, 1933.

The town of Upper Marlboro was surveyed in 1704, and became the county seat upon completion of the second courthouse in 1721. The third courthouse was erected in 1801 and remained in use until the building shown on this page was completed in 1880. The east and west courthouse wings were added in 1895. Although it might be hard to believe, this 1880 Victorian structure still stands in the town of Upper Marlboro. In 1940, the old courthouse was enlarged and remodeled into the structure that now is on Main Street. The old walls of the 1880 building can still be seen in some of the interior hallways of our modern courthouse.

Old courthouse photo courtesy of an unknown person

Remodeled 1940 courthouse.
Photo copied from an Upper Marlboro Town publication

Believed to have been taken at the rear of the old courthouse, this 1931 photograph shows the men originally assigned to police headquarters in Upper Marlboro. Sitting, left to right, are Sgt. Arthur Hepburn, Chief of Police Jeremiah Crowley, and Arnold Naylor. Standing, left to right, are Oscar Beall, Willie Gray, and Elon Turner. Note the fancy design on the ties worn by Naylor and Turner.
PGPD photo

Legislation enacted in 1931 required that the county furnish space in the Hyattsville area for a police court and county police substation. To comply with this mandate, the county commissioners authorized the lease of the First National Bank Building at a cost of $450 per month. The building, which still stands at Rhode Island Avenue and Gallatin Street, was renamed the Metropolitan District Building. It was used as a courthouse and police station until the County Service Building was dedicated in 1939.
Photo courtesy of Francis Geary

This poem, titled "Our Protectors," was clipped from an unknown Hyattsville newspaper by the family of Policeman Willie Clifton. The contemporary reader is left with the distinct impression that the citizens of the Hyattsville area held their county police in high esteem. Names of the policemen mentioned in the poem date the newspaper to between 1931 and 1933.
Poem clipping courtesy of Charles Ward

*These policemen were assigned to the Hyattsville
Substation in 1931. Sitting, left to right, are Claude
Reese, Sgt. Hervey Machen, Sr., and Ralph Brown.
Standing, left to right, are Willie Clifton and Arthur
Brown. Note the crossdraw holsters. This photograph
was probably taken inside the First National Bank
Building, because there appears to be a bank teller's
cage in the background.*
PGPD photo

THE COLONIAL TEA HOUSE MURDER

The date is November 23, 1931. A narrow column headline on the front page of the *Washington Star* reads, "One Slain, 5 Shot As Six Gunmen Raid Roadhouse." The incident, which the newspapers dubbed the Colonial Tea House Murder, occurred in an old and historic Bladensburg home. The home, just recently rented out, sat on a hill just south of Annapolis Road in Bladensburg. Evidence developed during the ensuing investigation indicates that the home was rented to a group of Philadelphia people who were using it for the sale of liquor, gambling, and prostitution.

The *Washington Star* reported that six holdup men entered the house shortly before 3:00 a.m. The bandits, as the newspaper called them, found four women and three men playing cards in the kitchen. After producing revolvers and a sawed-off shotgun, the holdup men ordered the victims to stand with their hands over their heads and their faces toward the wall. As one gunman stood by the victims, the others went through the house, corralling nine people into the kitchen. One of the gunmen started to complain about the victims' "holding out" after obtaining only $325 in cash. An argument ensued during which one of the gunmen panicked and started to fire his weapon. The other gunmen apparently "became alarmed and believing they were in danger of capture decided to shoot their way out." Grover Amick, a 28-year-old Washington man and customer was killed. Mr. Amick died of two gunshot wounds to the back, five other people were seriously wounded. Most of the gunmen drove off in their automobiles, but two were believed to have escaped on foot. It was later found that the holdup men had disabled all the cars outside of the house by removing their distributors. According to the newspaper this was done so that "none of the machines could be used to pursue them." The victims were transported to Casualty Hospital in the District of Columbia.

County police and volunteer election district constables from the Bladensburg area responded to the scene and immediately developed information connecting the robbery with certain people from Philadelphia. Prior to leaving the scene, county police authorities called the Philadelphia Police and requested that they arrest two individuals in connection with the robbery/murder.

Within several days of the crime, information was developed indicating that robbery was not the prime motivation behind the crime. The situation may have been precipitated by a feud between two rival Phildelphia vice gangs which were in the business of "trafficking pretty girls in a chain of establishments between Scranton, Pennsylvania and Washington, D.C." It was also determined that one of the shooting victims, Thomas Simone, was probably a member of the holdup gang who had

been accidentally shot by one of his compatriots. Another complicating, but interesting fact was that two of the Colonial Tea House robbery victims, John Bartlett, (alias "Man of War") and John Marche, were wanted by Pennsylvania authorities for two separate and unrelated murders.

Because the county police had no real investigative experience, a decision was made to request assistance from the more experienced Baltimore City Detective Bureau. Lt. Cornelius Roche and Sgt. William Feehley of the Baltimore City Police Department were assigned to complete all follow-up investigative work. It was a common state-wide practice for rural jurisdictions to call in more experienced city detectives when confronted with particularly complex criminal investigations. The Federal Bureau of Investigation also entered the investigation because of the White Slave Traffic Act (interstate transportation of women for purposes of prostitution). As a result of the initial contact between the county police and the Philadelphia Police, several people were arrested by the FBI and charged with violating the Federal Prostitution Law.

The local and federal investigation of this incident took place over an extended period of time. Official records of the case have never been located, but numerous newspaper articles report a large-scale investigation involving many arrests. These accounts reveal that most arrests were for investigative purposes and that only a few people were formally charged in connection with the Colonial Tea House Murder. Although the information is vague and confusing, it appears that those people charged with the Grover Amick murder asked for a change of venue and were actually tried in Charles County.

The Colonial Tea House Murder caused additional problems for the recently formed and somewhat inexperienced county police force. Maryland law, then in effect, required that a coroner's jury be convened to examine the facts of any suspicious death and that the jury submit a finding of facts to the state's attorney. Rumors circulated that the witnesses had been threatened and some were unwilling to testify.

A coroner's jury met at the Bladensburg Fire House on December 4, 1931. The federal prisoners, arrested for violating the Federal Prostitution Law, were among those summoned to testify. A number of local citizens and newspaper reporters gathered at the firehouse to hear the testimony. Because no photographs were allowed to be taken at the hearing, many of the newspaper photographers gathered outside the firehouse hoping to take pictures as the witnesses and suspects left the building. On duty outside the firehouse were County Policemen Ralph Brown and volunteer Election District Constable Howard Slater. These officers supposedly told the newspaper photographers that the U.S. Marshal did not want pictures taken of the federal prisoners. As the prisoners left the building after the hearing, several of the newsmen attempted to snap photographs in defiance of the police order. During the ensuing commotion, Constable Slater hit a *Washington Daily News* photographer over the head with his blackjack. According to one account,

Constable Slater grabbed a newsman's camera and "stamped upon and broke up the camera." In the meantime, Officer Brown was busy with another newspaper man attempting to snap photographs. Brown is reported as having confiscated the newsman's camera. The newsman Constable Slater encountered was arrested and charged with disorderly conduct and assault on a police officer.

A hearing on the charges against the *Washington News* photographer was held in Hyattsville Police Court on December 9, 1931. Judge J. Chew Sheriff, after hearing testimony from a number of witnesses, found the defendant not guilty. The *Washington Star* reported that the photographer was found not guilty by the judge "laying stress on the fact that the photographer was backing away from the officer holding his camera in one hand and flashlight in the other, at the time of the alleged assault."

Several complaints against the officers' actions were received by both the county commissioners and the governor. At the request of Governor Ritchie, a representative from the attorney general's office attended the news photographer's trial and forwarded a report to the governor stating in part, "Under the facts as developed in this case, I would unhesitatingly recommend that you request the County Commissioners for Prince George's County to take disciplinary measures against Officers Brown and Slater. I personally am inclined to think that they should both be dismissed from the force."

On December 22, 1932, the Board of County Commissioners held a hearing in reference to the complaints against County Policeman Brown and Constable Slater. According to the records, eight people gave testimony before the commissioners. After deliberating the commissioners voted "that the resignation of Constable Howard Slater, Berwyn District, be requested ... that County Policeman Ralph Brown be retained on the County Police Force, but that he be reprimanded; and that the Police Force be warned that the County Commissioners will not tolerate abuse of the public."

PARTHENON HEIGHTS

The Colonial Tea House was located to the south side of Annapolis Road. Situated on a hill between historic Bostwick (1746) and the new Bladensburg Elementary School, the old home was better known by its estate name of "Parthenon". Records reveal that the estate was known to some people as "War View," evidently because the home looked out over the fields where the Battle of Bladensburg was fought.
Photo courtesy of the Prince George's County Historical Society

County Policemen Claude Reese (left) and Willie Clifton (right) pose for this photo with a handcuffed moonshiner (center) following a raid on his still. Photo courtesy of Charles Ward

PROHIBITION

Prohibition was never well received in the state of Maryland. Within Prince George's County, the people seemed to be divided as to whether they were for or against the so-called wet laws. In a 1919 referendum, 3,010 county residents voted to adopt a local law to "forever prohibit" the sale and use of alcoholic beverages. The proposed legislation was narrowly defeated by a vote of 3,900 residents who were opposed to any such law. State-wide, the ten local jurisdictions affected by the legislation rejected the local option by a vote of 75,137 to 29,921.

In 1918, the General Assembly voted to adopt the Eighteenth Amendment to the U.S. Constitution. Although Prohibition was unpopular with most Marylanders, many local legislators succumbed to long-term pressure from the Women's Christian Temperance Union and Anti-Saloon League and voted for the amendment. A sufficient number of states reacted favorably to the amendment and it became law in 1920. Thus began what famous Baltimore newspaper man H. L. Mencken termed "Those Thirteen Dreadful Years."

Within a short period of time, legislation was submitted to withdraw Maryland's ratification of the amendment, with legislators calling the law "vexatious, iniquitous, and obnoxiously un-American." Governor Ritchie, a strong anti-Prohibition foe, was much milder in his rhetoric saying that "farmers should have the right to make cider and light wine, and that the laboring man and people in general want and should not be denied beer and light wines." However, Prohibition was now the law of the land, and those who had zealously fought for its adoption were not about to give up the fruits of their labor without a long hard fight.

Prince George's County found itself squarely in the middle of the fight over Prohibition. There was a good market for moonshine in both Washington and Baltimore and a lot of money could be made without much risk. The county's geographic location to the marketplace and its remoteness made it the ideal place to operate a moonshiner's still. Crain Highway became known as Bootleg Boulevard and proved to be a thoroughfare for the transportation of south county moonshine into the cities of Washington and Baltimore. Federal agents from the Bureau of Prohibition complained that they had very little cooperation in the Old Line State, and that their agents "were thrown to the wolves over there."

During the early years of Prohibition, no full-time local law enforcement agency existed within Prince George's County other than the sheriff and his one full-time deputy. Accordingly, the thrust of county efforts to enforce Prohibition laws came from volunteer deputy sheriffs and constables who were scattered throughout the county. To better deal with the problems of illegal liquor, the county commissioners appointed special constables who were solely responsible for enforcing Prohibition laws. On May 30, 1924, Special Constable Allen M. Chase was shot and killed during a raid on a moonshiner's still in the Tuxedo area.

It appears that county officials took a somewhat hard line with Prohibition enforcement. County records reveal that the state's attorney, Allen Bowie, was continually asking for additional funding to pursue his enforcement of the so-called wet laws. Available court records reveal that substantial fines were being imposed on those convicted of violating the liquor laws. It would also seem probable that local proponents of Prohibition lent a strong voice in supporting the creation of a full-time county police force. The formation of a full-time police force would act to suppress those who manufactured and sold alcoholic beverages.

Although the people of Prince George's County were evenly divided as to Prohibition, most other state residents had strong anti-Prohibition sentiments. Generally speaking, Americans did not like the idea of Prohibition and the law was in fact doomed. On December 6, 1933, the state of Utah joined thirty-six other states and voted for ratification of the Twenty-first Amendment, thus ending what the *Baltimore Sun* termed "13 years, 10 months, 19 days, 17 hours, 27 minutes, and 30 seconds of Prohibition."

THE SUN

Hegemony Over China Now
Occupies Powers, By
Wilbur Burton
—Page 2

VOL. 194—D.   PAID CIRCULATION NOVEMBER MORNING 173,011 / EVENING 98,091   270,542   SUNDAY 184,438   BALTIMORE, WEDNESDAY, DECEMBER 6, 1933   26 PAGES   2 CENTS

PROHIBITION ENDED
Lindbergh And Wife On Atlantic Hop

COUPLE LEAVE WEST AFRICA FOR BRAZIL

Flyers, Becalmed Since Saturday, Face 1,900 Miles Of Open Sea

HOMEWARD-BOUND AFTER LONG TRIP

The Great Game Of Politics
By FRANK R. KENT

Just Dumb

Washington, Dec. 5.
THE REPUBLICAN attack today upon the Roosevelt program is a fine illustration of the lack of political intelligence that characterizes the management of that befuddled and enfeebled party. It comes pretty close to the height of futility. They might just as well whistle in the face of an eigh...

HOUSE GROUP PLANS TO RAISE $237,000,000

Would Increase U. S. Receipts By Changes In Revenue Act Of 1932

INCOME TAX USED AS NEW SOURCE

Increase Made In Some Rates While Eight Loopholes Are Plugged

Text Of President's Repeal Proclamation
(By the Associated Press)

Washington, Dec. 5—The text of President Roosevelt's repeal proclamation follows:

Whereas the Congress of the United States in second session of the Seventy-second Congress, begun at Washington on the 5th day of December in the year one thousand nine hundred and thirty-two, adopted a resolution in the words and figures following, to wit:

JOINT RESOLUTION

Proposing an amendment to the Constitution of the United States.

Resolved by the Senate and the House of Representatives of the United States of America in Congress assembled (two-thirds of each House concurring therein), that the following article is hereby proposed as an amendment to the Constitution of the United States, which shall be valid to all intents and purposes as a part of the Consti...

States, as provided in the Constitution, within seven years from the date of the submission hereof to the States by the Congress.

Whereas, Section 217 (A) of the act of Congress entitled "an act to encourage national industrial recovery, to foster competition and to provide for the construction of certain useful public works, and for other purposes" approved June 16, 1933, provides as follows:

Sec. 217 (A) The President shall proclaim the date of:

(1) The close of the first fiscal year ending June 30 of any year after the year 1933, during which the total receipts of the United States "excluding public debt receipts" exceed the total expenditures (excluding public debt expenditures other than those chargeable against such receipts), or

(2) The repeal of the Eighteenth Amendment to the...

PRESIDENT PROCLAIMS REPEAL EFFECTIVE AFTER UTAH CASTS FINAL VOTE

Thirty-Sixth State Acts At 5.33 P. M., And Seven Minutes Later Phillips Certifies Ratification Of 21st Amendment

ROOSEVELT URGES PEOPLE TO BAR RETURN OF SALOON

Baltimore Sun *front page courtesy of Fred DeMarr*

These two photographs were contributed by Herbert "Fritz" Harrison. Chief of Police Jeremiah Crowley hired Fritz as his driver - not a perquisite for the new police chief, but a necessity because the chief did not have a driver's license.

In this early 1930s picture (right), Chief Crowley is shown overseeing the destruction of seized moonshine. Policeman Elon Turner prepares to throw a Ball jar of moonshine into the Western Branch as Sgt. Arthur Hepburn stands on the bridge railing. It is believed that this bridge stood near the present-day intersection of Routes 725 and 202 in Upper Marlboro.

With the introduction of Prohibition in 1920, bootlegging became the crime of preference for those who did not mind breaking the law to make a quick buck. When interviewed in 1981, Fritz Harrison, then a septuagenarian, recounted that as a young man he could clearly recall lying in bed on a hot summer night and hearing the whine of a Model A Ford as it traveled the road between Marlboro and Bladensburg. The natural quiet of a hot summer's night was only occasionally interrupted by the outburst of gunfire. Mr. Harrison indicated that the sound of an automobile's acceleration whine and gunfire usually meant that hijackers were attempting to waylay a load of moonshine making its way into the city.

Written on the back of this time worn picture (left) are the words "Herbert's car, waiting for Chief Crowley."

Photos courtesy of Fritz Harrison

County police cars were not equipped with police radios until the summer of 1934. Police officers on patrol duty remained in contact with their stations by periodically calling in from service-station telephones. Collins Service Station, located on Marlboro Pike in Forestville, was probably one of the places that the officers used to contact the Upper Marlboro Station. The site of this station is now occupied by a modern-day, self-service Amoco Gas Station. The old house still stands but has been moved back from its original location next to the roadway.
Photo courtesy of Willard Entwisle

Piscataway Tavern. While signs of urbanization were rapidly changing the north county's landscape, many south county communities were able to retain their rural nineteenth-century appearance well into the mid-twentieth century.
Photo by John Brostrup, courtesy of the Prince George's County Historical Society

Sgt. Hervey G. Machen, Sr., died in early June 1933. On June 5, 1933, the Board of County Commissioners promoted Ralph Brown to the rank of sergeant. The board then voted to cancel their next meeting so they could attend Sgt. Machen's funeral.

Shown left to right in this 1933 photograph are: Sgt. Ralph Brown, Chief of Police Jeremiah Crowley, and Sgt. Arthur Hepburn. Sergeant Brown, upon being promoted, was placed in charge of the Hyattsville Substation. Sergeant Hepburn remained in charge of the Upper Marlboro Station.
PGPD photo

Both of these newspaper photos, which date back to the mid-1930s, relate to what an unidentified newspaper called a "shooting, beating, and cutting." The sixty-five-year-old suspect used a gun, knife, and hammer to kill his sixty-year-old wife, twenty-one-year-old daughter, and twenty-six-year-old son. Another daughter was seriously injured along with her fiance'. The short news article accompanying the photos stated that the suspect was "apparently motivated by a sudden maniacal frenzy." The article goes on to say that the suspect later "leaped to his death beneath a freight train last night after the wholesale slaying at his home, one hundred feet across the District line on Queens Chapel Road." News clipping courtesy of Mrs. Harold Russell

This 1935 newspaper photograph captioned "Safe in the Arms of the Law" relates to an incident wherein two children wandered away from their home in the Sunnyside area of Berwyn. Police were called to conduct a search and found both children in a nearby swampy area.

Many social and technological changes have occurred to alter the nature of police work in the last fifty years. However, one aspect of the work that remains constant is that special gratifying feeling that an officer receives upon returning a lost child to his or her home.
Washington Herald *photo courtesy of Neva Reese*

Early photograph of Baltimore Boulevard or U.S. Route 1. Long established as a major north-south roadway, this state roadway was hard surfaced and well maintained.
Photo courtesy of the Prince George's County Historical Society

Taken in the mid-1930s, this photograph depicts Sgt. Ralph Brown wearing a three-quarter-length black leather uniform jacket.
Photo courtesy of Shirley Brown Teffeau

The county's early population growth occurred in several north-side incorporated towns near the District of Columbia line. Accordingly, those town governments were the first to hear a public hue and cry for increased police protection. The county government was able to distance itself from the demands for improved police services because most new residents resided within those municipalities already having a town police department.

On November 4, 1935, a young Mt. Rainier woman named Corinna Loring was reported missing from her Beach Street home. Miss Loring's body was found two days later on Saddleback Ridge. It appears that the victim had been "garroted" with a piece of twine. Although both the Mt. Rainier Police and county police were called to the scene, the actual criminal investigation was conducted by detectives from the Baltimore City Police Department. The case was never solved, although newspaper accounts reveal that information on a suspect was still being presented to a Grand Jury in late 1936.

Mt. Rainier Police Chief Eugene Plummer examines the crime scene. Saddleback Ridge is now the site of the Kaywood Garden Apartments.

Evidentiary photo with Miss Loring's home being circled as location No. 1. The crime scene is identified as location No. 2. On a present-day map, Beech and Cedar streets carry the respective names of Taylor and Upshur streets.

Photos courtesy of Shirley Brown Teffeau

	—1936—	—1937—
Commissioners (salaries)	$1,425.00	$1,500.00
Clerk to commissioners	2,375.00	2,500.00
Deputy clerk to commissioners	1,140.00	1,200.00
Secretary to clerk	1,560.00	1,760.00
Counsel to commissioners	900.00	900.00
Clerk to Circuit Court	1,560.12	2,291.88
County treasurer	9,750.00	11,160.00*
Transfer clerk	1,140.00	1,500.00
Keeper of Court House	1,350.00	1,350.00
Guard to jail	1,387.00	1,460.00
Almshouse	9,000.00	11,000.00
Supervisor of assessments	2,584.00	3,010.00
Clerk to supervisor	2,500.00	2,500.00
State's Attorney	2,375.00	4,200.00*
Sheriff	8,046.32	8,865.00*
Orphan's Court	1,641.60	1,728.00
County agent	1,800.00	1,800.00
Jail warden (for meals)	4,565.20	4,720.60
Jail physician	100.00	100.00
Fuel, Court house and jail	1,500.00	1,500.00
Bovine T. B. Eradication	3,000.00	3,000.00
Health officer	2,000.00	2,000.00
Home Dem. Agent	1,575.00	1,575.00
Messenger, Orphan's Court	144.00	144.00
Local Farm Agent (colored)	615.00	615.00
Public schools	439,488.00	467,800.00
Magistrates Acc'ts.	4,742.85	4,207.55
Fox scalps	252.00	564.00
Interest, lateral road bonds	11,577.50	11,577.50
Interest, court house bonds	1,850.00	1,750.00
Interest, jail bonds	1,800.00	1,800.00
Interest, school bonds	66,422.50	66,085.00
Interest, county road bonds	24,750.00	24,750.00
Interest, Edmonston road bonds	5,785.00	5,595.00
Jurors and Bailiffs	14,000.00	11,500.00
Stenographer for Cir. Ct.	1,140.00	1,200.00
Maryland Training school for boys	5,500.00	4,500.00
Defense of criminals	805.00	530.00
Expert witnesses, etc.	890.00	1,495.00
Registration, vital statistics	405.43	387.68
Out-pensioners	1,545.00	no levy
Jurors of Inquest	302.00	245.00
Hawk heads	110.40	87.90
Public printing	1,328.50	754.00
Store accounts	324.85	no levy
Taxes refunded	309.80	828.63
Burying paupers	875.00	670.00
Miscellaneous	4,068.98	3,243.40
House of Reformation	3,700.00	3,500.00
Trials removed cases	441.50	no levy
Police Department	36,000.00	56,000.00
Social worker	2,400.00	2,400.00
Redemption, school bonds	28,000.00	41,000.00
Redemption, ct. house bonds	2,000.00	2,000.00
Redemption, Edmonston road bonds	4,000.00	4,000.00
Md. Training school for colored girls	500.00	no levy
Montrose school for girls	600.00	no levy
Indigent blind	2,000.00	1,530.00
Md. Children's Aid Society	6,000.00	no levy
Exam., indigent mental patients	295.00	320.00
Old-age pensions	10,000.00	13,000.00
Aid to Dependent children	6,519.58	6,750.82
Roads	78,235.00	no levy
Surplus for emergencies	6,038.25	6,306.36
Total	839,035.38	$835,655.32

A comparison of the county government's budget for 1936 and 1937 notes a substantial increase in monies being allocated to the police department. An examination of the budget reveals some interesting information concerning the lifestyle of Prince George's County during the 1930s. Make note of the bounty money set aside for Fox Scalps and Hawk Heads.

This comparison was found in the Prince George's Post *of April 30, 1937.*

Allegations of police scandal, which the newspapers termed "The Bail Bond Racket," surfaced in the fall of 1936. Under state law, out-of-state motorists charged with traffic violations were not entitled to a personal summons; accordingly, the arresting officer brought them before a local justice of the peace. The motorists then posted a cash bond, or hired a bondsman to guarantee his appearance in court. If neither option was met, the motorists simply went to jail until the next available court date. The allegation in the Bail Bond Racket was that bond fees were being split between the bondsman, justice of the peace, and police officer. It was also alleged that some policemen and a bondsman had conspired to arrange "bargain fines" for motorists who were willing to pay a price to have some of their more serious traffic charges dropped.

In December 1936, the Grand Jury returned a criminal conspiracy indictment against policemen Warren Peake, Claude Reese, Arthur Brown, Albert Anderson, Maurice Hampton, and Howard Slater. Police desk clerk Frank Beall was also charged along with Hyattsville Justice of the Peace Herbert Moffat and bondsman Elmer Pumphrey. On December 15, 1936, the county commissioners suspended, without pay, all police personnel indicted by the Grand Jury.

Work on proposed legislation to create "a new police system" began shortly after the Bail Bond Scandal surfaced. The proposed law gave the county commissioners a second title of "Police Commissioners for Prince George's County," requiring that the new police commissioners meet at least once a month for the sole purpose of discussing police matters. Strength of the new police force was set at eighteen "police officers . . . one of whom . . . shall be designated Superintendent of the Prince George's County Police." Each police applicant was required to pass " a mental and a physical examination." Present members of the force were exempt from taking the physical examination. Education and "mental adaptability" were also factors to be considered when determining an applicant's qualifications to become a police officer. Each officer, including those reappointed from the old force, was to serve a six-month probationary period before receiving permanent employment status, thus, eliminating the old requirement that officers be reappointed every two years. For the first time, the chief, or now superintendent of police, had the authority to suspend, or otherwise discipline members of the force. Officers retained the right to appeal disciplinary actions to the county commissioners. The law further required that the county provide training for probationary officers, and that other officers receive periodic retraining. The superintendent's annual salary was set at $2,500, sergeants' at $1,900, and police officer's at $1,500. Probationary officers were to receive $100 per month and all officers were also allotted $60 annually for the purchase of uniforms.

The legislation, entitled Chapter 50 of the Acts of the General Assembly of 1937, received a strong endorsement from the Prince George's County Federation of Citizens Associations and was signed into law by Governor Harry W. Nice on March 17, 1937. On that same day, all nine of the actively working county policemen submitted their immediate resignations. The commissioners then recessed their meeting for the purpose of reorganizing the county police force. At four o'clock, the commissioners reconvened and reappointed eight of the nine members who had resigned. The commissioners, feeling that the force needed new direction, chose not to reappoint Chief Crowley.

The March 19, 1937 edition of the *Prince George's Post* reported that Chief Jeremiah Crowley was ousted from the force's top position and replaced by Sgt. Arthur W. Hepburn. The paper quotes Chief Crowley as saying that the actions of the commissioners did not surprise him. Other members of the force to receive appointments were Sgt. Ralph Brown, and "Privates" Jack Dent, Edward Merson, Elon Turner, Arnold Naylor, William Gray, and Oscar Beall. Melvin Kent was appointed as a desk clerk at the Hyattsville Station. Another six members of the force remained on suspension awaiting trail in connection with the Bail Bond Racket. During this period, Elon Turner was promoted to the rank of sergeant and placed in command of the Upper Marlboro Station. In May 1937, the police commissioners began conducting mental and physical examination of 117 men who had applied for employment as police officers. In late June, the *Washington Star* announced that effective July 1, 1937, ten new police officers would be appointed to the county force. Those receiving appointments were identified as Earl J. Huber, Charles N. Thomsen, Andrew J. Carrigan, Louis J.

Mackall, Lawson L. Peed, Richard J. Earnshaw, Richard A. Pearson, Edwin C. Cissel, Roscoe C. Sines, and Charles F. McGuire. The commissioners had now fully staffed the force and thus effectively prohibited the reemployment of any of those policemen on suspension because of the Bail Bond Racket.

The trial of those charged in the Bail Bond Racket began July 12, 1937, and lasted through nine days of testimony. The jury received the case at about 2:55 p.m. on July 22, 1937, and deliberated for forty minutes before returning a not guilty verdict. The *Prince George's Post* quoted jury foreman William McQueeney as saying that the verdict was "easy for the jurors." A comment in the *Washington Star* stated, "While the acquitted officers are now eligible to apply for their old jobs, no vacancies exist on the present force. Under a new county law applicants must pass a physical and mental test."

In August 1937, Sgt. Ralph Brown and Pvt. John Dent of the old force were selected to attend Session No. 64 of the Police Training School in Washington, D.C. Members of the new force selected to attend were Earl Huber, Louis Mackall, Charles McGuire, and Charles Thomsen. In 1938, Pvt. John Dent was selected to be the first county policeman to attend the FBI National Police Academy in Washington, D.C. Pvt. Dent graduated from the FBI Academy on November 19, 1938, and was thereafter used "as an instructor in the supplemental training courses for members of the force."

On September 1, 1937, Police Officer Edward D. Merson was killed in an automobile accident. Officer Merson was responding to a possible drowning at Blue Pond in Muirkirk when his automobile "left the roadway and struck a tree." Officer Merson was transported to Casualty Hospital in Washington, D.C., where he died of injuries received in the accident. Edward Dennis Merson was the first county policeman to die as a result of injuries received in the line of duty.

On September 3, 1937, the *Prince George's County Post* published a lengthy list of new county police regulations. The *Post* termed these rules as, "The Why, the How, and Don'ts of County Police Work." The paper further commented, "If county policemen are REQUIRED to live up to these regulations and are ALLOWED to live up to them, the county can have a police system to be proud of. Residents of the county, however, must know that they will have just so good a police service as they are willing to pay for, in money, and interest." It is believed that most of the county's new police regulations came directly from the MPDC's General Order Manual. During this time period, the term "police private" starts to make an occasional newspaper appearance when referring to county policemen. The term had been used by the Metropolitan Police for a number of years.

Notes of general interest found in the minutes of the Police Commissioners meetings are as follows:

On September 24, 1937, Henry C. Briscoe was hired as a police officer to replace Edward Merson.

As of December 24, 1937, the training of the force during their probationary period has been completed and each member has passed all tests creditably.

On March 25, 1938, the commissioners were invited to inspect photographic equipment and the paraphernalia for the identification of criminals recently set up at the Hyattsville Substation. (Note: This event marked the beginning of specialized police work within the county police force.)

In December 1938, Officer Oscar Beall left the force and was replaced by Francis A. Richards.

The December 8, 1938 *Prince George's Post* contained an article on a number of recommendations that the Chamber of Commerce had made regarding police department operations. One recommendation was that a rank of corporal be created, and that the corporal be placed in charge of the new Bureau of Identification in Hyattsville.

New legislation was enacted in 1938 increasing the department's strength to twenty-two police officers. On August 1, 1939, four new officers were appointed: Thomas Ray Blandford, Wilson Purdy, William C. Suit, and William R. Travers. John F. Dent and Louis Mackall were also promoted to the new rank of corporal.

Thus ended the decade of the 1930s. The police force had gone through a period of drastic change, but the promise of a new decade had rekindled the spark of professionalism and pride. The force had been rejuvenated with a transfusion of young police officers who looked to the future with enthusiasm and vigor.

Hepburn Gets County Chief Appointment

New Superintendent and Others Given Temporary Appointments for 4 Months

Arthur W. Hepburn was named superintendent of the Prince Georges county police by the board of commissioners, Wednesday, shortly after Gov. Nice had signed the bill creating a new police department set-up for the county.

Former Chief Jeremiah J. Crowley, who many thought might be re-appointed, refused to comment, other than to say: "I am not surprised."

The appointment of Superintendent Hepburn, who had been acting as a sergeant in charge of the Upper Marlboro sub-station, and others, was for a temporary period of four months. Appointments were made at a special session of the commissioners.

Among those named, other than Hepburn, were: Sgt. Ralph Brown and Private Jack Dent, Ed. Merson, Arnold Naylor, William Gray and Oscar Bell. Melvin Kent was reappointed desk clerk at the Hyattsville sub-station.

Merit System

The chief provision of the new law is for the establishment of a merit system. All new appointees to the force will be required to pass a standard test set up by the county commissioners, who are authorized under the new legislation, to act also as police commissioners.

One of the principal tasks confronting the commissioners is the selection of a superintendent to head the new force.

Under fire since a grand jury returned indictments against seven of his men in connection with an investigation of an alleged bonding racket,

12 Additional Men

In addition to a new chief, the commissioners also will be empowered to appoint 12 additional men to the department.

Although the law increases the force by only five men over the old act which fixed the number at 15, the indictment and suspension of seven officers leaves 12 positions to be filled.

The commissioners expect to complete reorganization of the force within a month.

This article from the Prince George's Post *of March 19, 1937, announced the appointment of Arthur W. Hepburn as the county's new superintendent of police. Courtesy of the* Prince George's Post

Page Twelve   THE PRINCE GEORGES PO

The PRINCE GEORGES POST

A COMMUNITY NEWSPAPER

Published Each Week by The Prince Georges Post, Inc., Business Office, 104 Maryland Ave., Hyattsville, Md. Entered as Second Class Mail, College Park, Md.

| Telephone Hyatt. 111 | Three Cents Per Copy One Dollar Per Year |

Adequate Compensation

Ten men have been selected for appointment to the county police force. These men have been chosen, at least in large measure, "without benefit of politics." At least they have been given an examination aimed at determining the degree of mental and physical fitness which they might bring to the job. That there has been some politics in the naming of these men may be admitted . . . it is difficult to keep what we term "politics" out of public office. Nor should it be so. It's the manner which politics is "played" by some that has given it the meaning more popularly applied to the term.

More important, however, than the politics of the thing is the thing itself . . . the county police force. An inspection of the men who have been named for appointment would indicate there will be a rather high type of citizen who will don the county police uniform the first of July. Some of them are outstanding. And there are outstanding men on the force now. These men will do much to raise the standard of the county police body to a level that will be a credit to themselves, and to the community which they serve.

But, more important even than the men who will make up the "rejuvinated" force is another factor . . . the attitude of the community toward the county police, not as individuals, but as an adjunct of the public life of the county. The police force will be just as efficient and trustworthy as the community will want it to be. And the future of the force will depend quite as much on the individuals of the county as on the individuals of the police force.

And the community must keep in mind that if it demands much it must be willing to give much in return. It must keep in mind that the county police force they might want cannot be maintained for long without adequate equipment with which to do the job required of them, and without adequate compensation to the men themselves. A police force that does function efficiently and judiciously is worth a lot more than it now receives. In other words, the time must come when the county will need match a worthwhile police force with worthwhile compensation.

Accounts in local newspapers supported the concept of improving and professionalizing the county police force. This editorial, espousing the county's need to "adequately compensate . . . the men who will make up the rejuvenated force," was published in the June 25, 1938 edition of the Prince George's Post. *Courtesy of the* Prince George's Post

COUNTY SEAT

News and Views of Prince Georges County From the County Seat

With the appointment of 10 men to fill the vacancies in the county police force, interest in the constabulary now simmers down to the selection of a superintendent.

Who this man will be, even the police commissioners do not know. But that each member of the board has his choice is certain. The reappointment of Acting Supt. Hepburn to serve during the six-months' probationary period was a stall, to allow the board to iron out its differences, according to well-informed circles.

Charlie Early, a former sheriff, whose widely-rumored candidacy for the job, was reported to have been viewed with favor by some of the more influential party leaders, appears now to be slipping out of the picture. Somewhat along in years, Early apparently was not overly anxious about the appointment. Had he been a keen aspirant for the office, most observers believe a way could have been found to effect his appointment.

In his present strategic position, Hepburn naturally is regarded as a strong possible choice for the position. Hale, hearty and well-met, "Hep" has a number of loyal supporters. Some possible significance may be attached to the fact that Hepburn announced his intention of attending the Washington police training school course beginning July 1.

Although these two candidates appeared at first to be the only ones under consideration, more recently other names have been rumored as possible appointees. Earl J. Huber, of Laurel, and Charles N. Thomsen, of Takoma Park, are the most prominently mentioned. Out of the 10 new appointees, these two were selected by the police commissioners to attend the Washington police training school. And we have it from reliable sources that these names were not merely drawn out of a hat.

During the 1930s, police cars were purchased and immediately assigned to an officer who was allowed to drive the vehicle back and forth to work. The officer also received an allowance for any maintenance work that was required. An interesting note from the commissioners' meeting of April 23, 1935, reads:
Ordered, that the report of J. J. Crowley, Chief of Police, with reference to the bill of Mr. Charles Beyer for repair to his automobile caused by a collision with the car of Officer Anderson, be accepted; and that the Clerk advise the Chief that the Commissioners do not carry property damage insurance on the County Automobiles and that Officer Anderson will have to take care of the bill in question. The 1937 Ford 2-door sedan shown here was assigned to Sgt. Brown of the Hyattsville Station. The radio-dispatched car was equipped with a one-way radio (note antenna on roof), siren, and spotlight. This particular photograph was probably taken at the Brown Farm, which was located on what is now the 6700 block of New Hampshire Avenue in Chillum.
Photo courtesy of Shirley Brown Teffeau

This police-related cartoon was published in the Prince George's Post on September 17, 1937. Ironically, directly next to the cartoon is a news story about the receipt of a letter of commendation for Police Officer Edward Merson. The letter, which addressed the officer's "courteous behavior and efficient performance of duties," was sent to the county commissioners one day prior to Officer Merson's line-of-duty death.
Courtesy of the Prince George's Post

Friday, September 17, 1937

THE GREAT AMERICAN HOME

BIG MOMENTS IN HISTORY.
REMEMBER WHEN YOU ACTUALLY GOT TOGETHER ENOUGH NERVE TO SPEAK TO A POLICEMAN.

R-R-R

NICE DAY, OFFICER !!!

COUNTY SEAT

News and Views of Prince Georges County From the County Seat

This is the story of how death intervened and robbed County Policeman Ed Merson of laurels that were due him.

Last May, the late Officer Merson was called to the home of Dr. W. M. Wooster in Berwyn on a report that someone had attempted to burn his home.

Merson's courteous behavior and efficient performance of his duties impressed the doctor. A week before the officer's sudden death, in an auto crash at Muirkirk, last week, Dr. Wooster penned a letter of commendation to the board of county commissioners. It read, in part:

"Especially do I wish to commend the good judgment and unusual official treatment accorded me by Officer Merson. He is a credit to your force and shows an excellent selection on your part."

The letter was received by Clerk James Heal, but the commissioners did not meet the following Tuesday and the letter received no public recognition. The next day Merson was killed.

Last Tuesday, when the commissioners met at Upper Marlboro, the letter was called to their attention —too late for the board to vote an official commendation.

EDWARD DENNIS MERSON

Killed in the line of Duty
September 1, 1937

Police Officer Edward Dennis Merson was the first member of the Prince George's County Police Department to be killed in the line of duty. Although a report of Officer Merson's death undoubtedly existed, it cannot be located. A verbal description of the incident, that has survived the passage of time, simply tells us that Officer Merson died in a single car automobile accident. More recently, several old newspaper accounts of the accident have been found, and they have shed some additional light upon the circumstances surrounding Officer Merson's death.

A lifelong resident of Laurel, Edward Merson was married and the father of two children. He served with the U.S. Army during World War I. After receiving his discharge, he worked for the Maryland Department of Roads. On June 3, 1935, he received an appointment to the county police force and was assigned to the Hyattsville Substation.

According to one unidentified newspaper, the incident resulting in Officer Merson's death occurred at 9:00 a.m., September 1, 1937. Officer Merson received an emergency call stating that a car was submerged in Blue Pond, and that it was thought that the occupants had drowned. The news account goes on to say that "Merson's police car left the Boulevard and crashed into a tree in Muirkirk." Merson was transported to Casualty Hospital located at Seventh and Constitution Avenue in northeast Washington by the Bladensburg Rescue Squad. At the hospital, it was determined that "he had been badly smashed, with severe cuts about his mouth and a fractured skull, causing his death a few hours later."

On September 10, 1937, the Prince George's Post reported that "Officer Merson was buried with military honors at Ivy Hill Cemetery in Laurel. Members of the county police acted as pallbearers and the Sons of the Legion were honorary pallbearers. The Laurel National Guard fired a salute."

On February 2, 1938, all members of the Prince George's County Police Department attended an advanced course in Red Cross First Aid. Shown in the front row of this photograph, from left to right are Chief Howard Homes of the Hyattsville Town Police Department, County Police Sgt. Ralph Brown, Supt. Arthur Hepburn, Sgt. Elon Turner, and George Gray. In the middle row are Edwin Cissel, Richard Pearson, Charles McGuire, John Dent, and Edwin Thompson. In the third row are Earl Huber, Richard Earnshaw, Charles Thomsen, Arnold Naylor, Roscoe Sines, and Lawson Peed. In the rear row are Pvts. Oscar Beall, Louis Mackall, and Henry Briscoe. Photo courtesy of Mrs. Edwin Cissel

It appears that no formal training of county police officers took place prior to 1937. With the addition of ten new patrolmen, the newly reorganized force made arrangements for six of its members to attend a three-month police training school at the Metropolitan Police Training School in Washington, D.C. Four of the attending officers were newly hired while the remaining two were from the old force.

MPDC Training Class 64 is pictured in front of the old Washington City Hall Building. Six county police officers attending the MPDC training stand to the far left of this photograph. Left to right in the first row are Sgt. Ralph Brown, Pvt. Louis Mackall, and Pvt. Earl Huber. In the second row are Pvts. Charles Thomsen, John Dent, and Francis McGuire. Photo courtesy of John Dent, Jr.

Four members of Class 64 stand next to Prince George's County police car No. 5. From left to right are Pvts. Earl Huber, Charles Thomsen, John Dent, and Louis Mackall.
Photo courtesy of John Dent, Jr.

John F. Dent of Piscataway received his appointment to the police force on June 3, 1935. Also appointed were Edward Merson, Maurice Hampton, and Warren Peake. In 1938, Officer Dent attended the twelve-week FBI National Police Academy in Washington, D.C. John Dent was the first county policeman selected to receive training at the FBI's National Academy.

Graduating members of Session No. 6, FBI National Police Academy, November 19, 1938. FBI Director J. Edgar Hoover is pictured in the middle of the front row. Officer John Dent is located in the second row, just behind Mr. Hoover's left shoulder.
Photo courtesy of John Dent, Jr.

The Dixie Pig was a well-known bar and eatery located at Peace Cross in Bladensburg. As shown in this photograph the area in and around Peace Cross was infamous for its flooding when anything more than a normal rain occurred. The Dixie Pig was also the victim of an occasional robbery, as detailed in this clipping from the June 2, 1938 issue of the Prince George's Post. *The news article refers to Officers Earl Huber and Edwin Thompson being inside a nearby restaurant "sipping coffee" when the "Pig Holdup" occurred.*
Photo courtesy of Francis Geary. News clipping courtesy of the Prince George's Post

Thursday, June 2, 1938

Police Find No Clues In Pig Holdup

ROBBERS ESCAPE WITH $600 IN CASH AFTER OVERPOWERING LONE ATTENDANT LAST THURSDAY.

County police were still searching at noon yesterday for a clue as to the identity of the two men who stuck up the Dixie Pig Barbecue in Bladensburg last Thursday and made a get-away with about $600 in cash.

Odell Hale, of Hyattsville, night counterman at the tavern, reported to police that he was alone in the establishment at the time of the robbery, which occurred about 5:30 a. m. He said a tall dark man entered and asked for aspirin tablets.

As Hale went to get some aspirins, the man stuck a gun in his back, hit him on the head and shoved him into a beer storage room. He stayed inside until he heard a car drive away, then bashed the door in and made his escape. He attempted to call police but found the bandits had cut the wires. He then ran across to the Del Rio where he found Officers Huber and Thompson sipping coffee.

Hale was questioned by the officers, taken to the Hyattsville station for further questioning, then taken to Washington to be queried by police there.

This Hyattsville photograph was taken in the late 1930s. Pictured left to right are Sgt. Ralph Brown, Justice of the Peace John Fainter, Supt. of Police Arthur Hepburn, Hyattsville Town Councilman William T. Jennings, and Officer Louis Mackall. Note the rabbit's foot in place of a whistle on Mackall's uniform.
Photo courtesy of Mrs. Ralph Brown

Down on the farm. Many of the policemen assigned to the Upper Marlboro Station in the late 1930s owned working farms. In this photograph, Officer Arnold Naylor and his partner Lawson Peed (with his foot on the front bumper) take a break form their patrol duties to say hello to Mrs. Peed and the children.
Photo courtesy of Elsie Peed

Firearms practice in the late 1930s. Left to right are Oscar Beall, Richard Pearson,
Supt. of Police Arthur Hepburn, Richard Earnshaw and John Dent. Note the cigarette
hanging from Chief Hepburn's mouth.
Photo courtesy of Mrs. Richard Earnshaw

Downtown Capitol Heights in the late 1930s. Although not as old as Hyattsville, the Capitol Heights and Seat Pleasant area developed as a working-class community of new homes in the early 1900s. Note the partially hidden sign advertising the cost of a haircut at thirty-five cents. Photo courtesy of an unknown donor

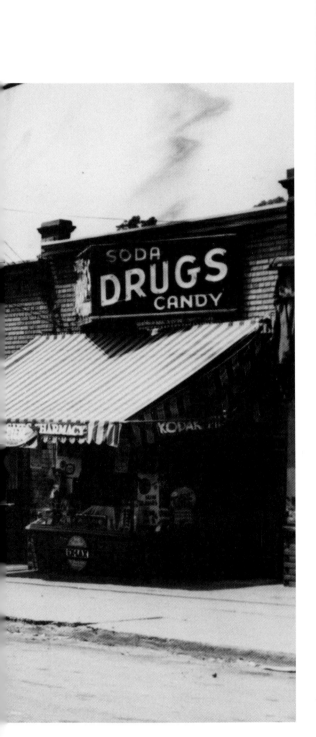

The County Police Boys Club was formed in the 1930s. Various teams from the entire county were coached by volunteers, including county and municipal policemen. Sporting events such as baseball, football, and boxing matches, were scheduled on a seasonal basis. Various events were staged in an attempt to raise funds for team equipment. One such event was a Magruder Park softball game between the members of the county police and the Hyattsville Volunteer Fire Department. This photograph was printed in a newspaper with the caption "Prince George's County Uniformed Forces Play." Left to right are Fireman Robert A. Baker, Colonel William Jennings of the Hyattsville Town Council, and county police Officer Edwin Thompson. Photo courtesy of retired Capt. Edwin Thompson

This photograph could be titled "Local Boy Makes Good." Taken in 1939, it shows one of the many Police Boys Club baseball teams. This particular team was coached by Mike Mulligan (standing at the far left) of the Colmar Manor Police Department. In the front row, second from the right, is a young man named Robert Baeschlin who later became a county policeman and played softball for the Fraternal Order of Police in the mid-1950s. Promoted to the rank of detective sergeant, Bob Baeschlin retired after more than twenty years of service.
Photo courtesy of Capt. Mike Mulligan, Jr., PGPD

Known as "Firwood," this beautiful old home and scientific laboratory stood at the present-day site of the County Service Building. The home was owned by James Harris Rogers, a famous electrical scientist who was instrumental in developing advanced wireless telegraphy systems.
Photo courtesy of Francis Geary

The County Service Building awaits the beginning of its dedication ceremonies on October 14, 1939. The entrance to the Hyattsville Station was located on the building's south side.
Photo courtesy of Francis Geary

The following story, which dates back to the late 1930s, was pieced together from several undated newspaper articles obtained from retired Lt. Richard Pearson.

Although the date of this incident is unknown, we do know that events precipitating the police department's involvement started at about 7:00 a.m. Police Officers Richard Pearson and Henry Briscoe were on routine patrol in the Hyattsville area when they received a radio call for a robbery at Jarvis' Filling Station in Beltsville. The MPDC dispatcher who placed the call also gave the officers a lookout for three white-male suspects occupying a 1938 Pontiac with Pennsylvania license 74-Z-9. The vehicle was last seen traveling south on U.S. Route 1.

As the two officers sped north along Route 1, they observed the southbound holdup vehicle as it approached Hyattsville. Officer Briscoe, who was driving the police car, turned the cruiser around and caught up with the suspect's vehicle near the Hyattsville Bridge. The suspects, observing the pursuing police, turned off onto Bladensburg Road. Driving toward the District of Columbia at a high rate of speed, several of the suspects started shooting at the police. Officer Pearson returned the suspects' fire, emptying his service revolver and then borrowing Briscoe's weapon.

The chase, reaching speeds of up to eighty-five miles per hour, continued into the District of Columbia for another five miles. According to Pearson the chase ended at 3rd and K streets, N.E., when "we pushed their car over to the curb and captured them, our guns were empty, but they didn't know it." Pearson is also quoted as saying, "The Washington traffic and pedestrians didn't pay much attention to our siren, but they scrambled when they heard the shooting." After arresting the three suspects, Pearson noticed that six of the twelve shots he had fired had gone through the rear window of the suspects' vehicle.

The suspects, all under nineteen years of age, had stolen the holdup car in Philadelphia and were headed south. Three handguns were removed from the vehicle: a .45-caliber automatic, a Luger, and a .32-caliber revolver. The suspects were taken to the Ninth Precinct, and later transferred to Hyattsville where they were jailed in lieu of a $5,000 bond. Photo courtesy of retired Lt. Richard Pearson. (Lt. Pearson served with the police department between 1937 and 1970. He was very ill at the time we interviewed him and has since passed away. His son, Richard Pearson, Jr., is also a retired county police sergeant.)

Two County Policemen Set Up Identification Bureau

181 Prisoners Have Been Photographed; $500 Spent; Equipment Valued at $2,000

Two Prince Georges County (Md.) policemen who refused to take "no" for an answer have succeeded in their aim to give their department a modern identification bureau.

Officer Mackall.

On several occasions, unsuccessful attempts were made to get money from the Board of County Commissioners to pay for the installation of cameras and fingerprinting devices. It was estimated the entire plant would cost approximately $1,500.

With the approval and co-operation of Supt of Police Arthur Hepburn, Officers Louis J. Mackall and Charles N. Thomsen started "picking up" spare parts of cameras. They acquired a box from one place, a lens from another. What they couldn't find at their own price they made themselves.

They set aside a room in the basement of the Hyattsville substation, painted it black and built their own developing equipment. With paint brush, hammer and saw and wiring tools, they worked day and night during their time off.

Although the Hyattsville police quarters are cramped at best, they were able to get a small room where they could set up their equipment. They had one counselor who worked tirelessly with them—John A. Styers, fingerprint expert of the Metropolitan Police Department, who shared their ambition of seeing a modern identification bureau established in the suburban area.

The work was started March 1 and additions are made with whatever equipment comes to hand. But the important work of identification is carried on with meager equipment.

Since the two policemen started the project, 181 prisoners have been photographed and fingerprinted. One amnesia and two accident victims have been identified by the bureau. Through co-operation with other bureaus, the two officers have collected 1,895 sets of fingerprints for their files. They also have made photographs at the scene of 20 serious accidents.

It was through the efforts of Officers Mackall and Thomsen that the notorious "pants burglar," who terrorized the metropolitan area for several months, was finally caught. He recently was sentenced to five years in the penitentiary by the Circuit Court at Upper Marlboro.

The two officers estimate their entire plant has cost them approximately $500, but they value it at $2,000.

After the bureau was established, the Board of County Commissioners finally appropriated $300 toward its cost.

Officer Thomsen.

This unidentified news clipping from the late 1930s relates to the formation of an Identification Bureau. The unit was the police department's first attempt at specialization; it was in fact the forerunner of the 1947 formation of a Detective Bureau. Duties assigned to the unit included the photographing and fingerprinting of prisoners, processing crime scenes for evidence, and conducting special investigations for the superintendent of police. Initially established to operate out of the Hyattsville Station (the busier of the two stations), the one-man unit soon expanded with a second identification officer being assigned at the Upper Marlboro Station.
Newspaper article courtesy of Dorothy Thomsen Barnes

CHAPTER IV

1940-1949
Professionalization/
The Development of a
Full-Service Police Department

*ancis A. Richards joined the police
partment in December 1938. The police
r shown here is a Chevrolet and the
otograph bears a handwritten date of
gust 25, 1941. Private Richards
signed from the department in 1945
d went into the construction business.
1951, he returned to the department as
newly appointed police chief.
hoto courtesy of Lt. William Richards*

*Patriotism is not a short and frenzied outburst of emotion, but the tranquil and steady
dedication of a lifetime.*

—Adlai Stevenson

The 1940 census revealed that 89,490 people resided within Prince George's
County. A particularly strong indication of the county's trend toward urbanization was the population increase of 29,395 people over the previous ten years.
The county police department entered the 1940s knowing that its twenty-two
sworn officers and six civilian desk clerks would, in all likelihood, be overwhelmed by
an ever-increasing number of calls for police service.

As the county's population increased so did the need to provide a more complete
police service. This is especially true considering that the police department offered no
in-depth follow-up investigative services until the late 1930s. Although the record is
vague and somewhat contradictory, it appears that the department initiated its first
"plainclothes" investigative service in 1939. A short departmental history written in
the mid-1940s states that, "During 1939 the Board of Police Commissioners designated two police officers to work plainclothes. One was assigned to the Hyattsville
Station, and the other to (the) Marlboro Station." It was the duty of these officers to
"investigate all serious crimes and perform such other duties as may be designated to
them by the superintendent of police." Several other references indicate that investigative services were not available until the early 1940s. In any event, all available
information points to the fact that the department's present-day investigative services
evolved out of the Identification Bureau which was formed in the late 1930s. Identification Bureau personnel took fingerprints and photographs of those charged with
serious crimes, processed crime scenes for evidence, took photographs at the scenes of
serious accidents, and conducted special investigations for the superintendent of
police.

When the Japanese bombed Pearl Harbor on December 7, 1941, all Americans
joined together in the one common goal of winning the war. The police department
found itself with some new priorities, which included preventing sabotage at any
number of sensitive war-related sites located within the county.

On April 16, 1942, the *Prince George's Post* announced that the county commissioners had allocated $13,350 for the purchase of a "two-way radio system" for the police
department. The system would replace the old one-way radio that still functioned on
the Metropolitan Police Department's radio frequency. The modernized system, which
called for a transmitter in both the Upper Marlboro and Hyattsville Stations, was
strongly supported by local civil defense leaders who stated that the two-way system
could act as an emergency back-up system if a telephone failure occurred. Cpl. Louis

Mackall, who had previously been assigned to the Identification Bureau, was reassigned as the officer in charge of police radio communications. Louis Mackall remained assigned to communications work until his retirement in May 1962.

Understaffing of the police department remained a problem throughout the 1940s. The April 2, 1942 edition of the *Prince George's Post* contained a story about "the present lack of adequate police protection" in unincorporated county communities. The paper reported that a representative from the Green Meadows Citizens Association said that "something drastic must be done and quickly . . . some kind of police protection." The association's spokesman went on to say "unincorporated areas are forced to depend on the county police. . . . The county force is all too small and overworked to give these areas the protection they should have."

In an attempt to rectify the understaffing problem, the superintendent of police made a yearly appeal for additional manpower to the Board of County Commissioners. The legal procedure to increase the department's size was time-consuming and awkward. Because the county had no charter, it was still a requirement that changes to local law be enacted by the Maryland General Assembly. Awkward as the procedure might be, appeals for additional manpower did not fall on deaf ears, as the record reveals that fifteen additional policemen were added to the force between August 1939 and July 1943. And, creating several additional station clerk positions also allowed an equal number of uniformed officers to be reassigned to patrol duties.

As the department grew it became more sophisticated in the ways of the outside world. On October 23, 1941, members of the force were instructed "to have telephones installed in their homes." A retirement fund was established in January 1942. The fund allowed the chief and desk clerks to retire at the age of seventy. Police officers were eligible to retire after reaching their sixty-fifth birthday.

During this time, most police officers within the state wore similar-colored olive-drab uniforms. In April 1943, Supt. Arthur Hepburn saw a need to distinguish the county police from other police agencies. Accordingly, the superintendent adopted a new uniform that consisted of a gray shirt with a cadet-gray hat, blouse, and riding breeches. The officers continued to wear their black Sam Browne leather gear and leather puttees.

On August 10, 1943, Superintendent Hepburn died of a heart attack at his home in Brentwood. An editorial in *The Prince Georgean* stated "Yes, the county has lost one of its most efficient and beloved officials, and the people have surely lost a sincere good friend." The Board of County Commissioners appointed Sgt. Ralph Brown, the officer in charge of the Hyattsville Station, as the county's new superintendent of police. Cpl. Roscoe Sines was promoted to the rank of sergeant and placed in charge of the Hyattsville Station.

As the war dragged on, it affected every facet of the American lifestyle including the police department. Although there was an obvious need for increased police manpower, little growth occurred because of the rate at which young men were being drafted into the armed forces. Because their work was classified as critical policemen were initially exempt from the draft, but this changed in 1944 when all exemptions were dropped for single men under twenty-nine years of age. Within a short period of time, two policemen, Roland Sweitzer and Wilmer Suit, were drafted into the service. Earlier, Officer Earl Huber, who had previous military service, had voluntarily gone back into the Army.

In late 1944, a Prince George's County Police Association was organized to "secure a closer official and personal relationship among the law enforcement officers within the county; to consider and discuss methods of preventing and combating crime; to secure unity of action in police matters and to advance and elevate the standard of police institutions. . . ." According to the association, another reason was to obtain a "sick and health benefit program that has been underwritten by the men themselves in the form of sickness insurance." At that time, the county government did not provide its employees with health insurance, and it was only through the formation of a police association that group health insurance could be purchased. The association remained active until December 27, 1955, when all eighty-nine members opted to join the Fraternal Order of Police.

A mid-1940s police association publication stated that in 1945 the county had a population of 132,000. The publication reported that the department's thirty-eight men ("1 superintendent, 4 sergeants, 5 corporals, 6 desk men, and 22 officers") responded to 12,744 calls for service and made 3,070 arrests. According to the publication, this was a "herculean task" when compared with "Montgomery County, which had a police force of more than one-hundred officers to serve 108,000 residents.

With the end of World War II, the police department again needed to modernize and expand. Because of dissatisfaction with the light gray blouses that were being worn, another uniform change had occurred in the mid-1940s. The light gray shirts, hats, and riding breeches remained, but the blouse color was changed to dark blue.

In 1947 the force was again reorganized and its strength increased to forty men. Sgts. Roscoe Sines of Hyattsville and Elon Turner of Upper Marlboro were promoted to the new rank of lieutenant. Sgt. Charles Thomsen, Identification Bureau, was also promoted to lieutenant and placed in charge of the newly created Detective Bureau. Cpl. John Dent was promoted to the new rank of detective sergeant and placed second in command of the Detective Bureau. Assigned as the department's first detectives were Earl Huber, Richard Pearson, Wilson Purdy, and John Siddall. Sgt. Louis Mackall, the department's radio and communications officer, was also promoted to lieutenant.

Urbanization continued to move east out of the District of Columbia and into Prince George's County. Changes within the county had been occurring for years, but at a rather slow leisurely pace. In the late 1940s, every indicator pointed to an accelerated rate of development. At the time, few people realized that the county's old lifestyle was about to begin a long journey toward extinction. Prince George's County desperately attempted to hold on to some semblance of its rural past. Officers assigned to the county's most populated northside communities routinely responded to neighborhood disputes and theft complaints, but they also continued to receive frequent calls from the motoring public about farm animals roaming at will, on now heavily traveled roadways. Occasional calls were also received which required the police to mediate disputes between property owners and the county government over public access to certain roadways. A news article from the late 1940s tells of two county officers who were given the assignment of removing a roadblock erected at Fifty-first Place in Edmonston. It seems that William B. Armstrong had built the roadblock on what he considered to be his privately owned roadway. The county government countered this claim by stating, "the road has been in use for more than two decades and that it is now a public way." The newspaper printed a picture of two county policemen and a tow truck driver removing a large roadblock that was intended to obstruct vehicular

traffic. The county's 250-year-old rural lifestyle wasn't about to disappear overnight, but the slide toward urbanization could not be stopped.

The county's rapidly growing population had increased the volume of routine calls being handled by the less-than-fifty-man police department. Although calls concerning violent crimes were few, the rapidly growing population increased the probability of their occurrence. The department was also under increased pressure to curtail the county's longstanding gambling and liquor violation problems. As the decade of the 1940s came to a close, the police department's ability to render an adequate service to the county's 194,000 residents was in question.

Roland B. Sweitzer became a county police officer on July 1, 1941. He advanced through the ranks and became the department's chief of police in mid-July 1971. Chief Sweitzer retired on May 1, 1975, with almost thirty-four years of dedicated service to county law enforcement. Photo courtesy of retired Capt. George Conner

Sgt. Ralph Brown poses with his new triangle-shaped shoulder patch. Prior to 1941, county police officers wore no distinguishing patch identifying them as county policemen. Photo courtesy of Shirley Brown Teffeau

Gasoline was readily available and inexpensive as can be seen from this ad found in a prewar issue of The Prince Georgean. *Tydol was a brand name gasoline with a large number of stations along the entire East Coast. The company went out of business in the mid-1950s.*
Newspaper courtesy of the Prince George's County Historical Sociey

The Japanese attack on Pearl Harbor, December 7, 1941, altered every American priority. The American people joined together, like never before, with a common goal of total victory.
Baltimore Sun *front page courtesy of Fred DeMarr*

Pvt. Roland Sweitzer stands next to his 1940 police car. Police vehicles were issued directly to individual officers who drove the cars to and from work. This particular 1940 Ford was the first county police car to be equipped with a gasoline heater for winter comfort.
Photo courtesy of retired Chief of Police Roland B. Sweitzer

World War II placed additional strains on an already overburdened police department. During the early years of the war, county officers acted as air raid wardens and enforced blackout regulations. The fear of sabotage was always present and officers were directed to pay special attention to war-related industries.
Photo courtesy of Shirley Brown Teffeau

Officer Lawson Peed at shotgun practice.
Photo courtesy of Elsie Peed

Early 1940s photograph of Pvts. Elmer Lee Pumphrey (left) and Edwin Cissel.
Photo courtesy of Mrs. Edwin Cissel

Today's police officers are, on occasion, directed to assume traffic and crowd control duties at the scene of large fires. Similar duties were also performed by members of the early police department. This photograph depicts Pvt. Richard Pearson at the scene of a fire in the Hyattsville area.
Photo courtesy of Francis Geary

On March 20, 1942, the county commissioners approved a two-way radio network for the police department, thus discontinuing the old one-way system that had served the county since 1934. The Hyattsville Station used the call letters WJLW, while the Upper Marlboro Station used the letters WJLU. Both stations broadcasted calls over the same single frequency network. In this photograph, Superintendent Hepburn dispatches a call from the Hyattsville Station, while Desk Clerk Melvin Kent (center) and Cpl. Louis Mackall look on. Louis Mackall spent twenty years in police communications, retiring in 1962 with the rank of captain.
PGPD photo

During the 1940s, the county and state police were responsible for patrolling the county's rural roadways. Both agencies were small and relied on each other for help. This photograph was taken around 1943. The state trooper's name is Lee Allers.
Photo courtesy of Elsie Peed

The Prince Georgean

The Rhode Island Avenue Press and The Suburban

AN INDEPENDENT NEWSPAPER
Published Weekly

FRANK B. SMITH .... Editor and Publisher
SHELBY B. SMITH .... Advertising Manager

Entered as second-class mail matter January 7, 1919, at the postoffice at Mt. Rainier, Md., under the Act of March 3, 1879. Additional entry as second-class mail matter authorized at the postoffice at Hyattsville, Maryland.

Editorial Office _____ 4009 Thirty-first street, Mt. Rainier, Md.
Publication Office _____ 5303 Baltimore Avenue, Hyattsville, Md.
Telephones _____ Warfield 1011, Hyattsville 0444; Night, Warfield 2111

FRIDAY, MARCH 26, 1943

A Much Needed Increase

There is a bill before the present session of the Legislature looking to increasing the size of the Prince Georges County Police force and making some changes in the present system. Now the police have twenty-five officers, including the Chief, two sergeants and two corporals. Besides these there are six desk clerks, whose duties are just what the names implies. However, the bill provides for an increase in pay for these clerks and it is hoped they will be given police authority to be used only in the station houses.

The bill provides for eight additional policemen and creates two more corporalcies, thus bringing the group up to a point of efficiency the increased population of the county demands.

It is understood the bill has the endorsement of the Board of County Commissioners, and it is difficult to find an good reason why it will not pass. In fact, considering the need and the immense growth the county has had during the past two years, the requested increase seems most conservative.

Taken as a whole, the county's police force has been most efficient, and Chief Arthur Hepburn and his two sergeants, Ralph Brown and Elon Turner, and Corporals Louis Mackall and John F. Dent can well be proud of the work they have accomplished. The Board of County Commissioners surely can feel that any support they give this group will redound to the betterment of the police system, which in the end gives the taxpayers of the county more for their tax dollar.

The Prince Georgean sincerely hopes this bill will pass, thus giving the police the much needed men they deserve permitting the Chief to arrange for a real police department.

Commissioners Appoint Seven To Police Force

Pvts. Naylor and Sines Promoted to Corporals At Substations

The Board of County Commissioners have appointed seven additional men to the police force. Pending final physical examination, the new appointees are Ralph Bond, Brandywine; Charles L. Perrygo, Oxon Hill; Arnett W. Cord, Landover; Charles F. Caldwell, Colmar Manor; Reginald R. Austin, Brentwood; James H. Burgess, Mt. Rainier; and Vincent S. Free, Clearview.

The commissioners at this time approved the promotions of Pvts. R. A. Naylor and R. C. Sines to corporal at the Upper Marlboro and Hyattsville substations, respectively.

William A. Carson, president of the commissioners, explained that several other applicants had been turned down because they had been deferred from the draft as essential farm workers. Appointing them to the police force, he added, might have made them subject to induction.

Authority to appoint up to eight additional men to the county police force was granted the commissioners by an act passed at the last session of the State Legislature.

The commissioners also appealed for volunteers to act as dog tax collectors in the Riverdale, Queen Anne, Piscataway and Marlboro districts. These men receive 25

An editorial in The Prince Georgean *of March 26, 1943, endorses a legislative bill to increase the police department by eight new officers, thereby bringing the department's total strength to thirty-three men.*

On July 9, 1943, The Prince Georgean *reported that the county had just appointed seven additional officers.*

Articles courtesy of the Prince George's County Historical Society

DRESSED TO KILL—Because 20 Prince Georges county residents are receiving Pasteur treatment for rabies, the police chief orders his men (left) to shoot on sight all stray dogs. Yesterday approximately 50 were killed, even those on private property. Now, asks little Milo Holt, of Piscataway (Prince Georges county), Md.: "Has anyone seen my Tippy?" The picture (right) shows them in happier days. The 7-month-old female pup is lost, and may be wandering around the county now. If you see her, notify us, please, NOT Prince Georges police.
Times-Herald Staff Photo

A rabies outbreak in the early 1940s led to an order for county policemen to shoot all stray dogs. Published in The Times Herald, *this photo obviously left a little something to be desired in the way of good police/ community relations.*
Photo courtesy of retired Lt. Pete Perrygo

This wartime news photo bears the caption, "Prince George's County policemen use their cruiser for protection as they await the horde of Nazi sympathizers during the State Guard-Minute Man maneuvers yesterday near the Queens Chapel airport." The officers are (left to right) James H. Burgess, Charles F. Caldwell, and H. E. King.
Photo courtesy of Martha O'Brien

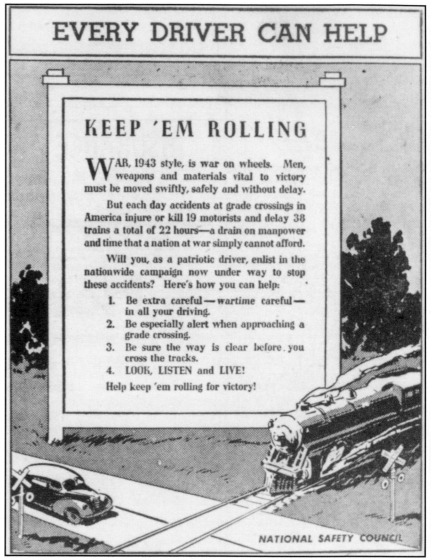

The war effort affected every facet of American life. This 1943 National Safety Council newspaper advertisement asked the "patriotic driver" to use caution when approaching railroad crossings, car/train accidents being a "drain on manpower and time that a nation at war cannot afford."
From The Prince Georgean, *courtesy of the Prince George's County Historical Society*

Three Cents a Copy—$1 per year

Ralph W. Brown Is Appointed to Head County Police Force

Will Succeed A. W. Hepburn Who Died August 10

FRIDAY, AUGUST 20, 1943

Arthur W. Hepburn

Prince Georges County lost one of its best officials last week when Arthur W. Hepburn, chief of the county police force, died. Those who knew him personally have lost a friend, for "Hep" was a friend to all who knew him, always endeavoring to help in any situation where he was involved.

He became chief of the police force in one of its most rtying times. While the force was small then, it just survived a scandal caused by conditions and lack of coordination of the several interests of the law enforcement group. Naturally, those who remained on the force were on "pins and needles" for a long time, and the chief had no easy job bringing order out of the then group chaos.

However, he went along in his even-going manner, gaining the confidence of his subordinates, always looking to their interests as well as to the efficiency of the force, until when he was taken he had perfected a police organization which stood second to none, considering its number, equipment and financial cost. He was most modest in his activities, always giving credit for success to the others involved.

During his tenure of office he had instituted many of the most modern of police methods and equipment. He had the confidence of his superiors, and his recommendations were usually heeded if there was any way possible. He had established a most enviable reputation with the police organizations of the city, State and country at large, having worked successfully with the F. B. I., in a number of important cases.

Having lived in the county for over thirty years, Chief Hepburn had been active in most of the civic and political affairs here. His family was reared here and had participated also in the county's activities, looking always to the betterment of the community in which they lived.

Yes, the county has lost one of its most efficient and beloved officials, and the people have surely lost a sincere and good friend.

Ralph W. Brown, sergeant in charge of the Hyattsville substation, was named early this week to succeed Police Superintendent Arthur W. Hepburn, who died on August 10.

Sergeant Brown, a member of the county force for 21 years, joined it under the late Chief J. J. Crowley and later was made head of the Hyattsville station.

A native of Prince Georges County, he attended the Takoma Park elementary school and McKinley high school in Washington. He is married and has three children, Ralph, jr., 17; Joseph, 14, and Shirley, 11. He lives at 6819 New Hampshire avenue, Chillum.

In announcing Brown's appointment, William A. Carson, chairman of the county commissioners, pointed out that although other members of the police force are picked on a merit basis, the position of chief is a political appointment and need not necessarily come from the civil service roster.

"There were a number of good candidates in the field for the job," Carson said, "but the board and county political leaders decided in Sergeant Brown's favor in view of his qualifications, experience and long service on the force."

Supt. Arthur W. Hepburn died on August 10, 1943. The county commissioners appointed Sgt. Ralph Brown as the new superintendent of police.
Newspaper articles from The Prince Georgean, *courtesy of the Prince George's County Historical Society*

This photograph of the department's upper echelon was taken between 1943 and 1944. Left to right are Sgt. Roscoe Sines of the Hyattsville Station; Cpl. Louis Mackall of Radio Communications; Supt. Ralph Brown; Cpl. Charles Thomsen in charge of the Identification Bureau; and Sgt. Elon Turner of Upper Marlboro Station.
PGPD photograph

This 1945 Evening Star newspaper photograph is a clear illustration that remnants of eighteenth and nineteenth-century justice still existed within Maryland law. Captioned, "Lashed Man Leaves Jail" the accompanying story tells of the conviction of a Dillon Park man for "wife beating." A circuit court jury sentenced the man, pictured here with his face covered, to receive ten lashes at the County Jail. According to the Star, the flogging was imposed by County Sheriff R. Earl Sheriff.
Photo from the scrapbook of retired Lt. Pete Perrygo

In 1946, the police department began to wear dark blue blouses and French blue breeches. This uniform color scheme is still worn today. To publicize the issuance of new uniforms, Superintendent Brown scheduled a photo session at the rear of the Upper Marlboro Courthouse. Pictured left to right, front row: Sgt. Elon Turner, Supt. Ralph Brown, and Sgt. Roscoe Sines; second row: Cpl. Jack Dent, Cpl. Edwin Thompson, Cpl. Boyd Hamilton, Sgt. Charles Thomsen, Sgt. Louis Mackall, Cpl. Arnold Naylor, and Cpl. Richard Earnshaw; third row: Desk Clerk Dowlin, Officers Reginal Austin, Arnett Cord, Pete Perrygo, Ralph Bond, Edwin Cissel, and Richard Little; fourth row: Officers Elmer Pumphrey, Wallace Baker, Joseph Hill, Raymond Blandford, Richard Pearson, Wilson Purdy, and Lawrence Riddlebarger; fifth row: Officers Adam Lindsey, Martin Keech, Earl Huber, Vincent Free, James Burgess, and Charles Caldwell; back row: Officers Benjamin Richards, Joseph Vincent, Roland Sweitzer, John Siddall, Charles Nalley, and Lawson Peed.

The following officers were also hired in 1946 (for some reason they are not shown in the photograph): James Kearns, Emmett Gray, William Wiseman, and John Tucker. Officer Horace King, also a member of the department, is not pictured.
PGPD photo

Personnel assigned to the Hyattsville Station. Pictured left to right, front row: Cpl. Boyd Hamilton; Sgt. Roscoe Sines, in charge of the station; Sgt. Charles Thomsen, in charge of the Identification Bureau; Sgt. Louis Mackall, in charge of Radio Communications; and Cpl. Edwin Thompson; second row: Officers Elmer Pumphrey, Wallace Baker, Reginal Austin, Arnett Cord, Edwin Cissel, and Richard Pearson; third row: Officers Adam Lindsey, Joseph Hill, James Burgess, and Charles Caldwell; back row: Officers Earl Huber, Roland Sweitzer, and Richard Little.

Because the Hyattsville Station was the busier of the county's two stations, both the Identification Bureau and Radio Repair Shop were located there. PGPD photo

Personnel assigned to the Upper Marlboro Station. Pictured left to right, front row: Cpl. Jack Dent; Sgt. Elon Turner, in charge of the station; Cpl. Arnold Naylor; and Cpl. Richard Earnshaw; second row: Desk Clerk Dowlin, Officers Raymond Blandford, Pete Perrygo, Ralph Bond, and Lawrence Riddlebarger; third row: Officers Benjamin Richards, Wilson Purdy, Vincent Free, Lawson Peed, and Charles Nalley; back row: Officers Joseph Vincent, Martin Keech, and John Siddall.
PGPD photo

Officers James Burgess (left) and John Siddall clown around after the formal picture-taking session. Police work never really changes. Hopefully, there will always be a couple of jokers around for a good laugh.
PGPD photo

County Police Force Changes, Raises Ordered

Reorganization of the Prince Georges County police force, authorized by the last session of the General Assembly, will become effective July 1.

Announcement of the changes was made by Norman H. Collins, president of the board of police commissioners whose membership includes the county commissioners.

The modernization program will include promotions for 19 policemen and increased salaries for all members of the force of 40 men.

Sgt. Charles E. Thomsen, former identification officer, will be promoted to lieutenant in command of a new detective bureau. Corporal John F. Dent will be named detective sergeant and second in command.

Sgt. Roscoe C. Sines, now commanding Hyattsville station, and Sgt. Elon Turner, commanding Marlboro, will be promoted to the new rank of lieutenant and will retain command of their respective stations.

Sgt. Louis J. Mackall, radio and communications officer, will be promoted to the rank of lieutenant. The new lieutenants will receive $3380 a year.

Superintendent of Police Ralph W. Brown will receive a salary jump from the present $3358 to $3820.

Plain-clothes Officer Edwin C. Cissel will become identification officer and Pvt. Earl J. Huber is assigned to the detective bureau as plain clothes man in his place.

Corporals Boyd A. Hamilton and Edwin R. Thompson of Hyattsville Station and Richard J. Earnshaw and Arnold Naylor of the Marlboro Station will receive promotions to sergeant with $3130 pay.

Privates Lawson Peed, Thomas R. Blandford of Marlboro Station; Roland B. Sweitzer, Elmer Lee Pumphrey and Reginald R. Austin, Hyattsville station, will be promoted to corporal at a salary of $2850.

In addition to Huber, present plain clothes men in the department will be named detectives and receive the same pay as corporals. They are Richard A. Pearson, Wilson J. Purdy and John W. Siddall. The identification officer also will receive corporal's pay.

The Prince Georgean of June 3, 1947, announced another reorganization of the police department. The "modernization program" included increased salaries, the official formation of a detective bureau, and the creation of several new ranks for the department's forty-man force.
Article courtesy of the Prince George's County Historical Society

This is a rare photograph of a patrol car with the triangular police seal, which was adopted for county patrol cars in 1947. Prior to this time, patrol cars were marked on the side doors with the words "Prince George's County Police."
Photo courtesy of Emmett Gray

The ever-increasing number of calls for service placed an unusually heavy burden on an understaffed county police department. Roland Sweitzer, in reminiscing about his police experiences, expressed his gratitude to the many volunteer firemen who continually offered their assistance to the police department. Sweitzer states that the volunteers always offered a helping hand in controlling traffic at the scene of an emergency situation, and that they frequently stood by, as a precaution, while a lone officer handled a disturbance call. In this mid-1940s photograph, police officers Charles Caldwell (left) and William Wiseman look on as a group of volunteer firemen prepare to evacuate an injured person.
Photo courtesy of Mrs. Donald Farran

CHARLES F. CALDWELL

Killed in the line of duty
June 12, 1948

Charles F. Caldwell was born in Washington, D.C. The Caldwell family moved to the Mt. Rainier section of Prince George's County in the mid-1920s where Charles Caldwell attended Mt. Rainier High School. Initially employed as a painter, Charles Caldwell became a Prince George's County policeman on July 13, 1943, and was assigned to the Hyattsville Station.

At approximately 6:00 p.m., Saturday, June 12, 1948, police officer Caldwell and his partner Wallace Baker responded to a call for a fight in the 5300 block of Nash Street in Fairmount Heights. Upon arriving at the scene, the officers arrested Jane Hall after being told that she had stabbed a neighborhood man. The man had already been transported to a Washington hospital.

According to a newspaper account of the incident, the suspect was arrested by the two officers and was being taken back to their "squad car" when she struck officer Caldwell. The newspaper goes on to report, "The girl's father pounced upon the policeman, grabbing his service revolver and fired. Pvt. Caldwell . . . fell at the first burst and Pvt. Baker started for the radio car for help. Using Pvt. Caldwell's gun, Hall exchanged shots with Pvt. Baker from a distance of about 10 feet. The policeman emptied his pistol, and fell wounded . . . Hall was (also) wounded." A witness is reported to have stated, "Hall and his daughter pulled Pvt. Baker up a hill at the rear of Nash Street and beat him with his blackjack."

Officer Caldwell was transported to Leland Hospital in Riverdale. According to the previously mentioned news account, Caldwell suffered from three bullet wounds to the chest, but was conscious when brought into the emergency room. He supposedly smiled and asked for Doctor Malin, the hospital director. Just after this request, he lapsed into a coma and was pronounced dead at 7:00 p.m.

Officer Baker was transported to Prince George's Hospital and admitted in good condition with bullet wounds to his left leg and right arm. Thomas Hall, the fifty-five-year-old, six-foot-six-inch stoneyard laborer, was treated for minor gunshot wounds and released into police custody. He was transported to the Hyattsville Station and charged with murder.

Officer Charles F. Caldwell was the first Prince George's County policeman to be fatally shot in the line of duty. He was survived by his wife and two young sons.

*The 1937 law reorganizing the police department required that all
county officers receive training. However, as already indicated only six
county policemen were sent to the Metropolitan Police Department's
recruit training school in Washington. No additional officers received
any formal recruit training until 1951. This photograph of a mock crime
scene training session seems to indicate that occasional inservice
training did take place in the late 1940s.
Courtesy of Emmett Gray*

Officer Emmett Gray and Lt. Roscoe Sines examine a revolver taken from a man who had threatened to kill himself. Two officers responded to an attempted-suicide call on Ardmore-Ardwick Road and were confronted by an armed suicide suspect who pointed his weapon at one of the officers. A shootout ensued during which the suspect was shot by the officers. Courtesy of Emmett Gray

Police Officer George R. Roland. In the late 1940s, many uniformed officers became disgruntled with the awkwardness of wearing riding breeches and leather puttees. Superintendent Brown agreed that the uniform was uncomfortable and approved the use of straight-legged pants. The superintendent also adopted the wearing of a gold hat band and white shirt for himself and his two station commanders.
Photo courtesy of retired Sgt. George R. Roland

In this late 1940s photograph, several police officers and some local citizens sit on the steps of the Hyattsville Station on a hot summer's night. Air conditioned buildings were a few years away, so the only way of catching a breath of fresh air was to go outside and take advantage of the nighttime coolness.
Photo courtesy of Emmett Gray

Downtown Hyattsville was in its prime during the 1940s. The county's northside population was still increasing rapidly, and the downtown area served as the commercial hub of business activity.
U.S. Bureau of Roads photo courtesy of the National Archives

The winds of commercial change began to stir in the late 1940s and would eventually whip up a firestorm and forever change the face of Prince George's County. At the time, most large commercial retailers were located in downtown Washington. With the exception of some five-and-dime stores, local retailers were small mom-and-pop operations offering a limited variety of merchandise. The large number of people now residing in the outlying suburbs of Washington offered a potential bonanza for commercial growth. The first to recognize and capitalize on this new market were the supermarket chain stores. This late 1940s photograph of a crowded supermarket opening depicts police officers Roland B. Sweitzer (left) and Joseph Hill on crowd-control duty.
Photo courtesy of Roland Sweitzer

Although they may not want to admit it, police officers have traditionally depended upon their "better half" for everyday support. Psychological stress factors placed on police officers can be so overwhelming that mental survival may very well hinge on the family support and understanding they receive. In many ways the unsung heroes of our day are those members of a police officer's family who exist in a state of uncertainty everyday of the year, year after year. The family knows, all too well, the dangers associated with a law enforcement career, yet they have no control over the twists of fate that can, at any given moment, devastate their lives.
Photo courtesy of Elsie Peed

On-scene photograph of a late 1940s fatal accident occurring on U.S. Route 1. Officer Emmett Gray, shown here in civilian dress, drove up on this accident while off duty. The two uniformed officers are Maryland state troopers.
Photo courtesy of Emmett Gray

An extremely close-working relationship existed between the county police and the various municipal police departments. Because there were so few policemen in the county, the departments, including the state police, depended on each other for back-up protection. Three county policemen were members of this 1948 Municipal Police Association's Pistol Team. Pictured left to right in the first row are county policeman Horace King, Riverdale policemen Bill Baxter and John Fitzhugh, along with Paul Leyendecker of Landover Hills. In the second row are county policeman Earl Huber, Dan Manuel of Mt. Rainier, Chief Henry Nebel of Bladensburg, an unknown officer from Riverdale or Edmonston, and county policeman Emmett Gray.
Photo courtesy of Emmett Gray

In 1940, Prince George's County had no hospital service available within its boundaries. To obtain emergency medical treatment, county rescue squads transported injured persons to hospitals located in Washington, D.C. In September 1942, Prince George's County's first hospital, Leland Memorial Hospital in Riverdale, became operational. Prince George's General Hospital in Cheverly (above) opened its doors on March 21, 1944. Originally a 100-bed hospital, it was built with funds obtained from the Federal Works Agency.

Prince Georges Police—Smallest Force in Area—Ask More Help & Pay

Prince Georges County's 160,000 inhabitants and its 500 square miles are policed today by a force of 42 men whose pay is some $500 per man lower than any of the three other suburban counties.

Police Chief Ralph Brown has again asked the Prince Georges County Commissioners to approve a bill to give him more men and money, but he hasn't the slightest hope of getting either. He could use 60 more men "easily," he says.

The News learned the commissioners have no intention of recommending the bill to the Maryland legislature. They feel an increase in the budget would necessitate new taxes.

Despite the rapid growth of the county, the police force has added only 10 men in the last four years. To be a policeman in this county you have to be in love with your work—there is little financial reward.

Here's how the county forces stack up:

138 IN MONTGOMERY

In neighboring Montgomery County, Chief Charles Orme has a flock of shiny new radio cars, four substations, 138 men whose basic salaries are some $630 higher per man than Prince Georges', fancy uniforms and what is generally regarded as one of the finest county forces in the country.

This high-powered outfit patrols only 10 square miles more territory than do their cousins in Prince Georges. Moreover, a larger number of low-income families live in Prince Georges, and statistics indicate the greater proportion of crimes are committeed by those in financial difficulty.

Arlington and Fairfax counties have around 70 men each. Arlington's population compares with Prince Georges', but its area is much smaller. Even so, Arlington has requested more men, and appointment of seven new policemen has been recommended in that county's budget for the coming year. Fairfax has a large area to cover, but is thinly populated compared with the other three communities.

Chief Brown said Prince Georges police can put only four cars into operation at one time—and this on Friday and Saturday nights when two of the three working shifts are doubled up. He figures it takes at least 15 minutes to get a squad car to answer a call.

PREVENTATIVE, TOO

A police force's mission is as much to prevent crime as to avenge it. The presence of squad cars on the road is a deterrent to traffic violations, and to crime of all sorts.

Also, suppose a fight broke out in a county tavern. A squad car doesn't get there for half an hour. Meanwhile, someone has been killed. What would have been simply disorderly conduct has become murder.

Moreover, if two or three disasters strike at once—a robbery, an accident and a fire—it means Chief Brown will have to summon some of his scant force from off duty.

He said his policemen draw no overtime, tho some put in 16 hours a day, twice a week, week after week.

NO INCREASE IN 2 YEARS

Failing to get more men, Chief Brown would like to see a $500 increase straight thru the ranks. There has been no increase in police salaries in the last two years, tho the cost of living has increased. County policemen now get a $120 raise every four years.

An alternative to increasing the county force would be for Chief Brown's organization to absorb qualified men from the county's many town police organizations.

There are approximately 100 town police in the county. Some of these men might qualify as county policemen, and Chief Brown said he would like to have those men incorporated into his force.

This Washington Daily News *article was found in the scrapbook of retired Lt. Pete Perrygo. Although undated, information within the article places it in the late 1940s. The article is particularly interesting because it compares salaries and other working conditions of the Prince George's County Police with several neighboring jurisdictions.*
Photo courtesy of retired Lt. Pete Perrygo

JIMMY LAFONTAINE'S GAMBLING CASINO, 1922-1948

As discussed in a previous chapter of this book, a man named Jimmy LaFontaine operated a large gambling casino near the intersection of Bladensburg Road and Eastern Avenue. The only known police raid on Jimmy's Place occurred in the mid-1920s. The disposition of that case is not known, but an *Evening Star* article on November 20, 1931, vaguely refers to a Grand Jury indictment that, for some unknown reason, was never served.

The article also refers to the disposition of a federal income tax evasion charge against LaFontaine. According to the story, LaFontaine went to court in Baltimore and pleaded guilty to one of several tax evasion charges. Apparently a deal was struck because several of the remaining evasion charges were nol-prossed. The U.S. attorney told the court that LaFontaine had paid the government $206,651 in back taxes and penalties on his income for the years 1924 to 1929. The payment wiped out LaFontaine's civil indebtedness to the government and left the court with the sole responsibility of determining the criminal penalty for income tax evasion. LaFontaine was later fined $1,000 and sentenced to serve nine months at the Ellicott City Jail in Howard County.

Numerous complaints about the casino can be found in the minutes of the county commissioners' meetings. One typical notation from a June 7, 1932 meeting reads: "Ordered, that upon the request of numerous clubs and organizations of this County, representatives of which appeared before this Board and presented verbal and written protests and complaints about the alleged gambling resort located on Bladensburg Road, at the District of Columbia line, allegedly known as 'LaFontaine's Place,' the Chief and all Prince George's County Police are hereby directed to investigate, close and keep closed this alleged gambling resort."

Another *Washington Star* article on November 17, 1936, reads, "In December of 1934, the Prince George's County Commissioners ordered the county police force to close LaFontaine's and to keep it closed. Hearing subsequent rumors that the establishment was running, the Commissioners themselves visited it about six months later, but found no evidence of gambling. The Grand Jury, which adjourned a few weeks ago, said the gambling situation in the county was well in hand."

The following article, written by Mr. Lou Swerda, was published in the *Prince George's Post* of July 1, 1976. Mr. Swerda obtained the information for the article by interviewing some of Jimmy LaFontaine's old patrons and a few local cab drivers who remembered when the casino operated. The information contained in the article is probably more legend than fact, but Jimmy's surviving reputation is that of a man who ran a clean gambling operation, a wealthy, but kindhearted man who wouldn't hesitate to lend a helping hand to someone in need.

Jimmy LaFontaine operated a notorious gambling casino in Prince George's County. Located near the intersection of Eastern Avenue and Bladensburg Road, the casino was a plush, high-class establishment with a reputation for clean-cut games of chance. In 1951, Jack Lait and Lee Mortimer wrote an expose titled Washington Confidential. *This book, which is about the seedy side of life in the nation's capital, described LaFontaine's casino as a place where "Men won and lost fortunes. Women never got past the front door, and no man who couldn't afford to lose was ever admitted again."*

This 1925 newspaper photo was found in the scrapbook of Claude Reese, and relates to the only known raid on LaFontaine's casino. Newspaper photos courtesy of Neva Reese

CARD TABLE

THREE ROULETTE WHEELS

"THE SWEAT BOX"

POKER CHIPS

CASINO IN THIS COUNTY?

(some of you may remember)
by Lou Swerda

It wasn't as in the musical *Guys and Dolls*, the oldest established permanent floating crap game around. It was more than that. For over 25 years, in an old house just inside Prince George's County where Bladensburg Rd. and Eastern Ave. now intersect, a man named Jimmy LaFontaine ran an honest-to-goodness old fashioned, down-home gambling casino.

From 1922 to around 1948, from 11 a.m. to 6 a.m., seven days a week, (except Christmas, or when the local tracks at Marlboro and Bowie were running, or when the grand jury was in session), a serious gambler could risk an entire bankroll on games of chance.

There were horse-betting, dice tables, a roulette wheel, and all the card games from poker to black jack, including solitaire. In solitaire, the deck was purchased for $52, a dol-lar a card, and the player won $5 for every card turned up.

Anyone who has seen the movie *The Sting* can easily picture the atmosphere of the place. There were six betting windows in the horse room, and a giant tote board where odds and results were posted. All the races were announced from wire to wire over a loudspeaker by a man reading a Western Union ticker tape.

There were no telephones. This was to discourage the practice of "past-posting," whereby a gambler would have a confederate at the track who would call in the results of a race, and the gambler could then get his bet down before the Western Union wire could come in.

More important to gamblers, LaFontaine's paid track odds. Bookmakers, especially today, generally limit their payoffs to 20-to-1. One man hit a $100, three-horse parlay for $13,000 and was paid, in cash, on the spot.

Naturally, to be successful, LaFontaine's clientele had to be assured the place was on the up-and-up. Not just anyone, for example, was allowed to enter. Firearms, women, and whiskey were taboo, and anyone entering, be he a congressman or street cleaner, was frisked by muscular ex-football players.

The easiest way to get in was to have a Maryland Athletic Club card, the "official" membership card of the establishment. Members could bring guests, who, after they became known, were also allowed entrance.

Once in, patrons were encouraged to behave themselves. The chief encouragement were employees posted in chairs up near the ceiling. When voices were raised or a commotion started, someone would soon be exiting. Seldom was there any trouble at LaFontaine's.

Raids were also rare. It is said that LaFontaine had paid off the state and local politicians, and while that is probably true, it is also realistic to say that gambling was an accepted form of activity in the county then. In fact, it was a way of life.

A horse player could find action at nearly any barber shop or pool hall. Slot machines, although LaFontaine never had any, were common throughout the county.

The District of Columbia police decided once in 1937 to crack down on the place, but then-county Chief of Police Arthur Hepburn thwarted the attempt. Eastern Ave. didn't exist at that time, and the road leading to LaFontaine's was in the District. The D.C. police posted men at the entrance one night to harass patrons leaving the place. Hepburn learned of the scheme, however, tore down part of the tall green fence surrounding the property and had his men direct traffic onto Bladensburg Rd. into Maryland. The D.C. police were left embarrassed and twiddling their thumbs.

Rumor has it that an Edmonston constable, known as "Two-gun" Wilson, used to over-imbibe, deputize his drinking companions, and raid LaFontaine's. The truth is that although he frequently urged such actions he never actually took it.

Undoubtedly, the best reason for LaFontaine's success was LaFontaine himself. He was a rare man with that rare quality known as "class"—a term at once nebulous and yet understood by all.

He took care of his customers and he took care of the community around him. Although he was a Catholic, he donated to all the charities. His employees all lived in the area, generally Mt. Rainier, Hyattsville, and Cottage City, thus providing employment through some pretty tough times. There were no gangsters or underworld types at Jimmy LaFontaine's.

During the Depression, in fact his employees would report any of their neighbors who happened to be in dire straits, and LaFontaine would send them groceries, clothing or a load of coal.

He also ran a limousine service for his customers, picking them up at 7th and E in the District and returning them later. If someone won big, he would be taken home in the limousine with a bodyguard. And if someone lost big, he would also be taken home, or given cabfare.

The most common story about LaFontaine is that of the distressed housewife whose husband lost his paycheck at LaFontaine's place. This was a common occurrence, and the usual procedure was that the money was sent to Charles Ford, LaFontaine's attorney. Ford would repay the money, in return for a picture of her husband, who would thereafter be barred from the establishment.

LaFontaine, a grey, portly man, took greatest pride in his flock of fighting gamecocks. Contrary to rumor, cockfights were never held in the place. He raised them there, but fought them elsewhere, usually in Laurel or Hagerstown.

As Prince George's County changed from a rural to an urban area after World War II, and the federal government began cracking down on gambling, LaFontaine's casino disappeared from the scene. Most old-timers however, look back longingly on those days, and with few exceptions, note that the odds on winning a few dollars at LaFontaine's were infinitely better than they are now on hitting the Maryland lottery.

LaFontaine died a few years after his place closed, and in 1954, the fire department burned it down. *The District News* office now stands in what was the casino's front yard. LaFontaine has been called affable, unpretentious, charitable. Perhaps the best testimonial is also the simplest, expressed by a county cab driver: He was a great guy; everybody liked Jimmy LaFontaine.

In his book, Prince George's County: A Pictorial History, *Mr. Alan Virta states that* The Evening Star *remembered Jimmy LaFontaine as "The dapper little man who directed a big casino." Mr. Virta's pictorial history goes on to say that "during the twenties, thirties, and forties Jimmy ran the preeminent gambling establishment in the Washington area. Located on the corner of Eastern Avenue and Bladensburg Road, it was just out of reach of District of Columbia law enforcement officials and safely inside more tolerant Prince George's."*
Washington Star *photo, copyright the* Washington Post; *courtesy of the District of Columbia Public Library*

For a great many years, the Prince George's County Police Force took a lion's share of the responsibility for permitting Jimmy's place to remain in operation. Superintendent Ralph Brown probably lost his job in 1951 because of political animosities stemming from long-term county gambling operations. But, to place the blame for LaFontaine's operation at the feet of the police department is an overly simplistic response to a complex enforcement problem. The casino, which was well established and professionally run, was operating long before the county police came into existence. The police department, once in operation, lacked the manpower, expertise, and some would say motivation to mount a prolonged enforcement campaign against LaFontaine's casino. Many people also thought that gambling was a form of entertainment, at worst a victimless crime. Elected officials would occasionally express some concern over county gambling operations and direct the police to mount an anti-gambling campaign. Jimmy LaFontaine, always a practical man, knew when to tone down his operation. For many years, he opted to close down the casino when the county Grand Jury came into session (for two weeks—twice a year). It appears that Jimmy's place was raided by law enforcement authorities on one or two occasions, both occurring before a full-time police force was formed. It would also be fair to say that Jimmy LaFontaine had many powerful friends, some of whom were in a position to influence the occurrence of events.

According to a recently published Mt. Rainier history, LaFontaine's casino was originally built as a home for John C. Rives (1795–1864), who founded The Congressional Globe, *the predecessor of* The Congressional Record. *This history states that Jimmy LaFontaine died on November 21, 1949, leaving $2,245,430 of which $1,818,763 was cash.*

*A police color guard leads off a
1951 District Heights parade. Left to
right are Officers Albert Butler,
Thomas Rogato, Edward Gryszkiewi[c]
and Douglas Maxfield. A county*

CHAPTER V

1950-1959
Specialization/Urban Growth/ Increasing Demands for Police Services

Old ideas give way slowly; for they are more than abstract logical forms and categories. They are habits, predispositions, deeply ingrained attitudes of adversion and preference.
—John Dewey

With the onset of the 1950s, Prince George's County entered into a period of dynamic growth. Urbanization was no longer a vague government term; it had actually taken place, at least in that portion of the county bordering the District of Columbia. The county government, realizing that it had no other choice but to modernize, hired the Public Administration Service (PAS) to conduct an evaluation survey of county services. The survey, when completed, indicated that while the population of Washington had increased 184 percent between 1900 to 1950, the population in Prince George's County had increased 548 percent—90 percent of the county's growth being located within those areas directly adjacent to the District of Columbia.

The PAS survey, describes the county police as, "The largest police organization in the county. . . . The present force of the department consists of 57 persons, two of whom are on detached service to the office of the sheriff and the state's attorney's office. The department is divided into two separate organizational units, the Marlboro Station and the Hyattsville Station. Each station operates its own radio dispatching unit, keeps its own records, and has its own detective personnel. Each station has a lieutenant in charge. The communications maintenance personnel attached to the Hyattsville Station maintain all the radio equipment in the department and the equipment of those towns having radio units."

A listing of personnel strength according to rank and station was as follows:

Rank or title	Marlboro	Hyattsville	Detached	Total
Major	1	0	0	1
Lieutenant	1	1	1	3
Sergeant	4	3	0	7
Corporal	2	2	0	4
Private	6	10	0	16
Detective Sergeant	1	1	1	3
Detective	2	2	0	4
Desk Clerk	3	3	0	6
Jailer	0	1	0	1
Civilian Clerk	1	1	0	2
New personnel not yet assigned				10
Total	21	24	2	57

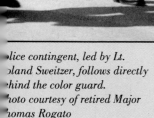

...lice contingent, led by Lt. ...oland Sweitzer, follows directly ...hind the color guard. ...hoto courtesy of retired Major ...homas Rogato

Political turmoil occurred as a result of the November 1950 elections. In a normally Democratic county, the Republican party made an unheard-of sweep and captured all five seats on the Board of County Commissioners. At their first meeting, the new Republican commissioners removed Superintendent Brown from office. F. Allen Richards, another Democrat, was appointed as the department's new superintendent of police. Mr. Richards, a county contractor, had served as a county policeman between 1938 and 1945.
Photo courtesy of Lt. William Richards

Additional police information found within the survey indicates that, "the desk clerks in the respective stations operate the 50-watt radio-telephone transmitter, which in turn activates a 250-watt transmitter to contact the radio-equipped mobile units. The Hyattsville Station also has a teletype transmitter and receiver which allows the County Police Department to be in immediate contact with all law enforcement agencies within the region."

The survey's most severe criticism of the police department was directed at the lack of a standard crime-reporting policy. According to the survey, each of the department's two stations maintained their own record-keeping systems, with neither system being compatible with the other. The study recommended that one single reporting policy be established and that all reports be filed in a Central Records Office at Hyattsville.

On November 9, 1950, the *Prince George's Post* heralded an unusually bold headline, "Republicans Win County Control." Traditionally, Prince George's County had been a Democratic party stronghold and according to the newspaper a "victory-starved Republican party emerged from a twenty-eight year hiatus" to win all five seats on the Board of County Commissioners. Allegiances within the ranks of the county government, especially within the police department, had leaned heavily toward the Democrats. This allegiance caused many police employees to predict that the new Republican commissioners would substantially change the police department.

The outgoing Democratic commissioners granted the police a pay raise on November 23, 1950. Starting salaries for probationary officers now began at $2,400 annually. After obtaining permanent status, an officer's salary was set at $3,200 annually. Desk clerks and detectives received an average pay increase of $300 per year. A new rank of "Private First Class" was also initiated with a starting salary of $3,300. Pvt. Adam Lindsay, the ranking private on the force, was advanced to the new grade. The commissioners failed to act on a proposal to reorganize the department stating that "it is best to leave this matter to the incoming commissioners."

On December 7, 1950, the *Prince George's Post* reported that the newly elected Republican commissioners had adopted a resolution whereby the police superintendent would now serve at their discretion. After approving the resolution, the new board "terminated the services of Superintendent Ralph Brown and designated Lieutenant Roscoe Sines as the Acting Superintendent."

F. Allen Richards was appointed as the new superintendent of police on January 9, 1951. A local newspaper described Richards as "a one-time police private—and a Democrat to boot. . . . the new Chief served as a private in the Marlboro Station from December 1938 until July 1945. He left the Force to enter private business as a building contractor." The new superintendent told one newspaper reporter that he intended to "enforce the laws of this county," apparently referring to his intention of strictly enforcing those laws prohibiting gambling. The superintendent also added that he would be aggressive in his attempts to have additional police officers appointed to the force, and that he had some definite ideas regarding certain organizational changes within the department.

The newly appointed superintendent thought that the police department was drastically understaffed and immediately issued an order for all officers to work a six-day workweek, twelve hours per day. He indicated that the extended schedule would remain in effect until twenty new police officers were hired and trained. Richards also disliked the title of superintendent and quickly began to wear a set of gold oak leafs on his uniform. Henceforth, all police personnel addressed the superintendent by his new military rank of major. The newspapers never did like the military title and continued to use the term "superintendent" or "chief of police" when referring to Richards.

Although the county did experience some violent crime, it

did not pose a serious problem to the safety of most county residents. In general, the public seemed more concerned about increased gambling activity and illegal liquor sales. Additionally, the public was asking that the police reduce the number of traffic-related deaths through a stricter traffic law enforcement policy. The public was also concerned about juvenile delinquency and asked for increased patrol activity at known juvenile hangouts. A Grand Jury note of October 30, 1952, stated that, "We have only six scout cars (on duty) to cover the entire county. . . . that number is hardly sufficient to patrol the Washington-Baltimore Boulevard, which claims more lives than any other highway in the State."

As the department expanded and additional patrol cars were needed, the longstanding practice of allowing senior patrol officers to take their patrol cars home was discontinued. Another tradition that disappeared around this same time was the two-man patrol car. An unidentified newspaper story quotes Major Richards as saying "About half of the Department's patrol cars now carry only one man in daylight hours. . . . eventually all will so operate." The chief went on to say that he would "never recommend nighttime solo patrols, that would be too dangerous."

In 1951, the police department reached a point where expansion and specialization could no longer be ignored. It was obvious that the department had outgrown its Upper Marlboro headquarters, and a project was initiated to find a more accessible location for a new headquarters building. To meet the increased public demand for stricter enforcement of the gambling and liquor laws, Officers Pete Perrygo and Ralph Bond were assigned to a newly formed Vice Squad. The officers were told to crack down on the widespread use of slot machines, bookmaking, and the many after-hours clubs that operated within the county. Det. Sgts. Vincent Free and John Siddall were assigned to the sheriff and state's attorney's offices to investigate some of the county's larger gambling operations. Police Officer Elmer Pumphrey was assigned to work as a one-man unit created specifically to handle check and fraud crimes. Six police officers: Pvts. Donald Forsht, Clarence Butler, Thomas Rogato, Thomas Irvine, Frank Noe, and Edward Gryszkiewicz were assigned to a special Accident Investigation Unit (AIU). Cpl. Roland B. Sweitzer was also assigned to conduct the department's first in-house Police Academy for training new officers.

An unidentified news article states that Central Avenue was the dividing line between the Hyattsville and Upper Marlboro Stations. The article further stated, "Working out of the Hyattsville Station are five beat cruisers and one accident investigation car. Four cruisers and an AIU car work out of the Marlboro Station. . . . The large number of cars on the road resulted in a substantial increase in traffic arrests." In 1952, county police officers made a total of 4,149 traffic arrests as opposed to 1,622 in 1951. During the same year, a total of 7,673 criminal arrests were made as opposed to 4,699 for the previous year. In an effort to release patrol officers from school crossing duties, Major Richards proposed hiring women as part-time school-crossing guards. The idea was initially turned down by the county commissioners, but became a reality in 1954. In

Numerous police departments within Maryland used some configuration of a triangular-shaped police shoulder patch. In 1951, Superintendent Richards adopted the use of a circular shaped shoulder patch to distinguish the county police department from other law enforcement agencies. Similarly designed collar ornaments, about the size of a bottle cap, were also adopted for use with the uniform shirt.
Washington Star *photo from the scrapbook of Supt. F. Allen Richards*

late 1953, Major Richards broke the sex barrier and made arrangements for the department to hire its first female station and record clerks.

Major Richards was, to say the least, a controversial man. He assumed office as a reformer and implemented many changes within a department that had experienced very little organizational change. He lobbied the county commissioners to modernize the department and successfully reduced a longstanding understaffing problem. Known as a straightforward and sometimes uncompromising man, his behavior was such that many people, both from within and outside of the department, failed to appreciate his true worth. Not afraid to speak out, he once complained that a group of reporters had misquoted him about the status of a gambling investigation. An unidentified news article quotes the superintendent as saying, "If I catch those men (reporters) I'll knock their Goddam heads off. . . . If they printed that they better get out of Prince George's County."

On December 12, 1953, *The Evening Star* reported that two county commissioners had completed a prolonged six-month investigation into several charges of administrative misconduct by Major Richards. According to the newspaper, three of the five commissioners had voted to "suspend a surprised Major Richards." After heated arguments, the commissioners decided to postpone a formal hearing into the misconduct charges. Another unidentified newspaper article reported that Major Richards made it known that he wanted a public hearing to allow him the opportunity to clear his name. The *Washington Post* later reported that Major Richards was "summarily fired" by the 3 to 2 vote of the county commissioners, and that the "action was taken without a public hearing which the Chief had requested." Pending the appointment of a new superintendent, the commissioners appointed Lt. Vincent S. Free as the acting superintendent of police.

In early 1953, a third police station was opened at 410 Addison Raod in Seat Pleasant. Besides being a neighborhood police station, this building housed all the department's specialty units, including headquarters. With the opening of Seat Pleasant another milestone was reached: the department could now boast that all its reports were filed in one central location. The building also housed a centralized radio dispatch room. All calls for police service were now dispatched from one central location rather than the individual police stations. A centralized Detective Division was also formed with all the department's detectives now working out of the new headquarters building.

In 1954, the department created the new rank of captain. Promoted to the new rank were: Vincent S. Free, who was still acting as superintendent of police; Charles N. Thomsen, chief of detectives; and Roland B. Sweitzer, who headed the Patrol Division. A Grand Jury report submitted on December 8, 1954, stated that the police department had in the six months between April 1, 1954, and September 30, 1954, driven 575,184 miles, answered 11,058 complaints, served 3,580 civil papers, made 5,660 arrests, and investigated 1,320 auto accidents. A police department annual report for 1954 also states that, "On September 7th, the opening day of school, we were able to place 15 uniformed female crossing guards at some of the hazardous intersections. On Monday, October 18th, we will be able to place 16 more uniformed female crossing guards at points needed to insure the safety of school children going to and from school. Before placing the guards on the street they are given 30 to 36 hours of instruction in first aid, and the handling of traffic, both in the classroom and at the particular crossing that they will guard." The department also reported that it had abolished the Accident Investigation Unit and created a one-man Traffic Safety Section.

On February 4, 1955, the county commissioners announced that they had appointed George J. Panagoulis as the new superintendent of police. Mr. Panagoulis, previously the director of public safety in the city of Greenbelt, succeeded Acting Supt. Vincent S. Free, who, in turn, assumed the new title of assistant superintendent. Major Panagoulis assumed control of the 112-officer agency at a salary of $6,000 per year. The new superintendent would remain as the department's chief executive officer for the next thirteen years.

Demands for additional and improved police services continued as the county's population increased. An article in the September 7, 1957 edition of *The Evening Star* stated that the Prince George's County Civic Federation had recommended three additional police stations be built, one on Indian Head Highway near St. Barnabas Road, another in or near Laurel, and a third on Route 301 near Route 50.

Violent crime, although slowly increasing, was still not a serious problem. Household and commercial break-ins were the county's most serious crimes, but the overall crime rate was comparable to that of other neighboring suburban jurisdictions. In 1956, the department's Detective Bureau investigated 660 breaking-and-entering offenses. In 1957, the assignment rate for break-ins climbed to 729 reported crimes.

The average Prince Georgian continued to be concerned about juvenile crimes, pinball machine payoffs, strip-tease joints, and the illegal sale of liquor. In 1957, the county experienced seven murders, thirty-nine rapes, ninety-six robberies, 729 breaking and enterings, 295 larcenies over $100, and 333 larcenies under $100. The department also responded to 52,310 calls for service; an increase of 25 percent over the previous year. The delivery of a quick and efficient police service, at least in the county's most heavily populated areas, was looked upon as a deterrent to the more serious crime that now plagued inner-city Washington.

In July 1958, Major Panagoulis submitted a report to the Board of County Commissioners for the calendar year 1957. This report revealed that the department's authorized sworn strength had increased to 150 men. The department indicated that it also employed "three clerk stenographers, one clerk typist, nineteen station clerks (two were part time), one jailer, and two janitors (one was part time)." A total of forty-one crossing guards were also employed under the supervision of Sgt. Thomas A. Rogato of the Traffic Safety Section. Two police officers had recently been assigned to assist Sergeant Rogato.

The salaries paid to county officers continued to lag behind those of other major jurisdictions in the Washington metropolitan area.

Rank	1st Year	7th Year
Private	$4,000	$5,200
Private First Class	4,100	5,300
Corporal	4,300	5,500
Detective	4,500	5,700
Sergeant	4,600	5,800
Detective Sergeant	4,800	6,000
Lieutenant	5,100	6,450
Captain	5,600	7,100
Inspector	5,800	7,600

In summary, the 1950s ushered in a period of increasing calls for service, but serious crime remained at a relatively low level. Urbanization, previously confined to the older northside towns, began to spread out into the unincoporated areas of the county. County government saw that future population increases would place new demands upon the police, and that there was a need to plan for future expansion. As the 1950s came to an end, the police budget was reported to be approximately $1,260,000. Just ten years earlier, the budget had been $326,106. During the same period, starting salaries had increased from $2,600 to

$4,000. Authorized strength had gone from approximately forty-two officers in the late 1940s to somewhat less than two hundred officers in the late 1950s. One new police station had opened in the densely populated Seat Pleasant area, and the need for additional stations had been publicly acknowledged. A centralized police records unit and central communications room were established in 1954 to better service the public and improve efficiency. The complexity attributed to some crimes caused the department to form a Vice Squad and Check and Fraud Unit. Public pressure over the escalating rate of juvenile delinquency also caused the formation of a two-man Juvenile Squad in 1958. Officers assigned to the Juvenile Squad also conducted formal parent/juvenile counselling sessions in minor law violation cases. Females, never before employed by the police department, were now hired as station clerks and school crossing guards. Police training, previously almost nonexistent, became an important part of the department's everyday operation. Training programs for new station clerks and school crossing guards were also established.

Prince George's County experienced a phenomenal rate of growth during the 1950s. The 1960 census reported that 357,395 people now called Prince George's County home; an increase of 163,000 residents in ten short years. History will reveal that Prince George's County was not fully prepared for the future growth onslaught. The tranquility previously associated with the largely semirural county of yesteryear would soon dissipate. Prince George's County was about to lose its country-like homogeneity and landscape to a conglomeration of housing developments, apartment complexes, shopping centers, and roads.

Records room at the Hyattsville Station. Prior to the 1954 creation of a Central Records Section, each individual station maintained its own recordkeeping files.
PGPD photo

Radio room at the Hyattsville Station. Until the creation of a Central Communications Division in 1954, each station had independent radio dispatch capabilities. Calls for service were received at the station and then dispatched to a patrol car by a station clerk.
PGPD photo

Photograph from the July 15, 1951 edition of The Evening Star *depicts Chief F. Allen Richards taking a sledgehammer to several slot machines that were seized in gambling raids. For many years the county police were criticized for what appeared to be lax enforcement of anti-gambling laws. One of the issues that helped elect a Republican-conrolled Board of County Commissioners was the promise of a crackdown on county gambling. Superintendent Richards, upon his appointment, promised to work with the sheriff and the state's attorney in a joint effort to stamp out gambling in Prince George's County. Photo courtesy of Lt. William Richards and retired Capt. Eddie Armstrong*

In the summer of 1951, the Senate Crime Investigating Committee, chaired by Sen. Estes Kefauver of Tennessee, was in the process of holding hearings on gambling operations occurring in and around the District of Columbia. One of the subjects being investigated by the committee was a Prince George's County bookmaker named Charles E. Nelson. On August 17, 1951, Prince George's County Sheriff Carleton Beall told the committee that Nelson had offered him $15,000 a month if allowed to open three gambling houses within the county. Mr. Nelson allegedly suggested that Sheriff Beall split the money three ways: $5,000 to himself, with the remaining money going to the police chief and state's attorney. According to the Post, additional testimony revealed that the sheriff had initially considered playing along with Mr. Nelson and then arresting him for bribery. The sheriff backed away from this plan after learning that county police detectives and congressional investigators were conducting a joint investigation into Mr. Nelson's activities.

Washington Post *front page courtesy of Fred DeMarr*

Shortly after assuming office, Major Richards assigned then Cpl. Roland Sweitzer to conduct the first in-house training school for rookie police officers. The county's first recruit training class received its instruction at Frederick Sasscer Junior High School. This class photograph was taken on the back parking lot of the courthouse in Upper Marlboro. The class is being inspected by Chief Richards and newly appointed Sergeant Sweitzer. Left to right in the first row are Douglas Maxfield, George Thornberry, Kenneth Embrey, Robert Cabral, and John Branzell. Left to right in the second row are George Clements, Buck Schaefer, James Vincent, Oliver Weekly, and Oral Husk.
PGPD photo

When Police Chief F. Allen Richards assumed command of the police department, he initiated a bimonthly policy of personally inspecting the officers at both the Upper Marlboro and Hyattsville Stations. Newspaper photo from the scrapbooks of Major F. Allen Richards and retired Capt. Edwin Thompson

The department continually upgraded its radio system. In this January 4, 1952 newspaper photo, Lt. Louis Mackall explains to Chief Richards the procedure by which the 50-watt signal leaves the Upper Marlboro Station and is transmitted to an antenna atop a 500-foot water tower in Suitland. The signal is then automatically boosted to 500 watts and relayed to patrol cars.
Evening Star photo from the scrapbooks of Major F. Allen Richards and retired Capt. Edwin Thompson. Courtesy of Lt. William Richards and retired Capt. Edward Armstrong

Early 1950s photo taken on the steps of Hyattsville Station. Left to right, in the first row are John Tucker, Major F. Allen Richards, Lt. Roland Sweitzer, and Officer Weaver. Second row: Jack Dent, Ray Blandford, Wade Beall, Edwin Thompson, and David Dudley. Third row: Boyd Hamilton, James Vincent, Lawson Peed, and George Clements. Fourth row: Charles Schaefer, John Branzell, Carl Keech, and Benny Richards. Fifth row: Bob Cabral, Oliver Weekly, and Richard Earnshaw. Sixth row: Lawrence Riddlebarger, Edward Bowser, Douglas Maxfield, Bill Wiseman, and Adam Lindsay. In the rear are Oral Husk, Emmett Gray, George Thornberry, Joseph Vincent, George Roland, and Kenneth Embrey (who is partially blocked from view).
PGPD photo

Officer Thomas Rogato, one of six policemen assigned to the Accident Investigation Unit (AIU), stands beside his 1952 Ford cruiser. The unit was formed to investigate all serious personal injury accidents, but the task proved to be beyond the unit's reach because of accident volume and area coverage problems. Other specialty units (Vice, Check and Fraud, and a later Juvenile Squad) prospered and generally improved police efficiency. Photo and patch courtesy of retired Major Thomas Rogato

Police Officer Edward R. Gryszkiewicz, a member of the Accident Investigation Unit, in his uniform blouse. During the late 1960s, the correct spelling of Lieutenant Gryszkiewicz's name was worth five points on every Police Academy final examination.
Photo courtesy of Corky Gryszkiewicz

The Hyattsville Station provided a police service to approximately one half of Prince George's County up until 1954. Police services during any one tour of duty were provided by four "area cars." One Accident Investigation Unit assisted the area cars on the day and evening tours of duty.
Photo courtesy of retired Sgt. Jimmy Miller

The manufacturing of illegal liquor continued to be a profitable venture in the county's southern region. County policemen, left to right, Dick Earnshaw, Charlie Nalley, Pete Perrygo, Ralph Bond, Lee Pumphrey, and Major Richards look on as Phil Kearns prepares to knock the top off a barrel of moonshine.
Photos courtesy of retired Lt. Pete Perrygo, the family of Sgt. Ralph Bond, and retired Lt. Phil Kearns

EXPANDED P.G. POLICE FORCE PROVES WORTH

But Even Larger Staff Is Held Unnecessary

BY ARTHUR MIELKE

It was 7:15 p.m. on a recent balmy evening. The shift was changing at the Hyattsville station of Prince Georges county police force, and more than a score of officers were on hand.

Suddenly, the station dispatcher's radio crackled with an alarm. A speeding car, said the Washington department's dispatcher, was careening out New Hampshire avenue, heading for Prince Georges.

Within a matter of seconds, six police cruisers had wheeled from the station parking area to set up the roadblock pattern designed to stop speeders and other such law violators.

The speeder was caught, in the fashion characterizing most such captures, but that isn't the point of this story. The main point is that the Hyattsville dispatcher, without fuss or bother, was able to get six police cars on the road at once.

Force Expanded

Little more than two years ago, the dispatcher would have been happy if he ould have sent two cruisers on such an assignment.

But during this interval the force has been expanded from a group of about 35 men to 72. Another factor which adds to availability of personnel is the two-shift schedule; each man works a 12-hour day.

Credit for development of this "new" county police force must go in large measure to F. Allen Richards, Prince Georges police chief, and the county's board of commissioners.

Richards has been hammering constantly for a larger force, for better equipment and for a suitable headquarters building, centrally located, where police records can be kept.

The commissioners, to a great extent, have gone along with Richards.

Fear Tax Increases

Despite pressure from some minority groups in the county, the commissioners have authorized a force of 93 men, have allocated $125,000 for purchase of a Seat Pleasant headquarters site and for erection of the building. Citizens opposing the changes said they "fear" tax increases.

The increase in personnel has shown some tangible results.

The "northern section" of the county—the area roughly north and west of Central avenue—has been divided into five patrol beats. The other portion of the county has four.

Working out of the Hyattsville station are five "beat" cruisers and one accident investigation car. Four cruisers and an A.I.U. car work out of the Marlboro station.

The total is satisfying when compared compared with the "old days"—only two years ago—when, during daylight hours, only three cruisers covered the county and only two patroled from midnight to 8 a.m.

The larger number of cars on the road has resulted in a substantial increase in traffic arrests. In 1952, county police made a total of 4,149 traffic arrests as against 1,622 in 1951. In over-all cases county police made 7,673 arrests last year, as against 4,699 the year before.

Regular Inspections

The county's detective squad has been expanded from seven to 13 since Richards took over on Jan. 15, 1951. The detective group has been "departmentalized" as well, with men specializing in check and fraud work, vice and identification.

The county force now is inspected regularly every month by Richards.

But Richards is not fully satisfied with the strides already taken.

In the budget he has submitted to the commissioners for fiscal 1953-54, he is asking for an additional 67 men, the number required to bring the force up to 150, which the recent grand jury cited as "the minimum" required properly to police the county.

The commissioners' decision on the request will be announced late in March.

This 1953 newspaper article identifies some of the new police services that Chief Richards implemented during his tenure as superintendent of police.
Courtesy of Lt. William Richards

Residential development, on what had previously been farmland, caused a host of unique public safety problems. During the 1950s, a series of potentially dangerous incidents occurred when children fell through decaying boards used to cover old farm wells. In this particular photograph, county detectives drain a well in search of a child. Nothing was found.
Photo courtesy of retired Lt. Phil Kearns

A negative vote by three of the five county commissioners forced Superintendent Richards from office in December 1953. The county commissioners appointed Lt. Vincent S. Free the department's acting superintendent and shortly thereafter promoted him to the newly created rank of captain. The commissioners had difficulty finding a new superintendent and Captain Free retained the title of acting superintendent for the next two years. On February 4, 1955, the commissioners appointed George Panagoulis as the department's new superintendent of police. Captain Free remained at headquarters as the assistant superintendent. He was promoted to the new rank of inspector in May 1956.
PGPD photo

The police department opened the Seat Pleasant Station in 1954. The first floor of the new building housed uniformed officers assigned to patrol the county's new central patrol area. The building's second floor housed headquarters, records, communications, and all detective personnel.
PGPD photo

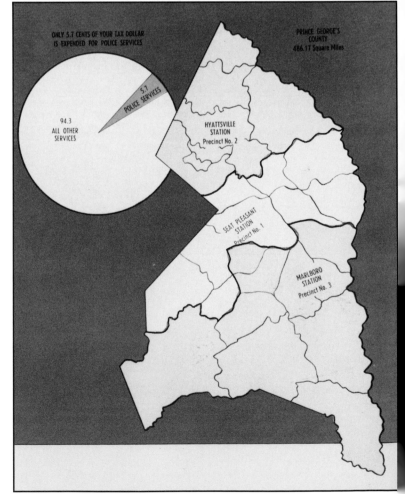

The police department's first Central Communications Room. Located on the second floor of the Seat Pleasant Station, the department's single-frequency police radio was used to dispatch all county police units. Most town police departments and the Maryland Park Police also functioned on this radio frequency. *PGPD photo*

On February 16, 1954, the department hired and began training twelve female clerks. The hiring of these female clerks broke the department's twenty-seven-year-old tradition of employing only males. After a two-week training period was completed, nine clerks were assigned to the three stations, two were assigned to the Detective Division, and one to the new Central Records Office. Left to right, in the first row, are Lorraine Armstrong, Dolores Tullis, Beverly Pierce, and Mae Ferguson. Second row: Capt. and Chief of Detectives Charles Thomsen, Thelma Baze, Frances Chisholm, Marion Voorhees, and Lt. Roland Sweitzer. Third row: Shirley Mangum, Maude Diggs, Arlene Thomas, Bernadette Howlin, and Diane Fowler.
PGPD photograph

Shirley Mangum, one of the original females hired in 1954, was initially assigned to the Seat Pleasant Station. She became a secretary to Roland B. Sweitzer when he was promoted to captain and placed in charge of the Uniform Division. Mrs. Mangum continued to work for Roland Sweitzer, serving as his personal secretary when he was appointed as chief of police in 1971. She is presently assigned to Central Records as an Administrative Assistant III, and is the department's senior employee with thirty-seven years of service.
Photo courtesy of Police Records

126

On May 13, 1954, the police department unveiled its mobile crime laboratory. A news article stated that the mobile lab enabled the department "to do everything on the scene of a crime that we now do at Headquarters except develop photographs." This photo was taken at the rear of the Seat Pleasant Station. The old house in the background is on county property at Addison Road and Eads Street. The house, which was later painted white, was converted into office space and used to alleviate some of the overcrowding in the Seat Pleasant Station. The building was torn down in 1968 and replaced with a temporary metal structure. The new building housed the Central Records Division and the police chief's office.
PGPD photo

Detectives assigned to the Identification Bureau responded to crime scenes and processed them for physical evidence. Det. Clarence (Moby) Vincent is shown here making a plaster of Paris cast of a shoe print found at a crime scene on Marlboro Pike.
PGPD photo

The department hired its first fifteen school crossing guards in the summer of 1954. Employed at wage rate of approximately $1 per hour, the crossing guards attended a training program prior to assuming their duties. Pictured, in the first row, left to right, with Capt. Roland Sweitzer are Frances Fauntleroy, Frances Goode, Martha Houchens, Betty Vollmer, Lillian Sesso, and Annie Edwards. Second row: Thelma Mabry, Beverly Mangun, Louise Miller, Cleo Hickman, and Gladys Rowles. Third row: Dora Hathcock, Eltrude Alvey, Pauline Shisler, and Jeanette Kans.
PGPD photo

The County Commissioners appointed George J. Paugoulis as the department's new superintendent on February 4, 1955. Mr. Panagoulis had previosly served seventeen years as the town of Greenbelt's chief of police. The new superintendent appointed Captain Free as his assistant superintendent.
PGPD photo

The new Central Records Section. This photo was probably taken in the mid-1950s. Florence Senes (a longtime police employee who retired in the mid-1980s) is shown completing some filing. Also pictured at their desks, left to right, are Marion Peaire, Dolores Tullis, and Mae Ferguson.
PGPD photo

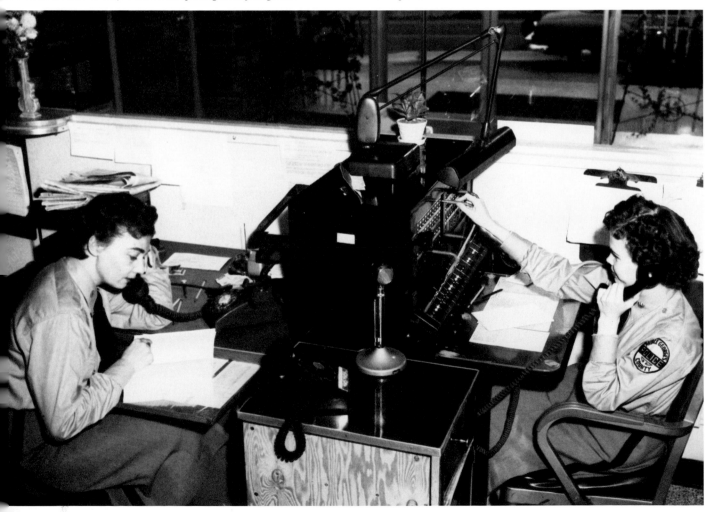

Working the police department's switchboard are Thelma Atkins (left) and Rose Bishop. All routine and emergency calls came through one main police number REdwood 5-5555. Although the operator was able to handle most situations, a surge of calls could bottleneck the switchboard. In 1955, a total of 36,411 calls for police service were received.
PGPD photo

THE SHOMETTE/RYAN MURDERS

"You could search the whole world over and not find a more pleasant strip of greenness than tree-shaded Northwest Branch Park, 10 miles northeast of Washington, D.C., in Prince George's County, Maryland. Designed for play the park provides ball fields, a picnic area with outdoor fireplaces and a small, meandering stream from which it takes its name. People who bought homes in the nearby Lane Manor development looked upon this park as an ideal place for a family to relax. On week nights teen-agers would sit at the picnic tables and talk until dark. Then they would cross West Park Drive to one of their houses and play records." The sublime tranquility of these words led off a magazine article about one of Prince George's County's most baffling, senseless, and brutal murders.

On Wednesday, June 15, 1955, two best friends, 16-year-old Nancy Shomette and 14-year-old Michelle Ryan left their West Park Drive homes and disappeared into the tree-shaded Northwest Branch Park. It was shortly after 8:00 a.m. in the morning. The first warm days of the year had arrived and both girls looked forward to a summer of fun. School had just recessed for the summer and both girls were headed for Northwestern High School in order to pick up Nancy's report card. Cutting through the park was a familiar shortcut for Nancy, who was just finishing her junior year at the school.

Sometime prior to 10:00 a.m, Nancy Shomette's parents became concerned when she failed to return home. Mr. Shomette drove to the school and was told that Nancy had never arrived to pick up her report card. Returning home Nancy's father was concerned, but not overly alarmed. He thought that Nancy and Michelle might have taken a bus into Washington and gone shopping in the downtown stores (the suburban shopping center had yet to make its appearance within Prince George's County).

At about 10:15 a.m, a 12-year-old neighborhood girl, walking through the park, discovered a body in some thick woods. Running home, the girl told her mother that there was a body in the woods with blood on it. The mother initially believed that her daughter had been watching too much television, but agreed to accompany the youngster back into the park. The woman took one quick look, and she ran home to call the police.

Privates E. G. (Denny) Husk and William Kreitzer of the county police department's Hyattsville Station were the first officers to arrive at the scene. They found a girl's body at the edge of some thick woods about eighty feet from a dirt road which ran through the park. The position of the body and the victim's disarrayed clothing gave the officers reason to believe that the girl had been murdered elsewhere and then dragged into the woods. Sgt. John Branzell, the shift supervisor, arrived a few minutes later. After examining the crime scene, the sergeant walked back into the woods and found the body of a second teen-age girl. The physical appearance of the second victim led the officers to believe that she also had been killed elsewhere and then moved. A large spot of blood found near the road and

three expended rounds from a .22 caliber gun would later lead investigators to believe that the double murder had actually occurred on the open roadway.

Chief of Police George Panagoulis was notified of the murder and, in accordance with the practices of the day, responded to the crime scene along with Capt. Vincent Free. The chief was briefed about the details of the double murder by Sergeant Branzell and Detective Sgt. Richard Pearson, Sr. Realizing that he had a particularly brutal and heinous double murder of two young girls on his hands, the chief placed one of his most experienced detectives, Lt. Earl J. Huber, in charge of the case.

The medical examiner, after arriving on the scene and examining the bodies told the detectives that both victims had been shot to death. Nancy Shomette's body revealed eleven bullet wounds, while Michelle Ryan had been shot three times. FBI analysis of the .22 caliber rounds found at the crime scene would later reveal that the murder weapon was a .22 caliber Marlin semi-automatic rifle. While detectives canvassed the neighbor-hood for information, Army engineers with mine detectors were called in to search for the weapon. The Chillum-Adelphi Volunteer Fire Department assisted in an "elbow-to-elbow search," but found no evidence of value. Metropolitan Police Chief Robert V. Murray assigned four of his best detectives to assist the county police in their investigation of the case. Michelle Ryan was the daughter of Metropolitan Police Officer Thomas W. Ryan.

An autopsy revealed no evidence that either victim had been sexually molested. In an attempt to find additional evidence a stream running through the park was temporarily dammed and a search conducted of the stream bed with negative results. A large pond in the park was also drained and searched in hopes of finding the murder weapon. Numerous suspects were picked up for questioning over the next few days. Several of the better suspects volunteered to take polygraph tests which were adminis-tered by the Metropolitan Police (the county police did not have a trained polygraph operator). All of those taken in for questioning were released. Detectives assigned to the case interviewed hundreds of people over the next several weeks without obtaining any information of real substance. Investigators assigned to the case surmised that the girls were initially shot near the park roadway and that the suspect then dragged their bodies into the woods in an apparent attempt to conceal the murders. Although the murders occurred in broad daylight, no witnesses came forth to indicate that they had seen anything suspicious on the day of the shooting. The police investigation revealed that the suspect had fired a total of seventeen shots, but no one reported hearing the girls scream or the sound of gunfire. A composite drawing of a possible suspect was later developed. This suspect, an odd-looking man, had been observed in the area on several previous occasions wearing a military type fatigue uniform with bandoliers and carrying a rifle.

The murders of Nancy Shomette and Michelle Ryan shocked the entire metropolitan area. The FBI later entered the case because it was believed that the suspect had fled across state lines and that he might also have been involved in a series of other murders. Never before, in the annals of county law enforcement, had so many law enforcement officers gathered together with the sole goal of identifying and arresting the person responsible for the senseless murdering two young teenage girls. The investigation continued for a prolonged period of time, but as substantial leads dwindled the case came to a stand still. Thirty-five years later the Shomette/Ryan case remains unsolved.

SIDE NOTES OF INTEREST: Most of the information furnished about the Shomette/Ryan murders was obtained from an old issue of *Master Detective Magazine*. That information was then matched with the personal recollections of retired Capt. E. G. Husk who was one of the first uniformed officers on the scene. Captain Husk also has a *Washington Daily News* clipping bearing the date June 15, 1956. This clipping contains information about two Maryland girls whose nude bodies had been found in Potomac Valley waters northwest of Washington. The newspaper story states, "The grim discovery came exactly one year after two other teen-age Maryland girls were shot to death in Prince George's County's Northwestern Branch Park. There is the chance that the same killer has struck again. A body tentatively identified as Shelby Jean Venable, 16, of Laurel, was found yesterday near Wheatland, Va. face down in a shallow stream which empties into the Potomac in Loudoun County. Another body, believed to be that of her friend, Mary Elizabeth Fellers, 18, of Beltsville, was found Saturday in the Potomac River near Brunswick, 10 miles away. . . . The girls were last seen alive in Beltsville on June 1 when Mary Fellers' 13-year-old brother saw them get into a light blue car driven by a young man. . . ." Although not specifically stated, the county police probably had no official involvement in this investigation because the girls had evidently been reported as missing to the Maryland State Police.

Word of mouth information that survived the passage of time indicates that a roving musician, who was born and raised in Hyattsville, had become a prime suspect in the Shomette/Ryan case and in a series of other murders occurring in both Virginia and Maryland. The suspect was supposedly involved in the slaying of four family members traveling through Louisa County, Virginia. The bodies of two family members were discovered in Louisa County, while the two remaining bodies were supposedly found in the Jessup area of Howard County, Maryland. A Virginia court ruled that the suspect was mentally incompetent to stand trial and confined him to a mental institution with the understanding that he would never be released. Many of the detectives who investigated the Shomette/Ryan murders are now deceased and the passage of time has somewhat tarnished the memories of those retired officers who still remain with us. In 1990, some thirty-five years after these brutal murders, several leads were developed which caused county homicide detectives to dust off and review the thousands of pages contained within the now thirty-five-year-old report of investigation.

BLACK HAIR

HEAVY BLACK EYEBROWS

CRISS-CROSS BANDOLEER

CANTEEN ON BELT

ROLLED GRAY BLANKET

WEB BELT

TWO CLIP HOLDERS

BAYONET HUNG FROM BELT

22 CAL. RIFLE

5 FT. 10 IN. TALL

WEIGHT 140 LBS

SHABBY FELT HAT

john McCormick

WORE FADED BLUE-GRAY COTTON SHIRT AND TROUSERS. LIGHT COMPLEXION AND THIN FACE. ABOUT 25 YEARS OLD -

The police circulated this composite drawing of a man they wanted to question in reference to the Shomette/Ryan murders. Nicknamed by the newspapers as "Poncho Villa," the man had been seen in the general vicinity of Northwest Branch Park on several different occasions by several different people. Unidentified newspaper clipping from official police file

131

Jerry's Hot Dog Stand on Bladensburg Road was one of several drive-in restaurants built to serve the county's growing urban population. The drive-in restaurant, an early forerunner to the fast-food industry, quickly gained popularity with the younger generation. Some drive-ins became a gathering place for teen-agers and presented the police with a new problem, teen-age loitering and juvenile delinquency. Taking everything into consideration, crime remained within bounds, and the 1950s turned out to be a relatively tranquil period of time.
Photo courtesy of Francis Geary

Officers from Hyattsville Station await an inspection.
PGPD photo

Officers from Seat Pleasant stand beside their police cruisers
ready for inspection.
PGPD photos

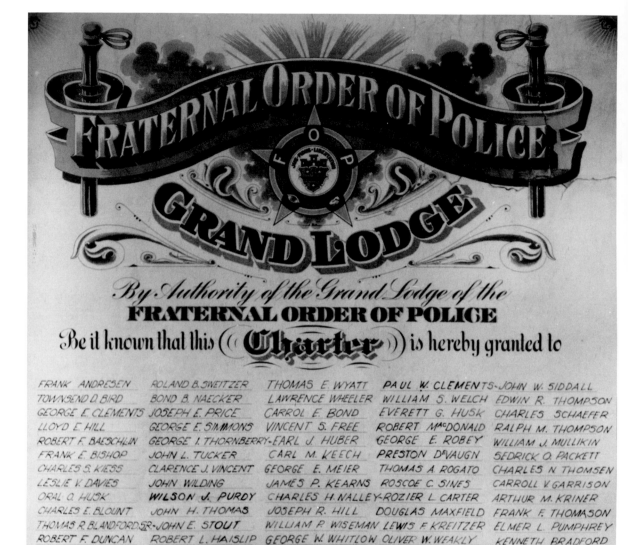

The Prince George's County Police Association disbanded when its members chose to join the Fraternal Order of Police, a nationwide fraternal police organization. Prince George's County FOP Lodge 89 received its formal charter on December 27, 1955. Charter courtesy of Prince George's County Fraternal Order of Police Lodge 89

Mid-1950s, FOP Lodge 89 softball team.
Kneeling, left to right, are Jack Magruder,
Jack Padgett, Bill Mathews, Walter Bosch, and
Wallace Hunter (Maryland Park Police).
Standing, left to right are Bob Baeschlin, Leroy
Collins, Townsend Bird, Henry Schoen, and
Denny Husk.
Photo courtesy of an unknown donor

Sgt. David Dudley conducts a roll call. Note that each officer is wearing his full Sam Browne gear
and uniformed blouse. The blouse was worn during the fall and winter months. The regulation
requiring the wearing of a hat was strictly enforced by supervisory personnel. The wearing of the
blouse continued up until the Blauer Jacket was issued in 1972. Today, the blouse is a special
occasion dress uniform and the wearing of a hat is considered optional under most circumstances.
PGPD photo

Concern over increased juvenile crime became an issue in the mid-1950s. Some people believed the violence portrayed in certain comic books contributed to the increased rate of juvenile delinquency. Detective Emmett Gray and Assistant State's Attorney Woody Shiver review comic books that were seized in a raid as being "lewd and lascivious."
Photo courtesy of Emmett Gray

Officers Jimmy Miller (who retired as a sergeant) and Everette "Denny" Husk (who retired as a captain) stand next to their 1958 Ford police cruiser. The object on the vehicle's right front fender was called a "stop light." An officer would pull along side the traffic violator's left front fender and activate the light, which reflected the word "stop" in red letters.
Photo courtesy of retired Sgt. Jimmy Miller

Remarkable County, Prince Georges

By Hal Willard

THE CONTRAST between the two large Maryland counties bordering on the District of Columbia was emphasized last week as never before.

Prince Georges knocked 5 cents off its tax rate and Montgomery added 12 cents.

The Prince Georges rate fell from $2.15 per $100 of assessed valuation to $2.10 —saving taxpayers about $292,000, or $4 for a man whose house is assessed at $8000.

Montgomery raised its rate from $2.03 to $2.15 at a cost to taxpayers of $1,-116,000—or $9.60 to the man with the $8000 assessment.

Willard

Both counties adopted record budgets for operations and new construction during the year starting July 1. The Montgomery County budget is $53.4 million while the Prince Georges budget is $28.6 million. The Prince Georges budget lags far behind that of its neighboring county even though Prince Georges is larger. Current population estimates give Prince Georges 325,000 persons—about 25,000 more than Montgomery.

The new tax rates also underscore the big disparity in services provided to the public in the two counties. Montgomery, already spending more on services than its neighboring county, raised taxes to provide even more services. Prince Georges, in cutting its taxes, fell that much farther behind Montgomery.

The tax rates are predicated on yearly expenditures, but it is difficult to compare the budgets of the two counties b e c a u s e the Prince Georges budget does not include capital outlay.

The operating budgets for the school systems in both counties afford some basis for comparison. Enrollments are roughly equal—in the vicinity of 53,000-55,000. The Montgomery budget is $19.2 million and the Prince Georges budget is $16.2 million.

What are the differences? Montgomery has kindergartens and a junior college. Prince Georges has neither.

There is more emphasis on special types of education in Montgomery County, which is generally considered to have one of the most advanced and effective educational systems in the Nation. This requires teachers with special training and consequently costs more.

In another field of comparison, Montgomery County has 227 policemen and their starting salary is $4100 a year. Prince Georges has 130 officers and the budget authorized 20 more at a starting salary of $3600 a year.

Prince Georges County Police Chief George J. Panagoulis had asked for 36 more men. A grand jury report last week recommended that the county have 200 policemen by the end of this year.

BUT THE MOST STARTLING THING about the Prince Georges tax cut was the fact that the Board of Commissioners made it.

Members of the board had said, publicly and for months, that the county would be hard pressed to find enough money to meet its budgetary obligations. After some early talk of a tax raise, which was emphatically dismissed, three fiscal developments apparently convinced the Commissioners that a tax cut was justified. They were:

• The $400,000 in real estate transfer tax revenue authorized by the Legislature.

• Some $1.2 million more the county will receive from its tax rate, despite the reduction. There is a $50 million hike in the assessable base. Last year it was $526 million; now it is $584 million.

• Some $800,000 shaved from departmental budget requests.

While the Prince Georges County Commissioners were slashing budget requests and reducing the tax rate, their opposite numbers in Montgomery County were doing exactly the opposite.

The Montgomery County Council added thousands of dollars to the budget recommended to them by County Manager M. L. Reese. They did this partly in response to the demands of citizens who appeared at a public hearing and said they were willing to pay larger taxes to obtain added services which they felt were essential.

These citizen demands again underscore the difference between the two counties. Hundreds of vocal citizens turn out for budget hearings in Montgomery. In Prince Georges County 50 or 60 persons show up for the budget hearings.

The Montgomery County heads rarely hear a demand for a tax cut. But the Prince Georges lawmakers say they are under constant pressure from the citizenry to hold the tax rate steady or to reduce taxes.

This mid-1950s article is from an unidentified newspaper. Written by Hal Willard, the article is especially interesting because it compares the tax rates and spending priorities of Prince George's and Montgomery County.

In 1958, two additional officers were assigned to the Traffic Safety Unit. In addition to supervising school crossing guards, the unit was also responsible for conducting traffic safety classes at both public and private schools. Standing beside their cars, from left to right, are Pvt. George Whitlow, PFC George Robey, and Sgt. Thomas Rogato.
PGPD photo

PFC George Robey of the Traffic Safety Unit conducts a safety inspection at an elementary school bicycle rodeo.
Photo courtesy retired Cpl. George Robey

This aerial shot of Forestville was taken in the mid-1950s before Donnell Drive, Pennsylvania Avenue, and Penn-Mar Shopping Center were built. The large light-colored plot of land in the upper center of the photograph is O'Donnell's Farm (present site of Penn-Mar Shopping Center). Marlboro Pike, the main east-west roadway through the central county, can be seen at the farm's northern boundary. Andrews Air Force Base can be seen in the background.
Photo courtesy of retired Major Thomas Rogato

The General Assignment Squad of the Detective Division came into existence with the completion of Seat Pleasant Station. The centralized bureau was responsible for all follow-up criminal investigations concerning criminal matters other than vice and fraud cases. Pictured in the first row, from front to rear, are Detectives Emmett Gray, Denny Husk, and Bill Rutherford (the last detective just outside the office is unidentifiable). The rear office with the open door belonged to the Detective Division Commander Capt. Francis Thomsen. In the middle row, from front to rear, are Detectives John Wilding, Larry Wheeler, and Charlie Nalley. Lt. Earl Huber is sitting at the desk between the doors. The detective facing the wall in the third row of desks is unidentifiable, the detective sitting in the far right corner is believed to be Bob Cabral. The closed door at the right led to a prisoner interrogation room.
PGPD photo

Until the late 1960s, the police department maintained its own radio repair shop in a garage behind the Seat Pleasant Station. In this late 1950s photograph, Capt. Louis Mackall (left), Lt. Reginal Austin (middle), and Sgt. Duerell Seitz prepare to install a Dumont multi-tube radio into a police cruiser.
PGPD photo

This March 19, 1959 photo depicts a recruit class receiving firearms training at a range in Greenbelt. The class was instructed by FBI Special Agent Robert Hickman (left rear) and county police Inspector Vincent Free (right rear). Note the hand-on-hip or hand-in-pocket shooting stance that was taught at this time. This particular class was made up of Prince George's County police recruits and military personnel assigned to the armed forces police.
PGPD photo

Officers Frank Bishop (left) and Rodney Brewer reported that while driving down a newly resurfaced county road they found an owl with its talons embedded to the still-hot tar. The officers came to the bird's rescue and freed it after posing for this photo.
Photo courtesy of retired Sgt. Frank Bishop

1959 photograph of the Maryland National Capital Park and Planning Commission Police. The small park police department was formed in 1954 to police those areas controlled by the Park Commission. Left to right are: Chris Kreitzer, Wallace Hunter, Donald Leslie, and Hugh Robey.
Photo courtesy of Maryland Park and Planning Commission

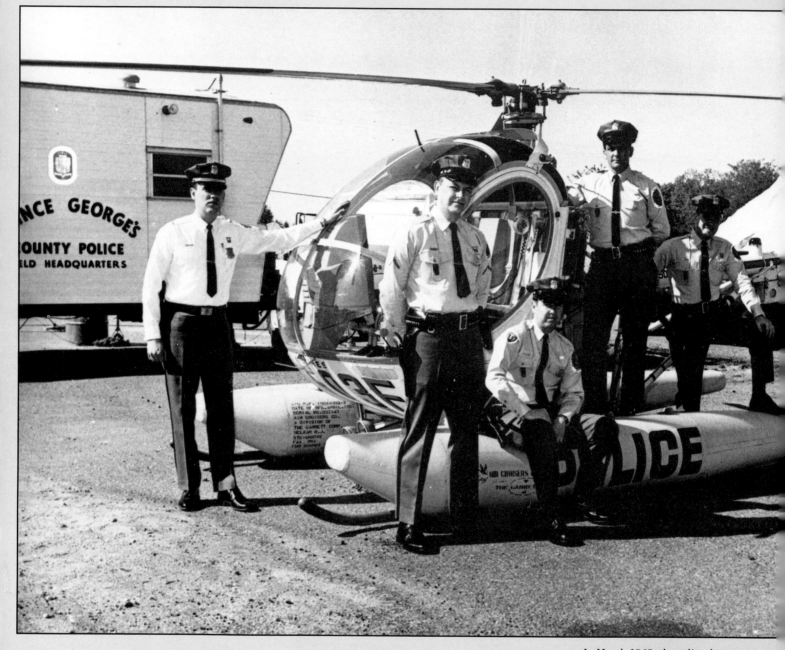

In March 1968, the police department entered into an experimental program with Hughes Aircraft to test the effectiveness of rotor-winged aircraft in everyday police patrol work. The project was titled *OPERATION ALERT*, an acronym for *Aerial Law Enforcement Reconnaissance Technique*. Hughes Aircraft supplied the helicopter and a pilot. The police

department supplied all of the necessary police equipment and an officer/observer for each flight. The plan was to have one helicopter on flight or standby status for approximately ten to twelve hours per day, alternating between day and night patrol. A total of two helicopters were assigned to the project.
PGPD Photo

CHAPTER VI

1960-1969
A Population Explosion/
Increased Crime

The essence of nostalgia is an awareness that what has been will never be again.
—Milton S. Eisenhower

The relative tranquility of the 1950s carried over into the early 1960s. Prince George's County's most severe problem appeared to evolve around how the county might best prepare itself for the anticipated increases in both population and developmental growth. A large volume of relatively inexpensive and undeveloped land made the county particularly attractive to those who advocated unrestricted development. The proliferation of planned single-family homes and large garden-type apartment complexes placed a tremendous burden upon the county to build new roads and schools, along with the necessity of expanding other vital governmental services.

In 1960, the 204-man county police department used a fleet of seventy-seven police cars to service the county's 357,395 residents. Traveling 1,956,280 miles the police department responded to more than 30,000 calls for service and made 10,934 criminal arrests. The six-year-old Seat Pleasant Station was composed of four patrol areas (11 through 14), the older and still more heavily populated Hyattsville area had seven area patrols (21 through 27), while the rural Upper Marlboro area had only three patrol areas (31 through 33). Countywide, the average number of officers on duty at any one time varied according to tour of duty: Shift One (midnight to 8 a.m.)—twenty officers; Shift Two (8 a.m. to 4 p.m.)—twenty officers; and Shift Three (4 p.m. to midnight)— twenty-six officers. Patrol officers worked a seven day, forty-eight-hour workweek, with short changes from shift to shift. The starting salary for officers had recently been raised to $4,500 annually.

The problem of serious crime continued to remain relatively low in 1960 with the department reporting:

Criminal Homicide	5
Rape	13
Robbery	73
Aggravated Assault	58
Burglary/B&E	1,336
Larceny	
Over $100	379
Under $100	1,011
Auto Theft	856

County officers also issued 7,101 traffic citations and investigated 3,877 motor vehicle accidents. Forty-four people were killed in traffic accidents during 1960.

One of the first 1960-style changes to occur within the police department was the adoption of a new and especially attractive police shoulder patch. The idea for the new patch, which incorporated the use of the county seal, came from Capt. Edwin Thompson. The county commissioners and Chief Panagoulis thought that the idea of a new county seal police patch improved the uniform's general appearance, and they authorized its use in 1961.

The police department broke another longstanding tradition in the fall of 1961 when Major Panagoulis informed the county commissioners that Carol Ann Polley had been selected from a long list of candidates as the department's first female police officer. The major stated that Carol Polley, a college graduate, had been specifically hired to work with juveniles and that he felt she would prove to be a valuable asset to the department. Officer Polley graduated from a five-week police academy training program, along with seventeen male officers, on December 29, 1961, and was assigned to the Juvenile Bureau.

In November 1961, the department announced that two officers had been assigned to a new K-9 unit and that plans were underway to form a "Tactical Squad." A news story issued a few weeks later said that "ten of the department's very best men had been hand-picked to become members of a specialized Tactical Squad. The squad, working in unmarked police cars, would be assigned to "work where there's a heavy incident of crime or a particular problem. . . ."

As a means of providing more effective neighborhood service, the police department opened its Bowie Station on November 1, 1962. The Oxon Hill Station opened eight months later to serve the county's extreme southern region. During this same time, a special three-man "Radar Unit" was created to enforce speed laws on those roadways that were experiencing an increasingly high accident rate.

Following a long-established tradition, each county Grand Jury submitted a final report on county government operations. Each department within the government was either praised or criticized by the Grand Jury. One such report, bearing the date March 12, 1963, bears the following comments in reference to the police department.

Prince Georges Police May Get Shorter Week

(See Editorial on Page 22)
By FRANCIS PORTER

Prince Georges police may get their long-sought 40-hour week this year, but they have little prospect for a pay raise.

Veteran members of the department said today that a reduction in the six-day work schedule may head off further resignations, but only a substantial pay boost can stabilize morale.

The 171-man department serving Washington's largest suburban jurisdiction is the only major force in the area on a six-day schedule. It also has the lowest—by at least $400—pay scale, and is the only one without a personnel merit system.

DISCONTENT

A News survey last week disclosed that the department also has the largest resignation rate in the area. Many members admit applying for police work in higher-pay shorter-hour jurisdictions, and up to 80 per cent of the Prince Georges policemen grab part-time jobs when they can get them.

Because their police shifts rotate each week—starting hours are midnight, 8 a.m. and 4 p.m.—three men sometime, take the same part-time job. Each works at it during the hours he is off duty.

"About the only ones who don't do extra work are the bachelors, and the guys with working wives," an officer who splits a fuel truck driving job with two other men said.

A private starts at $4000 in Prince Georges and in six annual steps, moves to $5200. In contrast, neighboring Montgomery pays rookies $4555, boosts them to $5545 in five years, then gives four per cent longevity raises every three years.

STILL HIGHER

District privates start at $5800. A District corporal gets more to start with than a Prince Georges inspector.

The recent snowstorm brought real gloom to the entire department. It halted racing for four days at Bowie.

The three race tracks in the county hire off-duty detectives to watch for gambling violations when they're operating and take on uniformed men to regulate traffic. Each man gets $15 per day. The part-time work schedules are made up by the department and posted on bulletin boards in all three stations.

"This means my bills will have to wait another month," said a detective who had been slated to "work the track" three of the stormy days.

EXTRA JOB

One veteran detective sergeant who once was noted for his night and day devotion to duty, now spends his off-duty evenings on a super market payroll watching for shoplifters. He would be getting at least $1000 more from any other area department.

"My wife can't work and I've got kids to send to school," he said. "I had a choice to make — a reputation or my family—and I made it."

Chief George J. Panagoulis last week submitted a budget to the County Commission asking for 38 more officers.

He said it did not include provisions for a cut in hours for the department. But the next day, he was in a budget conference with the county heads and one Commissioner said the 40-hour week was being discussed.

"We have got to do something for these guys," the Commissioner said.

Our inspection of the County Police Department led us to believe it is an efficient and well-run organization. The testimony we received from the Police Officers and Detectives was complete and well presented. The number of men employed by this department does not by any means, come up to recommended standards set by the FBI. Contrary to a well-publicized statement by a county official, that one percent of all Prince George's County Police are crooked, no evidence was presented to the Grand Jury to substantiate this statement. The Police Department appears to be doing as good a job as possible with the facilities at hand. We

Impoverished Police

3-14-60

NEATLY framed and hanging on the wall of Prince Georges County Police Chief George J. Panagoulis' office is a poem entitled "Loyalty."

It is most appropriate. There must be some good reason why policemen continue to work for Prince Georges County and "loyalty" is the best one we can think of. Certainly it's not the hours or the pay. As Francis Porter points out in his story on Page 5 today, they are by far the worst in the Washington area.

An undermanned, underpaid, overworked police force in a jurisdiction the size of Prince Georges is humiliating to the men and unhealthy for the county.

Sooner or later, a policeman paid a sub-standard wage for a six-day week is either going to quit, or he's going to become the target of grafters.

It's to the credit of Prince Georges policemen that so many have managed to stay both honest and on the job.

Chief Panagoulis can only do so much. His modest request for 38 additional men this year is a reflection of what happened last year, when he asked for 50 men and had his ears pinned back by the County Commission. He got 15.

He won the present piddling pay scale three years ago only after a real scrap with the Commission.

The fault lies with the County Commissioners. Prince Georges' appalling highway death rate, its booming burglary business and flourishing gambling trade will not be stopped as long as present policies are followed.

The county's citizens are entitled to have these problems corrected if they want them corrected. An efficient and effective police department would help. The citizens can get one if they want it enough to use their collective political voice.

● The police should be taken out of politics by establishing a firm merit system for them.

● To bring the department up to recommended standards, it should be just about doubled in size.

● The men should be put on a professional basis with a pay scale and hours which would insure that the department doesn't just get rejects from other jurisdictions.

Titled "Prince George's Police Department May Get Shorter Work Week," this news article (left) was printed in the Washington Daily News *of March 14, 1960. The newspaper also contained an editorial titled "Impoverished Police." The editorial (above) addressed the problems of an "undermanned, underpaid, overworked" police force.*

recommend that the County Commissioners give special consideration as to enlarging the facilities and personnel of the Seat Pleasant Station.
[Note: The comment pertaining to crooked policemen was probably made by the county sheriff, who at the time wanted to assume a more in-depth law enforcement roll.]

On May 2, 1963, after a fifteen-year lull, the realities and dangers of a career in law enforcement became apparent when Officer Alfred Steinat, of the Bowie Station, was shot to death by a suspected tire thief. If, in fact, the county police had become complacent, the death of Officer Steinat woke them with a startling sense of reality as to the dangers of police work. The county police responded to 55,159 calls in 1963 and according to an annual report, provided police services in more than 90,000 situations. With an authorized budget of $2,288,444, the department employed 256 officers. The last vestiges of a tranquil environment were disappearing from many of the county's urban-type communities.

Jurisprudence was turned upside down in 1963 when the U.S. Supreme Court rendered several landmark decisions concerning the admissibility of evidence in state courts. The court ruled, for the first time in the nation's history, that the Federal Constitution was applicable to those cases being tried in state courts. Henceforth, the federal court system would play an increasingly important appellate role in deciding what types of evidence would be admissible at the state court level. With the court's new activist roll, most local and state police agencies had to learn a whole new set of rules concerning the admissibility of evidence. Although the new rules made the officer's job more difficult, they also forced law enforcement to adopt new and more sophisticated methods of solving crime. The increased complexity of police work now required every police department to place additional emphasis upon the hiring of better-educated officers.

On December 28, 1964, the county signed a $21,000 contract with the International Association of Chiefs of Police (IACP). The contract called for the IACP to conduct an indepth study of the police department's general operational procedures and to make recommendations concerning the improvement of police services. In order to attract better-qualified officers, Prince George's County increased the starting salaries of officers from $5,200 to $6,100, the highest police salary in the metropolitan area. Officers up to the rank of sergeant received $860 per month increases. Lieutenants and above received a 5 percent pay raise. County Commissioner Bayne Brooke, the police liaison commissioner, noted in a press release that the department had a recruiting problem and that the county had a choice of easing up on its hiring requirements or increasing salaries to attract qualified police candidates. Commissioner Brooke stated, "We decided to increase the salaries, and we feel this will attract the caliber of men we want and need." The department also announced that the Detective Bureau would open up branch offices in the Hyattsville and Oxon Hill Stations. Previously, all detectives had worked from the bureau's main office in Seat Pleasant.

The Board of Education transferred ownership of the old Forestville Elementary School to the police department in 1965. Renovation of the building commenced immediately with the Police Academy, Driver Improvement School (traffic school for motor vehicle law violators), Traffic Safety Unit, Radar Unit, and K-9 Unit moving into the facility. Police headquarters continued to function from the still overcrowded Seat Pleasant Station. The burgeoning recruiting problem motivated the police department to implement a Police Cadet Program as a means of drawing younger people into a law enforcement career. The program began with three cadets: Gary Prediger, George Herl, and William Gullett, Jr.

In 1966, the department attempted to improve the working conditions of its patrol officers by implementation of a policy which required that all new police cars be purchased with air conditioners. Thus, Prince George's County became the first metropolitan area police agency to consider the summertime comfort of its patrol officers. Chief Panagoulis had long ago established a demanding policy concerning the military appearance of all uniformed county police officers. Realizing that his officers were hard-pressed to maintain a neat appearance during the hot, humid, summer months, the chief waited until one particularly sticky summer day before calling several of the county commissioners and asking that they go for a ride with him. Driving down the road, the chief talked to the commissioners about the difficulty that his officers had in maintaining a neat personal appearance after driving for several hours in a sweltering police car. After riding around for a couple of hours, in an oppressively hot police car, the chief made a plea for air-conditioned police cars. Chief Panagoulis later recounted that he was somewhat shocked when the commissioners readily granted his request. The department also announced that it was changing its policy concerning the use of two-door black police cars and would henceforth purchase white, four-door sedans as uniformed patrol cars.

The year also brought tragedy to the police department. On February 19, 1966, Sgt. Joseph K. Brown, of the Hyattsville Station, was shot while serving an indecent exposure warrant. Two other police officers were wounded during the attempted service of this warrant. Sergeant Brown, the son of former Police Chief Ralph Brown, died from his wounds.

The department's overburdened and antiquated single-channel radio system was replaced in 1967 with a modernized four-channel system. The police radio room moved out of the main Seat Pleasant building and into the old radio repair shop located just to the rear of the station house. The building had been extensively renovated to accommodate the new four-channel system.

The county also took a major step toward true professionalization when it placed all police promotions under the county's merit law. Henceforth, all promotions would require the receipt of a satisfactory promotional evaluation report, the passage of a written exam, and an appearance before a promotional board. Before this time, the only real criteria for promotion was that a slot exist and that the chief of police wanted to make the promotion.

The IACP completed its year-long study of the police department in November 1967. The 364-page survey rated the Prince George's County Police as "above average when compared with other suburban police departments in the Southern region of the country." The survey report went on to state that, "The administration of the department is, by and large, effective although at times unorthodox and controversial. The professional attitude and appearance of most members of the command staff and the force are apparent even to the casual observer." The study then went on to make a number of recommendations, indicating that, "There is a need for the introduction of additional management techniques to assist the department in its pursuit of excellence."

According to the 1960 census, Prince George's County was home to 324,714 white and 32,681 black or other racial minority residents. Although some black residents owned their land, many others acted as tenant farmers and worked the land in order to support their families. Many other black residents, especially those professionals who worked in the District of Columbia, lived in the older black communities of Fairmount Heights, North Brentwood, Lincoln-Vista, and Lakewood.

The 1960s had ushered in a period of social and judicial sensitivity toward the plight of minority Americans. Alan Virta, in his book *Prince George's County: a Pictorial History* writes, "The 1960s are remembered as years of social change . . . in the area of race relations." Mr. Virta goes on to state that demonstrations occurred at the Levitt Homes in Bowie after sales agents refused to sell a home to a black couple. He also states that protests and sit-ins occurred at a Route 1 segregated restaurant. Although slow to act, the police hierarchy realized that there was a need for black representation within the department. On November 6, 1967, the long-standing color barrier which prohibited blacks from the sworn ranks of the police department was broken with the hiring of two black police officers. Officers Alonzo D. Black and Luther V. Waktins were the first blacks to wear the county police uniform. It is important to note that the entire Washington, D.C. region was racially segregated by tradition and culture. The institution of segregation appears to have been so deeply ingrained into our culture that very few people took the time to question its appropriateness.

The United States entered an extremely difficult period in the mid-to-late-1960s. Fuming resentment over previous racial injustices, racial anti-establishment sentiment, the war in Vietnam, increased crime, and a general disrespect for authority made the mid-to late-1960s a difficult and sometimes volatile period for law enforcement. Major cities across the country, including Washington, D.C., experienced dramatic increases in violent crime. The District of Columbia, with its large and effective police force, drove some inner-city crime out into the suburbs of both Virginia and Maryland. Prince George's County was particularly hard hit by the "crime spillover" because it shared such a large unobstructed boundary with the District of Columbia.

The ever increasing rate of armed robberies and the seriousness of the crime caused the county to form a special squad of detectives to investigate these crimes. A county news release dated November 8, 1968, states, "a new, carefully programmed system of aggressive patrolling by uniformed and unmarked police cars is showing results in nabbing bank robbers. . . . Since May 20th, when a new Robbery Squad was established to supplement the accelerated patrol system, there have been fifteen bank robberies where county police were involved. Of the fifteen, eight were closed by county officers, in three other cases arrests were made by the Federal Bureau of Investigation after specific identification of the suspects by Robbery Squad detectives. . . . A grand total of $65,758.50 has been recovered during the period and eighteen suspects have been apprehended."

Ever mindful of the need to consider employing new techniques, the police department entered into a three-week experiment to evaluate the effectiveness of helicopters in police patrol. On the evening of March 21, 1968, Officer John

Officer Howard Kinports admires the police department's new car decal. The department began using the county seal as its new shoulder patch in late 1960. The word police was not included on the original patch because the department started out as the only county agency using the seal for identification purposes. Several years later the chief decided that it was necessary to include the word police because several other county agencies had begun to use the seal for identification purposes. Photo courtesy of retired Lt. Howard Kinports

Leatherbury, riding as a police observer, and a Hughes Aircraft helicopter pilot were assisting several ground units who were securing an unlocked bank door. As the helicopter prepared to clear the scene, it struck a high-voltage wire, plummeted to the ground, and exploded in a ball of flame. The crash killed Officer Leatherbury and the pilot.

On April 4, 1968, the Reverend Dr. Martin Luther King, Jr., was assassinated in Memphis, Tennessee. News of the assassination resulted in disturbances on the streets of the District of Columbia and other large cities. What began as a small-scale disturbance turned into three full days of massive rioting. A total of 11,600 troops and the entire District of Columbia Police Department were called out to quell the riots. Many areas of the city lay in ruin, devastated by fire. The number of fires burning within the city were so numerous that fire department assistance was called in from neighboring jurisdictions, including Prince George's County. Massive looting of business establishments also occurred throughout the city. The strong law enforcement stance taken by the county commissioners probably helped to save Prince George's County from serious looting and riot damage. A number of disturbances took place just inside the District of Columbia, but Prince George's County survived with only minor damage.

The county commissioners voted to formally abolish the old title of superintendent of police in 1968, adopting the more commonly used title "chief of police." A county government brochure for 1968 reports that the police department had an authorized strength of 441 officers, although actual employment was just slightly more than 400 officers.

Recently enacted federal legislation entitled The Omnibus Safe Streets Act allowed the federal government to financially assist local and state law enforcement agencies through the creation of a Law Enforcement Assistance Administration (LEAA). The primary purpose of LEAA was that of identifying, funding, and evaluating special crime reductions programs. The department's Research and Development Section (formed in 1967) was assigned the primary responsibility of creating and monitoring all LEAA grant projects. Another important LEAA goal was that of assisting law enforcement personnel in furthering their college education. At one time, more than half of the police department's officers, with LEAA financial assistance, were enrolled in college classes at either the University of Maryland or American University.

Increased concern over the issue of police discipline led to the formation of an Inspectional Services Unit in May 1968. The two officers assigned to the unit, Sgt. Rice Turner and Cpl. Eddie Armstrong had a number of responsibilities, but were primarily assigned to conduct administrative investigations into allegations of excessive police force.

Chief of Police George Panagoulis, a graduate of Georgetown Law School, had passed his Maryland Bar Examination in 1963. Deciding to go into the practice of law, Chief Panagoulis announced that he intended to retire effective July 1, 1968. The county commissioners immediately announced that they would appoint Deputy Chief Vincent Free as the department's new chief of police. The commissioners also stated that Inspector Roland Sweitzer was to be promoted to the rank of lieutenant colonel and assigned to the duties of deputy chief of police.

The shock and sorrow of another police death occurred on November 30, 1968, when County Police Officer Robert Yeszerski and Seat Pleasant Town Officer William Clements were shot and killed as Officer Clements prepared to tow away an automobile. The vehicle's owner, who had been previously warned to move the car, became enraged and shot both policemen.

A step toward improving patrol car comfort was announced on October 11, 1968, when the department decided that uniformed officers were no longer required to wear their hats while inside a patrol car. This move was taken because some taller officers were said to be experiencing "noticeable discomfort" while sitting in the newer model automobiles. A strongly worded statement was also issued to the force, reminding each officer to, "Put that cover on when you get out of the vehicle."

On February 16, 1969, tragedy again struck the department when County Police Officer William Gullett, Jr., one of the three original police cadets, responded to a call of a loud radio on Markham Lane in Kentland. Officer Gullet and his partner Pete Parrish encountered an armed man at an apartment doorway. The officers talked the suspect into holstering his weapon, but he drew the weapon for a second time without warning. An exchange of gunfire took place between both officers and the suspect. Officer Gullett and the suspect were fatally shot during the exchange. Officer Parrish escaped injury.

A previously unheard of event occurred within the ranks of the county police department in 1969. Tradition and a lifelong adherence to quasi-military rule had always been accepted departmental procedure. A member of the police force never spoke disrespectfully to a superior officer, and subordinate personnel never questioned the authority of a supervisory officer. Grumbling from the rank-and-file had always been a fact of life, but very little thought was given to correcting employee grievances. Police associations, including the FOP, were primarily formed for social purposes, or in the case of the old County Police Association, for obtaining hospitalization benefits that the officers paid for themselves. Unionism, even in its weakest form, was a concept beyond the imagination of most police officers.

The first signs of labor discontent began to surface within the county police in the late 1960s. An undated 1969 issue of the *Washington Star* reported that, "Four Prince George's County policemen are suing the County Commissioners, claiming they are forced to work overtime without compensation in violation of the U.S. Constitution's prohibitions against slavery and involuntary servitude." Privates Edward Staniek, Eldred "Al" Fox, William Kreutzer, and Charles Marcellino contended that they were regularly required to work more than their normal forty-two hours a week and must take compensatory time off instead of money for the extra duty. The officers also contended that the county "discourages them from actually using the compensatory time they earn and will not permit them to carry over more than ten days of the time owed them from one year to the next." Most older policemen looked on in amazement, never imagining that anyone would be bold or audacious enough to ask for paid overtime. The litigation against the county was dropped when the county government agreed to initiate a policy concerning the payment of wages for overtime.

In retrospect, the 1960s represented a decade of death and tumultuous change. Five county and one town policemen were shot to death in the 1960s, another county policeman died in a tragic helicopter accident. Nationally, incomplete FBI records reveal that more than 528 law enforcement officer were feloniously slain between 1961 and 1969. Another 324 were accidentally killed in the line of duty. During the same time, President John F. Kennedy, the Rev. Dr. Martin Luther King, Jr., and presidential candidate Robert F. Kennedy were assassinated. Fuming social discontent had resulted in violent riots in many of our nation's largest cities, including the District of Columbia. Prince George's County entered the 1960s with a population of 357,395 and a relatively small 200-man police force. Initially, there were very few concerns about the police department's ability to control the spread of crime, but that feeling of confidence disappeared in the mid-1960s. An unpopular war in Vietnam, civil disobedience, mind-altering drugs, and an increasing rate of violent crime tore the country apart. As the 1960s came to an end, the police department employed approximately 500 officers, 163 civilian support personnel, and 163 school crossing guards. The necessity of maintaining administrative control over the files of the department's 800 employees had caused the formation of a Police Personnel Office in the late 1960s.

Prince George's County had matured and come of age in the 1960s. It was now a major urban county, whose population had increased by more than 304,000 new residents in the past ten years. Unfortunately, violence had become almost commonplace within the inner beltway and people began to wonder if the police department employed sufficient officers to control the ever-increasing rate of crime.

Pictured here, with the exception of Superintendent Panagoulis, is the upper echelon of the police department during the early 1960s. Left to right are Capt. Charles Thomsen, Detective Division commander; Capt. Roland Sweitzer, Uniform Division commander; Inspector Vincent Free, deputy superintendent of police; Capt. Wilson Purdy, Headquarters Division commander; and Capt. Louis Mackall, Radio Maintenance Division commander.
PGPD photo

On November 8, 1961, Pvts. Edwin Stahl and Lester Rackey of the Seat Pleasant Station were on routine patrol when they received a call of a house fire at Glenarden Parkway and George Palmer Highway. The officers were within a block of the address when the call was received and reached the fire scene within seconds. According to their supervisor's report, "Upon arriving they found the house a blazing inferno and, disregarding their own safety entered the dwelling to remove the occupants trapped inside. The officers, making several trips in and out of the flaming house, brought out seven small children. After their last trip they checked with the mothers whose families occupied the home and were told all of the children living there were saved. A few minutes later the mothers double-checked and frantically told the policemen two more children were still inside in a crib. The two officers tried again to enter the building but were blocked by the flames. Moments later the Fire Department arrived but even firemen in asbestos suits could not get to the trapped children, and were forced back by fire, heat, and falling debris." Officers Stahl and Rackey were the first county police officers to receive Officer of the Year awards.

The county commissioners commended the officers with a citation for heroism "above and beyond the call of duty." Acting Board Chairman Herbert Reichelt, in presenting the award stated, "There is little we can say or do to express our pride in your accomplishment. Your brave deeds in this instance were above

and beyond the call of duty and I am extremely proud of you. Had it not been for your unselfish actions, these children would have surely perished."

Pictured left to right are Officers Edwin Stahl, Lester Rackey, County Commissioner Herbert Reichelt, and Chief George Panagoulis.
PGPD photo

On November 29, 1961, Chief Panagoulis announced that the department was forming a special Tactical Squad to deal with upsurges in crime. According to a press release, "the squad will not be assigned to any specific substation or area, but work on a day-to-day basis, concentrating wherever there are outbreaks of larcenies, holdups, or burglaries."

This Tactical Squad photo was taken in February 1962. In the first row, left to right, are K-9 PFC William Hicks, Pvt. Ewing Northcutt, Pvt. Albert Kulle, Pvt. Frank McQuain, Cpl. Louis Kreitzer, and K-9 PFC Albert Frank. In the second row are PFC Andre Gerard, Pvt. Richard Salter, Pvt. Howard Kinports, Pvt. James Burch, and PFC Charles Flynn.

The Tactical Squad and K-9 Unit were the forerunners to what is now the Special Operations Division (SOD).
PGPD photo

The first K-9 Corps, shown here with Capt. Edwin Thompson, are PFC William Hicks (left) and his partner, Blitz, along with PFC Albert Frank with his partner, Sport. According to a December 21, 1961 news article the dogs and officers attended a fourteen-week course of training by the Metropolitan Police K-9 Corps.
PGPD photos

A press release dated December 29, 1961, stated, "Nineteen new police officers joined the Prince George's County Force this week following graduation ceremonies. All privates, the graduates completed six weeks' training in basic police work and will be on probation for one year. Included in this class is the county's first policewoman, Pvt. Carol Ann Polley, who will be assigned to the Juvenile Squad." In the first row, left to right, are Bernard Schwartz, Charles Boteler, Donald DeSantis, Maj. George Panagoulis, Carol Polley, Andrew Panholzer, Joseph Dove, and Ralph Baker. Center row: Samuel Seger, Edwin Riegal, Rice Turner, Robert Greco, Hollis Jordan, and Robert Rollins. Third row: Raymond Reinhart, Duane Beeler, John Davis, George Robey, and Robert Harrison.
PGPD photo

Bureau of Public Roads photo; courtesy of the National Archives

Spanning the Potomac River between Virginia and Maryland the Woodrow Wilson Bridge was dedicated in 1961. The bridge was somewhat unusual because it spanned three jurisdictions: Maryland, Virginia, and the District of Columbia. The county's portion of the Washington Beltway did not open to the public until late 1964. Before the beltway's completion, a trip from Hyattsville to Oxon Hill could be a rather cumbersome and time-consuming ordeal, taking an hour or more on narrow traffic-clogged roadways.

PGPD photograph

Published in a 1961 police department brochure, the caption under this photo read: *"READY FOR INSPECTION - Prince George's County policemen stand along side of their shiny new cruisers ready for inspection. The County has 77 such cars to patrol its 487 square miles. The Police Department rolls up enough miles every week equal to the Earth's circumference."*
PGPD photo

In June 1962, several cars of a freight train carrying hazardous material jumped the track and turned over near Landover Road and Route 50. A round-the-clock cleanup project was commenced by the fire and police departments. A county press release relating to this incident states, "Personnel of the police and fire departments say a special thanks to McDonald's Hamburger System for food service provided during the recent railroad disaster in Kent Village. All personnel at the scene of the accident, as well as those at outlying traffic posts, were provided with food during the entire four-day period. . . ." Accepting a plaque from Major Panagoulis is McDonalds General Manager Oscar Goldstein. Left to right are Restaurant Manager Theodore Hazzard; Inspector Roland Sweitzer; Major Panagoulis; Mr. Goldstein; FOP president, Sgt. Henry Stawinski; and Mr. Kennard of McDonalds.

Note the 1962 food prices: a hamburger cost fifteen cents; french fries, twelve cents; and drinks, ten cents.
PGPD photo

On October 16, 1962, the county commissioners announced that Chief George J. Panagoulis had received his law degree from Georgetown University Law School after attending three years of night school. The commissioners praised Chief Panagoulis, stating that he "had developed a force second to none in the state in effectiveness and esprit de corps." The commissioners cited a number of accomplishments the chief had achieved since taking over the department in 1955. Specifically mentioned were the doubling of the department's sworn strength to 225 officers, and salary increases that allowed a senior police private to earn as much as $6,400 annually.
Drawing by Inspector Dick Mansfield of the Metropolitan Police Department

On November 1, 1962, the Bowie Station opened in the east wing of the old Belair Mansion in Bowie. Sgt. John Haas was placed in command of the thirteen police officers assigned to the new station. Also assigned as shift supervisors were PFC Joseph Thornberry, PFC William O'Neil, PFC Stanley Headley, and PFC Robert Zidek. Assigned to work the patrol areas were Pvts. Alfred Steinat, Edward Brink, William Lindsay, Gerald Morrissey, John Travers, Sam Seger, John Cicala, and Harold Wilson.
PGPD photo

ALFRED WALTER STEINAT

Killed in the line of duty
May 2, 1963

Alfred Walter Steinat, a Marine Corps veteran, became a Prince George's County policeman on May 16, 1962. After completing a six-week training program, Officer Steinat was assigned to the Upper Marlboro Station. In November, he was reassigned to the newly opened Bowie Station.

On May 2, 1963, Officer Steinat reported to duty at midnight and immediately received a call for a tire theft at Mitchellville Esso on Route 301. Upon arriving at the gas station, Officer Steinat was informed that a suspect had driven off without paying for a recapped tire. The suspect, a white male, was operating a black Falcon bearing Virginia tags. At about 12:15 a.m. Officer Steinat left the gas station, telling the attendant that he was going to look for the suspect's vehicle.

At about 1:25 a.m., Officer William Donovan of the Anne Arundel County Police Department saw Officer Steinat's cruiser on the northbound shoulder of Route 3, just inside the county line. The cruiser was unoccupied with its emergency lights activated. Using Steinat's radio, Officer Donovan notified the Prince George's County dispatcher of his findings. Officer Donovan then walked into the wooded area alongside the highway where he found Officer Steinat's body. Examination of the body revealed that the officer had been shot once in the back with a 45-caliber automatic handgun. A motorist advised the police that he had seen a black Falcon drive away from the murder scene at a fast rate of speed.

A police search of the crime scene turned up a wallet containing identification papers belonging to Thomas A. Hadder of Richmond, Virginia. A state of Virginia registration card to a Falcon was also found at the scene. Shortly thereafter, law enforcement contacts in Richmond developed a witness who had recently seen the Hadder suspect with a .45-automatic. As a result of this information, a warrant was obtained charging Thomas Hadder with the murder of Officer Steinat.

Thomas Hadder was arrested by the Maryland State Police on May 2, 1963, at about 7:30 p.m. The suspect, after leaving the crime scene, had driven to a nearby gravel pit where he remained until his arrest. During interrogation by county detectives, Hadder admitted to pulling a gun on Officer Steinat as they sat in the police car, and that the gun went off during a struggle.

Baggett Hails County Police Dept. And Chief as Among Best in Area

A police department "as effective as any in the area" was saluted this week by Chairman Jesse S Baggett of the Prince Georges County Board of Commissioners, who at the same time called Police Chief George Panagoulis "one of the best qualified and most capable police officers I have known —bar none."

Commissioner Baggett's remarks were directed to members of the County Police Association at their meeting last Monday night.

Recognizing the police officer as "the direct representative" of the County government to the men on the street the Commissioner said he was proud of the record, "both yours and ours."

He cited increases in manpower which have doubled the size of the police force in recent years and noted that with the recently-opened substation in the Bowie-Belair area and the soon to be completed new substation in Oxon Hill facilities have doubled, too.

"We feel the department has reached the point, like the County itself," the Commissioner told the policemen, "where old fashioned methods are no longer adequate for the type of community we have."

He said he felt that recent reorganizations within the department have brought the force "up to a point where it is as effective as any police force in the area."

Recognizing that an expanding County creates a need for "more stations and more officers", the Commissioner told the police officers "there is a direct benefit to you officers" in this expansion, which brings promotions "at a more rapid rate than in the past."

Commissioner Baggett cited recent innovations such as the K-9 Corps, the Juvenile and Traffic Safety Units and the Tactical Squad as "a credit to you officers as well as to us."

"We couldn't make these expansions and innovations," he said, "without the personnel who could handle them. And we couldn't do it without a chief of police of the caliber of Major George Panagoulis.

"I want to tell you here and now." the Commissioner added. "I think he is one of the best qualified and most capable police officers I have known — bar none. I sincerely hope and believe he will be with us for a long time."

The November 22, 1962 Prince George's Post *printed a news release made by Jesse Baggett, chairman, Board of County Commissioners.*

On February 21, 1963, Prince George's County joined five other metropolitan area jurisdictions in a direct-line police teletype network. The teletype network was just one of many police-related projects that had been coordinated by the Washington Metropolitan Area Council of Governments. Pictured at the teletype machine is Police Clerk Elaine Doman, in the middle is County Commissioner Frank Lastner, holding the teletype message is Chief Panagoulis. Prior to this time all interstate teletype contacts had been initiated through the Maryland State Police teletype system.
PGPD photo

157

Officers assigned to the Seat Pleasant Station had initially provided the Oxon Hill area with a police service. With the opening of the Woodrow Wilson Bridge in 1961, the population of the Oxon Hill area increased so dramatically that the county decided a new station was needed to service both Oxon Hill and Clinton. On June 22, 1963, the Oxon Hill Station opened in a renovated two-story frame home. Sgt. George Simmons was placed in charge of the new station, assisted by shift supervisors PFC Jim Kinnaman, PFC Ted Peters, PFC Vernon Herath, and PFC Harold Russell. Working in the patrol areas were Pvts. Jim Rash, Robert Ross, Robert Eflin, Bob Rollins, Joe Dove, Bob Mossburg, Al Alexander, Fenton Hinson, Hugh Chinn, Don Knepp, and John Albert.
PGPD photo

PFC Al Fox and his partner, Falco, graduated from the Metropolitan Police Department's K-9 School on November 22, 1963. While in training with the MPDC, they obtained a record-breaking training score of 659 points, the previous high score had been 622. PFC Fox and Falco, upon assuming their patrol duties, were assigned to work on nighttime school security.
PGPD photo

In 1965, the Seat Pleasant Station had five patrol areas. Car No. 11 was a two-man unit covering Fairmount Heights, Landover, Palmer Park, and Glenarden. Patrol areas twelve through fifteen were staffed by one-man units. Each station was commanded by a lieutenant. Patrol squads were supervised by a sergeant and one corporal. In this 1965 photograph, Pvts. Danny Olds and Mike Ariemma pose alongside their Plymouth Fury patrol car.
Photo courtesy of retired Sgt. Danny Olds

Taken in 1965 this photograph depicts a squad of officers assigned to the Seat Pleasant Station. Left to right are Dick Pearson, Jr., Sgt. Doug Maxfield, Ron Cook, Bud Conner, Eddie Armstrong, Russell Ferguson, and Jerry duCellier. The department's 325 officers handled 130,000 requests for service in 1965.
Photo courtesy of retired Sgt. Danny Olds

159

TODAY: 2 Full Pages of High School Basketball—Pages A-12-13

Weather Forecast
District and vicinity—Fair and cold tonight, low 20 to 25. Fair and cold tomorrow, high in lower 30s. Today's high, 52, at 1 p.m.; low, 35, at 5:40 a.m.

Full Report on Page A-2

The Evening Star
WITH SUNDAY MORNING EDITION

NIGHT FINAL

114th Year.   No. 50.   The Evening Star Newspaper Co. Copyright © 1966   ★★5   WASHINGTON, D. C., SATURDAY, FEBRUARY 19, 1966—40 PAGES   Phone LI. 3-5000   10 Cents

Policeman Dies in Adelphi Battle

Marines Airlift 4 Battalions To Seek Enemy

Drop Into Valley In Effort to Force Viet Cong to Fight

SAIGON, South Viet Nam (AP)—Four battalions of U.S. Marines, acting on intelligence reports of a sighting of the Viet Cong's hard core 1st Regiment, surged by helicopter today into the Phuoc Valley 350 miles northeast of Saigon. Initial contact was light.

Two Marines were wounded by ground fire on the helicopters as they were landing in the valley, which lies west of Tam Ky, between Leatherneck bases at Da Nang and Chu Lai. Field reports said nine Viet Cong were killed and the Marines seized a hastily abandoned Viet Cong arsenal.

Cavalry in Skirmishes

Down the coast, troopers of the 2nd Brigade of the U.S. 1st Cavalry, Airmobile, Division engaged in several new skirmishes with Viet Cong elements 10 miles southwest of Bong Son. Communist fire downed two American helicopters. The cavalrymen said they killed 37 Viet Cong, captured one and seized two dozen weapons.

U.S. B52 jets, using a new technique of hitting their targets twice in a row, struck at Viet Cong concentrations only two miles short of the Cambodian border.

The giant eight-engine warplanes hit three areas of western Tay Ninh Province about 75

Kennedy Favors Talks With Viet Cong Front

Says U.S. Alternative Is at Heart Of Hope for Negotiated Settlement

By ROBERT K. WALSH
Star Staff Writer

Sen. Robert F. Kennedy, D-N.Y., suggested today that the United States seek a negotiated settlement of the Viet Nam war by offering the Viet Cong's National Liberation Front a share in peace talks and in a possible coalition government.

Advocating a "middle way" move by this country between the extremes of unilateral withdrawal from South Viet Nam and a complete military victory over North Viet Nam, Kennedy said a negotiated settlement "means that each side must concede matters which are important in order to preserve positions that are essential."

He said the Senate Foreign Relations Committee hearings and the current Senate debate provide a good opportunity to specify U.S. objectives in the Viet Nam war and define concrete proposals as a basis for a negotiated settlement.

"Must Accept Fact"

"Whatever the exact status of the National Liberation Front, puppet or partly independent," he said, "any negotiated settlement must accept the fact that there are discontented elements in South Viet Nam, Communist and non-Communist, who desire to change the existing political and economic system of that country.

"There are three things you can do with such groups—kill or repress them, turn the country over to them, or admit them to a share of power and responsibility. The first two are possible only through force of arms.

"The last—to admit them to a share of power and responsibility—is at the heart of the hope

would have to be on the basis of a clear-cut negotiated settlement.

"Should Not Be Controlled"

"But the policy of the United States should not be controlled by the South Viet Nam government," he added. "I favor making our position clear in advance of negotiations that the National Liberation Front might be permitted to participate in a coalition government."

Kennedy conceded that NLF participation in any negotiated settlement would not be "the easy way or the sure way."

"It will require enormous skill and political wisdom to find the point at which participation does not bring domination or internal conquest," he said.

"It may mean a compromise government fully acceptable to neither side. It certainly means that we must take considerable risks in the expectation that social and economic success will weaken the appeal of communism and that sharing the burden and the satisfaction of helping to guide a nation will attract hostile elements toward a solution which will preserve both the independence of their country and their new-found share of power.

Fulbright Ends Open Hearings On Viet Policy

Indicates Chance Of Calling Others In Closed Session

By RICHARD FRYKLUND
Star Staff Writer

The Senate Foreign Relations Committee hearings on Viet Nam policy apparently have ended—with the hawks and doves and the agonizers in the middle still unchanged in their views.

Yesterday's session was the final one unless, as chairman J. William Fulbright, D-Ark., said, some other witnesses turn up.

"I personally don't see any need for further public hearings," Fulbright declared. But he said he would let the committee decide if it would like to ask Secretary of Defense Robert S. McNamara and Vice President Hubert H. Humphrey to appear at closed sessions.

Heard Almost 6 Hours

Yesterday's witness was Secretary of State Dean Rusk, who spent all but a few minutes of his almost six hours calmly explaining administration policy all over again.

There were only a few tension-filled minutes when Fulbright seemed to put all the blame on the Johnson administration for the failure of negotiation attempts and Rusk let his exasperation show.

Fulbright said the leaders on the Communist side are rational

For the second time in less than three years tragedy strikes.
Courtesy of retired Cpl. John Cicala

Two Officers Are Wounded Man, 41, Hel

Service of Warra Triggers Shootin Suspect's Son Hu

A Prince Georges Cou police sergeant was killed ea today and two officers w wounded in a gun fight at Adelphi, Md., apartment, wh they had gone to serve a w rant.

A 41-year-old mainten man the police sought with warrant was arrested afte dramatic search in a nea building about an hour and half after the shooting charged with murder and counts of attempted murder

The wife of the man charged with assaulting a lice officer and a juvenile of the couple also was held.

Police said the mother son fought with the off during the attempt to serv warrant.

Son of Ex-Chief

The dead officer was Joseph Kelly Brown, 36, of Dunbar Ave., Randolph Vill Prince Georges County. He the son of a former chie the Prince Georges County lice, Maj. Ralph W. Brown Brown was chief betw 1943 and 1950 and now is tired.

Brown was pronounced d at Washington Sanitarium Takoma Park.

Wounded in the gun f were Detective 1c Karl Nel Milligan, 34, of Mangum Ro College Park and Pat

JOSEPH K. BROWN

Killed in the line of duty
February 19, 1966

Joseph Kelly Brown was the second son of former County Police Supt. Ralph Brown. Born on the family farm, in what is now the 6800 block of New Hampshire Avenue, Joe Brown was educated in the Prince George's County Public School System. After graduating from high school, Joe attended the University of Maryland but decided to enlist in the Marine Corps with the outbreak of the Korean War. Joe was later prohibited from Korean combat duty when his older brother, a Naval Academy graduate and pilot, was lost at sea. Advancing to the rank of sergeant, he was assigned to Camp Pendleton as a drill instructor. After receiving his honorable discharge, Joe returned home and later joined the Takoma Park Police Department receiving his entry level training at the Prince George's County Police Academy in 1958. On March 16, 1958, Joe Brown transferred to the county police and was assigned to the Hyattsville Station. Advancing to the rank of sergeant in 1965, Joe Brown was known as a knowledgeable, no-nonsense supervisor who expected his officers to deliver a high-quality police service.

During the early morning hours of February 19, 1966, Sergeant Brown and PFC Buddy Boteler met with Det. Karl Milligan. All three officers, armed with an indecent exposure arrest warrant for 41-year-old Carl Knicley, drove to Knicley's apartment at 2211 University Boulevard. The suspect's wife answered the officers' knock, but slammed the door on the officers after being told of the warrant. After shutting the door, the wife was heard to say "They have a warrant for you, what have you done now?" Sergeant Brown obtained a pass key from a janitor, but upon attempting to open the door someone from inside again pushed the door shut. Mrs. Knicley then called out, "All right, the man you want is coming out." At this point, Knicley's seventeen-year-old son came charging out of the apartment and began to fight with the officers. As the officers fell to the floor grappling with the younger Knicley, the suspect came out into the hallway armed with a small-caliber automatic handgun. Sergeant Brown saw the weapon and yelled, "Watch it, he's got a gun." At this point Knicley fired the weapon several times hitting Detective Milligan in the left arm and Sergeant Brown in the chest. The suspect then ran back into the apartment and slammed the door shut. As the officers attempted to call for an ambulance, the armed suspect ran to an adjoining apartment house in an apparent escape attempt. Although wounded, Detective Milligan fired several shots at the suspect, but missed. Carl Knicley was arrested a short time later, hiding in the attic area above 2213 University Boulevard.

Sergeant Brown was transported to Washington Sanitarium Hospital where he was pronounced dead. He was survived by his wife and young son, his mother and father, and a sister.

On February 21, 1967, Marcia K. Stepnitz was hired as the department's second female police officer. After her police academy training, the college-educated officer was assigned to the Juvenile Bureau.
PGPD photo

On March 28, 1967, Lt. Thomas R. (Ray) Blandford, Sr., retired from the force with twenty-seven years of service. A lifelong resident of the county, Ray Blandford joined the force in 1939 and rose through the ranks to corporal in 1947, sergeant in 1953, and lieutenant in 1954. For many years, Lieutenant Blandford was in charge of the Upper Marlboro Station.
Police Department retirement photo

Early 1940s photograph of Police Officer Thomas (Ray) Blandford, Sr.
Photo courtesy of retired Lt. Tommy Blandford, Jr.

On June 20, 1967, twenty-four new county
policemen graduated from the police academy
as part of Training Session No. 1-67. During
the graduation inspection, Maj. George
Panagoulis, along with County Commissioners
Gladys N. Spellman and M. Bayne Brooke
examine the weapon of Officer James Wiseman.
PGPD photo

After graduation ceremonies, Richard Raley,
the six-year-old son of Officer John Raley, does
the honor of pinning on his dad's new badge.
PGPD photo

Crime intensified and became a more serious problem as the 1960s progressed. Pocketbook snatching and street rapes in the Langley Park and Adelphi areas became a particularly troublesome problem. In an effort to arrest the perpetrators, a special decoy detail of volunteer officers was organized. These photos were taken just before the decoys hit the streets. Pictured, left to right, are Bill Bailey, Jimmy Fitzpatrick, Scooter Kozlowski, Jimmy Ross, and John Lloyd. Kneeling in front is Joe Vasco. Dressed as they were, these officers had more than a few interesting stories to tell after walking the streets for a few hours. The unit was later to receive a letter of commendation from State's Attorney Arthur Marshall for its imaginative crime suppression techniques.
Photo courtesy of Cpl. Scooter Kozlowski

Officer John Lloyd dressed as a female decoy.
Photo courtesy of Cpl. Scooter Kozlowski

Officer Scooter Kozlowski prepares to walk the streets of Langley Park.
Photo courtesy of Cpl. Scooter Kozlowski

With the number of serious incidents occurring in the county increasing, the police department saw the need for a mobile field headquarters capable of quickly responding to the scene of unusually large emergency situations. In May 1967, the department acquired such a capability: a thirty-two-foot trailer, which was partitioned to provide two interrogation rooms, a communications room, and a combined map and reception room. A tractor, equipped with a gasoline-powered electrical generator for remote operations, was used to tow the trailer. PGPD photo

The department began the process of phasing out its black, two-door police cars in 1967. Henceforth, all uniformed patrol cars would be white, four-door vehicles, equipped with a special police package. The vehicles were also purchased with air-conditioning, the county police being the first metropolitan area police department to consider the summer time comfort of its officers. The department split its bid for new cars in 1968, purchasing both Ford and Plymouth automobiles. A 1968 Ford, custom 4-door air-conditioned sedan, wimbledon white in color, with a police package (390-cubic inch engine) cost the department less than $4,000 per vehicle. In this 1967 photograph, Officer Gerry Vitteck stands election day guard duty at a warehouse used for the storage of voting machines. Photo courtesy of retired Det. Gerald Vitteck

The increase in calls for service caused a virtual gridlock on the old single-channel police radio. In March 1967, the county commissioners announced plans for a new four-channel police radio communications system. It was also announced that a new communications center would be constructed in the old communications maintenance shop at the rear of the Seat Pleasant Station. Costs for the purchase of new equipment and renovation were estimated at $205,000. Design plans were completed when the project was announced, and the new communications center became operational in 1968. Photo from a police department annual report

On November 6, 1967, Class No. 3-67 began a fifteen-week basic entry-level training course at the County Police Academy in Forestville. The class consisted of twenty-nine Prince George's County police recruits, seven Maryland Park Police recruits, one Hyattsville City recruit, and one military policeman from the Armed Forces Police. From the very first day, Class No. 3-67 was different from all previous academy classes by virtue of the fact that two of the twenty-nine county policemen were black. Police Recruits Alonzo D. Black, Jr., and Luther V. Watkins were the first minority officers to be hired as Prince George's County Police Department. A first step had been taken towards equal employment opportunity within the police department.

On February 19, 1968, all thirty-eight members of Class No. 3-67 graduated at a police academy ceremony. Gladys Noon Spellman, then Chairperson of the Board of County Commissioners, was the commencement keynote speaker. Chief George Panagoulis pinned the police shield on each officer, a proud moment for each new officer as well as the wives, fathers, mothers, and children who were in attendance at the graduation. A large scroll on the academy's stage proclaimed, "The Future Holds That For Which You Prepare," and the future must have looked exceedingly bright to those young energetic officers, so eager to begin their careers in public service.

Class No. 3-67, as already mentioned, was a unique gathering of people from all walks of life. Twenty-one years after their graduation, a roll of their names reveals some startling realities about the hazards and uncertainties of a law enforcement career. Five of the original twenty-nine county officers are still on active duty with the department: William Johnson holds the rank of captain, James Ratherdale and Gerald Howard are sergeants, Oliver "Pat" Grogan and Harold "Gene" Wiles are corporals. Five members of the class retired as a result of duty-connected disabilities; another four took advantage of normal retirement. One of the Maryland Park Police officers later transferred to the county police, but has since retired. For one reason or another, twelve officers resigned prior to reaching their retirement eligibility.

Class No. 3-67 suffered more personal tragedy than any other Prince George's County training class with three of its members having made the ultimate sacrifice: losing their lives in the line of duty. The utter senselessness of their deaths clearly illustrates the hazards of police work and society's propensity toward useless acts of violence:

On November 30, 1968, just nine months after graduating, Officer Robert E. Yeszerski and a Seat Pleasant Town policeman were shot to death while impounding an automobile left on the street for repairs.

On February 16, 1969, one year after graduating, Officer William W. Gullett, Jr., was shot to death while handling a loud stereo call.

On November 28, 1983, fifteen years after graduating, Police Capt. Richard J. Beavers was shot to death while attempting to thwart a robbery. At the time of his death, Captain Beavers was commander of the Oxon Hill Station.

The members of Class No. 3-67 left behind an honorable legacy of police service. Their time of service came about during a period of social upheaval, when violent crime was reaching dangerously high levels, and when many people looked down upon police service with contempt. Undaunted by adversity and bolstered by a strong tradition of departmental esprit de corps, the members of Class No. 3-67 prevailed. Their devotion and commitment to duty clearly illustrate the highest traditions of police service.

To upgrade the quality of police service, many members of the class, along with numerous other officers, made a commitment to improve the law enforcement profession by pursuing a college degree during off-duty hours. For example, Alonzo Black obtained a law degree and resigned from the department to work in the state's attorney's office. Space does not allow us to present a detailed statement of the many unheralded achievements and acts of bravery by members of Class No. 3-67; like the time Det. Fritz Zimmer was shot while pursuing a holdup suspect, or the twenty-four-hour homicide investigations worked by detectives such as Sgt. Tommy Nylund, or the endless number of off-duty hours that Cpl. Pat Grogan spends in his many charitable and humanitarian endeavors. On February 19, 1968, the thirty-eight members of Class No. 3-67 raised their right hands and took the oath of office.

Member of Class No. 3-67, first row, left to right, are Elwood Ward, Newell Rand, Richard Beavers, Chief George Panagoulis, William Gullett, Walter McGinnis, and James Ratherdale. Second row: Jack McMillan, Leo Schiek, George Paine, Andrew Beall, Eugene Mitchell, and Marshall Mayberry. Third row: Robert Yeszerski, Richard Bonkowski, Roger Burnette, Lon McKamey, Oliver "Pat" Grogan, Charles Spencer, and Gerald Howard. Fourth row: Joseph Gray, Alonzo Black, Donald Smith, Lawrence Miller, John Booth, and Edward Wright. Fifth row: Thomas Gorman, Arthur Leveille, Edward Forbes, William Johnson, Harold Toren, and Daryl Fuller. Sixth row: Ronald Osbourn, Harold "Gene" Wiles, Luther Watkins, Frederick Zimmer, Frank Mione, and William Seminuk. Center rear: Thomas Nylund. PGPD photo

Officers from the Hyattsville Station responded to the Adelphi home of Lee D. Gerhold on the evening of February 8, 1968, and took a missing person report on the complainant's forty-year-old wife. Circumstances surrounding the disappearance led the reporting officer, Richard Donnelly, to believe that foul-play was a possibility. Mrs. Gerhold's body was found in her station wagon a few hours later; she had been shot in the head. Although the police believed that Mr. Gerhold was responsible for his wife's death, no evidence was developed to justify an indictment. The case remained unsolved for more than twenty years. In November 1988, an informant contacted the Baltimore City Police and told them that Mr. Gerhold was attempting to make a contract on the murder of his third wife. An ensuing investigation by the Baltimore City and Prince George's County Police Departments led to an arrest, indictment, and conviction of Mr. Gerhold for the murder of his first wife.

The Gerhold murder occurred when the county police were in the process of converting from solid black to all white police cars. This is the only known photograph of an old black and a new white police car together. The light-colored station wagon in the foreground contains Mrs. Gerhold's body.
PGPD photo

JOHN W. LEATHERBURY

Killed in the line of duty
March 21, 1968

I n March 1968, the county police department and Hughes Aircraft entered into a three-week "Eye in the Sky" program to evaluate the usefulness of a helicopter as an everyday crime-fighting tool. The agreement stipulated that Hughes would furnish a Model 300 helicopter and pilot for routine police patrol duty. The helicopter would alternate between day and night service, remaining on flight or standby status for approximately ten to twelve hours per day. When on patrol status, one of five volunteer officers would accompany the pilot.

On March 21, 1968, one week into the program, a tragic accident occurred. While on night patrol the helicopter, piloted by Mr. William Hanley, responded to the call of an open door at a bank in Hillcrest Heights. County policeman John W. Leatherbury, Jr., riding as the observer, overheard the radio call and directed the pilot to the bank. The helicopter came in low and hovered over the scene, lighting the immediate area with its high-intensity searchlight. The ground units stated that the door appeared to have been left open accidentally, and that they would clear the call after securing the door. The helicopter pilot revved the craft's engine to gain altitude, but one of the main rotor blades struck a nearby powerline. The craft immediately plummeted to the upper-level deck of the Montgomery Ward parking garage and exploded into a ball of fire. Both the pilot and police observer died on impact.

The pilot, Mr. William Hanley, a northeast regional sales manager for Hughes Aircraft, was a former Marine Corps pilot who had logged more than 2,000 hours of helicopter flight time. Twenty-six-year-old Police Officer John Leatherbury, the observer, had joined the department in 1965 and was assigned to the Seat Pleasant Station when he volunteered to participate in the helicopter program. Born and raised in Anne Arundel County, John Leatherbury entered the U. S. Navy after graduating from high school. After being honorably discharged he worked for two years as a fingerprint clerk for the FBI. In 1965, he reached a lifelong goal of becoming a police officer with his appointment to the Prince George's County Police Department. Officer Leatherbury was married, but had no children.

The headline for the Washington Post *of Friday, April 5, 1968, announced the assassination of the Reverend Dr. Martin Luther King, Jr. The newspaper also reported that various cities across the country were experiencing riots, looting, and fires. On Saturday, April 6, the Post headline read, "6,000 Troops Move Into District." Sunday's headline indicated that a total of 11,600 troops were now enforcing a curfew, and that 3,263 people had been arrested. Six persons were reported to have been killed during the disorders.*

Ben W. Gilbert and the staff of the Washington Post *later wrote a book about the Washington disorders. Titled* Ten Blocks From The White House, *the book tells us that very little activity spilled over into the Washington suburbs. In Prince George's County "an elementary school was set on fire, and three stores were looted during the rioting. . . On Saturday night, Washington police and federal troops set up checkpoints on nearly every major street leading in and out of the District on the Maryland and Virginia borders. They checked outgoing cars for contraband and all incoming vehicles to see if the occupants had legitimate reasons for being in Washington after the curfew. . . ."*

The book's authors go on to say that, "One of the large fires, still burning at nightfall, Saturday, was consuming a shopping strip of five stores on Southern Avenue, S.E., right on the borders between the city and Prince George's County, Maryland. As firemen fought the blaze that spread through all the stores, cars of Prince George's County policemen were parked just across the boundary line. The suburban policemen had gas masks, tear gas, canine corps dogs, shotguns, and rifles. Two State policemen, with high-powered rifles, were stationed atop a liquor store on the Maryland side of the line. Others poked gun barrels out from behind store walls. They were watching about 300 people, mostly youngsters, looting a grocery store, delicatessen, and liquor store, just inside Washington, half a block from the Maryland line. The Prince George's County Police had specific authority from County Commissioner Gladys Noon Spellman to shoot, if necessary, to stop any looting that spilled over into the county." The book goes on to read that "D.C. National Guard Major Robert Donlan remembered `being scared stiff' when he saw the police across the state line, `armed to the teeth, just waiting.' As Guard MP's under his command tried to disperse the crowd, Donlan went into the intersection with a bullhorn. `I told the people of Washington to stay within the city limits and go home. I told them if they crossed into Maryland they would probably be shot. Nobody crossed the line.'"

Photos courtesy of the Washing-*ton Post*

The rising rate of violent crime in the late 1960s caused the county government to increase the size of its police department. Inspector Roland Sweitzer and Sgt. Daniel Robertson are shown here inspecting the members of Training Session No. 1-68 just prior to their graduation. PGPD photo

When Chief of Police George J. Panagoulis announced his intention to retire effective July 1, 1968, the county commissioners immediately announced the appointment of Deputy Chief Vincent S. Free, a twenty-five-year police veteran, as the department's new chief of police.
Upon hearing of Chief Panagoulis' impending retirement an unidentified local newspaper editorialized that, "Mr. Panagoulis has given intelligent direction to the county force as it weathered growing pains of its most intensive development period. . . . The retiring chief has thrived on controversy. He is outspoken, and sometimes unorthodox. He has, however, above all, been human. . . . It may be that in this increasingly impersonal world, a touch of human interest may take a cold edge from the burgeoning bureaucracy we call government. It is this departure of the human element so colorfully displayed by Mr. Panagoulis that will —among other things—be missed."
PGPD photo

Chief of Police Vincent S. Free.

ROBERT E. YESZERSKI

Killed in the line of duty
November 30, 1968

On November 30, 1968, Seat Pleasant Town Police Officer William R. Clements had a conversation with a fifty-nine-year-old man named Willis Underwood. Officer Clements informed Mr. Underwood that the town police had received several complaints about his inoperable automobile being parked on Grieg Court for a long period of time, and that the vehicle would be impounded if not moved. Mr. Underwood responded by telling the officer, "You touch my car and I'm going to kill you."

Officer Clements reported the threat to his superiors within the seven-man town department and, in turn, was told to issue a traffic violation notice and impound the vehicle. Returning in the afternoon with a tow truck and county policeman Robert E. Yeszerski as a backup, Officer Clements prepared to impound the vehicle. As the tow truck hooked up to the vehicle, the suspect approached both officers from the rear. According to the tow truck driver, Underwood yelled something such as, "I told you I was going to blow your head off." He then pulled a gun from beneath his coat and began shooting. Both officers were apparently taken by surprise as each was shot three times. Officer Yeszerski was able to draw his weapon and fire two shots, but both rounds went into the ground. Immediately after the shooting occurred, a second county policeman, accompanied by an off-duty Seat Pleasant town officer, arrived on the scene and ordered Underwood to drop his gun. When Mr. Underwood refused to drop his gun, the town officer fired his service revolver striking the suspect in the side. Mr. Underwood was later tried and convicted of murdering both officers.

At the time of his death, Seat Pleasant Town Officer William R. Clements was twenty-four-years-old, married, and the father of one child. Prince George's County Police Officer Edward E. Yeszerski was twenty-three-years-old, married, and the father of two children.

The Courier, a local newspaper, published several pictures of Officer Yeszerski's funeral in its December 5, 1968 edition. Emblazoned upon one of these photographs was the following tribute: "Valor is often disguised by the courage to go about daily routine. Now the courage belongs to the families of two slain policemen who must go on living with the empty void that was once a husband and father."

A yearly report for 1968 revealed that the department received 93,332 requests for police service, and that an additional 99,301 services were also provided without formal request. The department's new four-channel radio communications system and a number of recently hired civilian dispatchers allowed the department to unravel the backlog of calls that had been associated with the old single-channel radio system. A new Washington Area Law Enforcement System computer terminal also became operational, thus allowing the department's 502 officers instant access to information concerning wanted persons, stolen automobiles, stolen property, and other information pertinent to the Washington area law enforcement community.
Photo from a 1968 Yearly Report

WILIAM W. GULLET

Killed in the line of duty
February 16, 1969

William W. Gullett, Jr., was born in St. Louis, Missouri, but moved to the College Park area of Prince George's County when he was two years old. After graduating from Northwestern High School, he joined the Prince George's County Police Department, becoming one of the first three members of a newly initiated cadet program. Completing several years of duty as a police cadet, Bill Gullett entered the police academy on November 6, 1967. After completing a fifteen-week training program, Officer Gullett was assigned to patrol duty at the Seat Pleasant Station.

On February 16, 1969, Officer Gullett and his partner PFC Harlan (Pete) Parrish received a 1:00 a.m. radio call for a loud stereo in an apartment at 2910 Markham Lane in Kentland. After arriving at the scene, the officers were directed to the apartment of Mr. James F. Jarred. The officers after knocking on the door were met by Jarred who immediately drew a large-caliber handgun and pointed it at the officers. The officers spoke with Jarred for about five minutes, persuading him to holster his weapon. As the situation calmed, the officers attempted to ease their way into the apartment, but Jarred suddenly drew his weapon and fired three quick shots. Both officers were able to draw their weapons and fire a total of nine shots. Officer Gullett and Jarred were mortally wounded by the exchange of gun fire. Officer Parrish, although directly in the line of fire, was not injured.

At the time of his death, Officer Gullett was twenty-two years old and single. He resided with his mother, father, younger brother, and two sisters at the family home in College Park. Officer Gullett's father, active in local politics, was the mayor of College Park. The senior Mr. Gullett would later be elected as the first county executive when a new County Charter was adopted in the early 1970s. William W. Gullett, Sr., described his son as being totally dedicated to a law enforcement career. "He was heart and soul a policeman, completely wrapped up in his work."

In response to an IACP recommendation, the department adopted a Watch Commander Patrol System in 1969. The system placed all patrol officers under the command of a "Watch Captain" who had command of all patrol officers during an eight-hour tour of duty. The occasional shifting of officers from one station to another, shift overlaps, early cars, late cars, and patrol beats that expanded or contracted with each tour of duty proved to be very confusing and unsettling to a police department that prided itself on inter-personnel cohesiveness. In less than two years, the department decided that the Watch Commander System was too cumbersome and returned to the more traditional system of administering patrol services through local stations.

Standing in the center are: Watch Commander Capt. John Tucker and Police Clerk L. Piazza. Kneeling, left to right, are Sgts. James Ritter, Ernest Riess, James Miller, and Cpl. Harold Wilson. Standing in the rear row are Sgts. Richard Pearson, Jr., James Godbold, Charles Flynn, Frank Bishop, James Rash, and Cpl. Jack Smith.
PGPD photo

Joseph McCaffrey's *Commentary* and *The Service Wife* By Rosemary Start Today

STAR ★ LEADER

Serving Southern Prince George's County

VOL. 5, NO. 31   10 CENTS PER COPY   CLINTON, MARYLAND   WEDNESDAY, AUGUST 13, 1969   12 PAGES

POLICEMEN TO MARCH ON COURTHOUSE

Fair And Showcase Opens Today With Thousands Expected

by Sam Sullivan

The Prince George's County Fair and Showcase opens today at the Fairgrounds in Upper Marlboro. Expected to be the "Biggest and best" ever, according to Bill R. Hunter, the fair director, the exposition has something for all of the expected crowd of 150,000.

For the children, there are myraids of rides, including the old stand-bys, the Ferris wheel and the merry-go-round, and for the adults, there are exhibits and booths show "Hee Haw." Owens will appear, along with the Buckeroos, on Friday and Saturday nights at 7 and 9 P.M.

Appearing on Sunday evening will be the other star of "Hee Haw," Roy Clark. Clark, a native of Prince George's County, will perform at 5:15 and 7:30 P.M. Appearing with Roy Clark will be Dub Howington and the Tennessee Haymakers, a local band which has sent several performers on the big time.

Officers Press Pay Increases

by Del Malkie

Over half of the members of the Prince George's County Police force have voted to march on the Courthouse in demand to the Commissioners for overtime pay and payment for hours of off-duty time spent in courtrooms.

Approximately 360 uniformed officers, about two-thirds of the non-commissioned policemen in the department, signed a petition listing their demands and voted at a meeting on July 23rd to march on the Courthouse the following Tuesday, July 29th.

Only the fact that three of the five Commissioners were

AREA HOME RIFLED BY BURGLAR

in Portland, Oregon, at a national convention of county officials on the 29th stopped that march.

Another meeting has been set for tonight, for the membership to confirm a new target date for the march on August 26th.

Det. Sgt. Pete Cissel, president of the local chapter of Fraternal Order of Police confirmed that the vote march stands.

"The vote has been taken and this week's meeting is only to confirm the date," Cissel said.

Reaction at Police Headquarters and at the Courthouse was similar in favor of the principle of the

An article on the front page of the Star Leader *for August 13, 1969, states that 360 county officers had threatened to stage a symbolic march on the courthouse in a demand for overtime and off-duty court appearances. A subsequent, but undated* Washington Post *article quotes Police Chief Vincent S. Free as saying, "the executive board of the Fraternal Order of Police, which is leading the drive for extra money, had been warned that a demonstration would be regarded as a breach of discipline." The article goes on to say that plans for the "demonstration. . .failed to materialize. . ." Internal change, concerning labor/management relations, had started to take place within the police department.*
Newspaper article courtesy of retired Cpl. John Pumphrey

1941-1951

1951-19

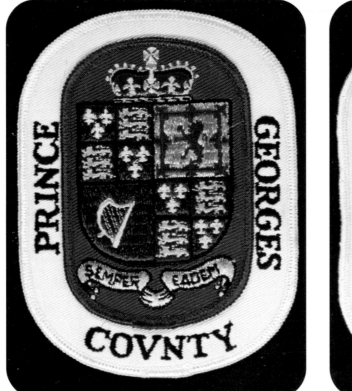

1961-1967

1967-pr

178

CONTEMPORARY LAW ENFORCEMENT
1991
An Overview

Photo courtesy of David Mitchell

Various duty uniforms worn by the department.
Photo courtesy of Henry Jones

Photo by Jack San Felice

180

*Recently found and extremely rare
original police badge from the 1930s.
Courtesy of P. Duncan*

*This old country barn, surrounded on three sides by new homes, stands
as a symbolic representation between the old and the new Prince
George's County. Boasting a population in excess of 700,000 people the
county is served by more than 1,500 police department employees.
Photo courtesy of Jack San Felice*

Morning inspection at the police academy.
Photo courtesy of Jack San Felice

Patrol duty.
Photo courtesy of Keith Evans

Police academy graduation inspection by Chief Mitchell.
Photo by Phil Masturzo, courtesy of the Prince George's Journal

Traffic enforcement.
Photo courtesy of Jack San Felice

Crime scene processing.
Photo courtesy of Jack San Felice

Meeting and conferring.
Photo courtesy of Jack San Felice

Located in Palmer Park, the new Police Services Complex serves to house Patrol District III, Headquarters, Educational Services, the Drug Laboratory, Narcotic Enforcement Division, and the Criminal Investigations Division.
Photo courtesy of Jack San Felice

The Hyattsville Criminal Justice Center serves to house Patrol District I and a Department of Corrections Work Release Site.
Photo courtesy of Jack San Felice

Members of the Community Orientated Policing Unit from District III are joined by County Executive Glendening and Chief Mitchell at the opening of a satellite police office in Seat Pleasant.
PGPD photo

Detectives investigate a murder.
Copyrighted photo by Phil Masturzo, courtesy
of the Prince George's Journal

A departmental chemist conducts an analysis of some suspected drugs.
Photo courtesy of Jack San Felice

Firearms training.
Photo courtesy of Mark Reinstein

Computerized judgmental Shoot/
No Shoot Training at the police
academy.
Photo courtesy of Keith Evans

More than 422,000 calls for
service were dispatched in 1990.
Photo courtesy of Jack San Felice

K-9 Patrol.
  Photo courtesy of Henry Jones

The police department and a number of community
organizations join together each year to sponsor a Christmas
Party for Deserving Children.
PGPD photo

United States Attorney General Dick Thornburg presents
County Executive Glendening and Chief Mitchell with a $1.2
check. The money was returned to the county coffers from the
Justice Department's Drug Asset Forfeiture Fund.
PGPD photo

Drug Abuse, Resistance, Education (DARE) training for children.
Photo courtesy of Jack San Felice

Motorcycle patrol.
Photo courtesy of Jack San Felice

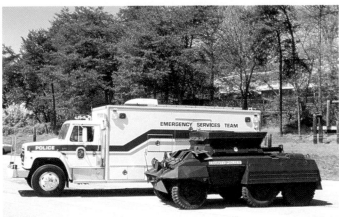

Special equipment used for barricade/hostage situations.
Photo courtesy of Jack San Felice

Computerized fingerprint equipment used to classify inked prints and to search for unidentified latent prints found at crime scenes.
Photo courtesy of Jack San Felice

Photo courtesy of Donald Downs

In May, 1695 a Council consisting of eight men sat down with a group of representatives from the House of Burgesses to map out the province of Prince George's County. They determined the boundaries and on May 22, 1695, the act was passed and the province became known as Prince George's County, to be "erected" on April 23, 1696.

In October 1696, the justices of Prince George's County applied to the Honorable Sir Thomas Lawrence Barronet, secretary, Council of Maryland, for a seal for the county. It was ordered that a seal be provided at the expense of the county and that Mr. Charles Beckwith of Patuxent be engaged for this purpose.

In the meantime, until the seal was ready, they could make use of the private seal belonging to the chief justice of the court.

The seal illustrated is a copy of the impression found upon legal papers coming from Prince George's County for the years ranging from 1704 to 1740. It shows beyond question that the designer chose to favor Anne of England, or waited until she had ascended the throne before striking the seal. Anne was the second daughter of James II and held the throne from 1702 until 1714.

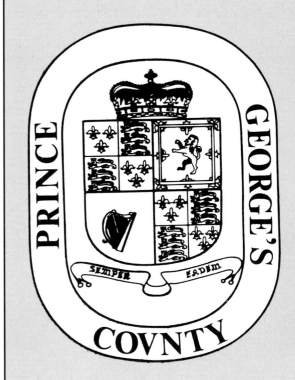

> Crest: *The Imperial Crown of England -*
>
> > *"St. Edward's Crown"*
>
> Arms: *Anne, quarterly, first and fourth grand quarters:*
>
> > *France modern and England quarterly; grand*
> >
> > *quarter, Scotland; third grand quarter, Ireland.*
>
> Moto: *Semper Eadem - "Ever the Same"*

The grand seal was reaffirmed as the original seal by the County Commissioners on November 25, 1958.

The original seal was officially altered in 1971 when the old English-style "u" was replaced and an apostrophe was added to "Prince George's County."

CHAPTER VII

1970-1979
Departmental Growth/
A Time for Change

Chief Sweitzer prepares to inspect the service revolver of newly appointed police officer Janet Brown.
PGPD photo

Tradition is often the reason one carries on when there are so many reasons not to.
—*Patriot Games*
Tom Clancy

The District of Columbia and its suburban neighbors entered the 1970s with the unique distinction of being America's most rapidly growing major metropolitan area. Prince George's County was identified as the area's fastest-growing jurisdiction. The Maryland National Capital Park and Planning Commission reported that "Between 1960 and 1970 the county's population increased by over eighty-five percent from 352,800 to over 658,000, thereby ranking the county as the area's most populated suburban jurisdiction." In 1970, the county police department functioned within the framework of an austere $10,748,026 budget, employing 502 sworn police officers, 189 civilian support personnel, and 165 crossing guards.

Violent crime within the District of Columbia became a serious problem and President Nixon's budget package for 1969 recommended that the Metropolitan Police be authorized to increase its strength to 5,100 officers. Experience showed that previous increases in the strength of the MPDC had tended to drive some crime out into the lesser protected suburbs. Because Prince George's County shared a 17.4 mile-long common boundary with the District of Columbia, it caught a lion's share of the spillover crime problem. In March 1969, County Board of Commissioners Chairman Francis J. Aluisi appeared before the U.S. Senate District Committee and asked the federal government for help in combating the ever-increasing county crime rate. Mr. Aluisi told the committee that "a great majority of the criminal activity along our common boundary is a direct result of conditions in the central city, and that increased anti-crime activity there will result in increased criminal activity in Prince George's County." Mr. Aluisi also cited recent crime statistics, noting that in the past nine months nearly 70 percent of the persons arrested in the county's 400 armed robberies were Washington, D.C. residents. Some 90 percent of these robberies had occurred between the District of Columbia line and the Capital Beltway.

In January 1970, Mr. Aluisi made a second appearance before the congressional committee stating that the federal government's "War on Crime" had been a "War of Words—Slogans," and that Prince George's County needed "help in confronting the gap between what needs to be done and what, in fact, is being done. Mr. Aluisi also stated that in 1969, narcotics arrests increased 96 percent over similar arrests for 1968. Violent crime, murder, rape, robbery, and aggravated assault also increased at an alarming rate. In 1967, there were a reported 1,109 such crimes in the county compared to 1,361 offenses reported in 1968. In 1969, the rate again increased, with the county experiencing 2,005 such crimes. According to Mr. Aluisi, these figures represented an 80 percent increase during the past three years. The armed robbery rate was of particular concern because it exemplified the spillover theory. In 1969, the county experienced 756 robberies for which 263 people were arrested; 129, or 40 percent of these individuals were District of Columbia residents.

County Police Chief Vincent S. Free also addressed the Senate committee stating "As the District Police force becomes larger and better, more is the tendency of the criminal to come to Prince George's." Lt. Col. C. V. Miller of the Montgomery County Police Department told the committee, "Senator, if you want to help us, build a forty-foot chain link fence along the District line and put barbed wire on top."

On November 3, 1970, the citizens of Prince George's County voted to adopt a charter form of government. Charter government, or home rule as it was sometimes called, did away with the county commissioner form of government and allowed the county to be governed by an elected county executive and county council. The newly adopted County Charter also gave the county additional autonomy from the state's General Assembly, thus eliminating the old and awkward requirement that local laws be enacted in Annapolis. The charter further specified that the chief of police be designated as the county's chief law enforcement officer. Prior to the charter's implementation, the sheriff, because he was a constitutionally identified officer, had technically been the county's chief law enforcement officer.

Law enforcement within Prince George's County experienced some particularly difficult growing pains in the early 1970s. The population explosion and increasing rate of crime placed a severe strain on the already understaffed police department's ability to keep pace with the continually rising demand for services. In April 1970, the Detective Bureau's General Assignment Section was reorganized into two major investigative units. The Crimes Against Persons Unit, which consisted of a Homicide/Sex Squad and Robbery Squad, operated from the Seat Pleasant Station. A Crimes Against Property Unit was also formed to investigate burglary and grand larceny offenses. The Crimes Against Property Unit operated from the Hyattsville and Oxon Hill Stations.

A fiscally lean county budget, serious overcrowding at every police facility, and an increasing rate of crime caused the department many problems. Overcrowding at headquarters in Seat Pleasant became so critical that the department had no other choice but to seek out new office space for the Homicide/Sex, Robbery, Juvenile, and Check & Fraud Squads. On January 1, 1971, these units moved into rental space at 8005 Cryden Way in Forestville. They remained in Forestville until March 1989, when a new Police Services complex was opened in Palmer Park.

Population growth and a decade of social change had a telling affect on the still small county police department. The rural simplicity of yesteryear was almost totally gone, replaced by the complexities of a modern twentieth-century urban lifestyle. The high rate of crime and a series of recent landmark court decisions forced the police to adopt new and more complex procedures for fighting crime and gathering the type of evidence that would stand up in court. Several newly developed theories about the type and quality of police service also caused police departments across the country to reexamine some long-established procedures. High technology, previously confined to the private business sector, now began to find a wide open marketplace within the law enforcement community. Increases in personnel strength, attrition, and the need to employ skilled technical workers placed each area police department into a competitive employment marketplace.

In 1972, the county government created a County Human Relations Commission with authority to conduct independent investigations into complaints of police harassment, demeaning language, and excessive force. If the commission found that an officer had acted improperly, it could request that the county executive ask the police chief to convene a trial board. The department continued to conduct its own misconduct investigations and to convene trial boards when necessary. In 1972, Police Chief Roland Sweitzer and County Executive William S. Gullett, Sr., announced that all future police trial boards would be open to the general public. Previous to this change in policy, all disciplinary proceedings had been closed to the public.

One aspect of police work that remained constant was the need for regulatory policies. The original twelve-paragraph set of rules and regulations adopted by the county commissioners on June 9, 1931, mushroomed into a voluminous three-inch-thick book of general orders. The Prince George's County Police Department was particularly proud of its quasi-military tradition. But society was changing, and some of the department's younger officers were now willing to question the department's authority to make questionable policy. The newly adopted County Charter permitted county employees, including the police, to be represented by a bargaining unit of their choice. The Fraternal Order of Police (FOP) Lodge 89, was chosen as the agent for the department's rank-and-file police officers. As events later proved, the county government was entering into a time period during which its labor/management relations would be strained to the very limit.

On June 28, 1974, the county government signed its first labor contract with the 750-member FOP Lodge 89. The initial contract was short term and the county quickly found itself involved in a bitter labor dispute with an increasingly militant FOP. The police department's pay scale was a key factor in the dispute. According to the *Washington Post* of October 16, 1975, "the average midpoint base salary for Prince George's [was] $12,615; District of Columbia, $14,153; Alexandria, $12,905; Arlington, $14,015; Fairfax, $14,260; [and] Montgomery, $13,384." The newspaper also inferred that the police were particularly upset with the county's chief negotiator, Donald Weinberg, whom the FOP accused of bad-faith bargaining. The FOP implemented a work-to-the-rule slowdown on October 15, 1975, protesting that the county was bargaining in bad faith. The *Washington Post* reported that "only emergency calls—those involving crimes in progress or persons whose lives were endangered could be assured of quick police response." The FOP, which termed their actions an "expression of dissatisfaction," also asked its members to turn in all police cars that were in need of repair. According to newspaper accounts, "more than one-third of the force's approximately 800 cars were listed as out of service."

On October 20, 1975, the county obtained a Circuit Court injunction prohibiting the police officers from "engaging in any job action or concertedly withholding or refusing to perform services . . . for which they are employed." The dispute between the county and its police officers was sent to a fact-finder who, according to The *Enquirer Gazette* of January 15, 1976, submitted a report stating that Prince George's County Police "are paid appreciably less than their counterparts in surrounding communities for comparable if not more demanding public safety duties." The *Washington Post*, of the same date, reported that County Executive Winfield Kelly had announced a settlement of the longstanding salary dispute between the county and its police officers. As a result of the settlement, the police received a pay raise that averaged out to 14.5 percent over a two-year period.

Issues such as poverty, racial discrimination, and the Vietnam War fueled strong anti-establishment sentiments throughout the 1970s. The rate of violent crime, which began to increase in the 1960s, continued its upward spiral during the 1970s. Inner-city riots with racial overtones continued to occur in many of the nation's older cities. Large-scale anti-Vietnam War demonstrations became commonplace in many cities, including Washington, D.C., with similar demonstrations occurring on many of the nation's college campuses. Prince George's County was not immune. On several different occasions in the early 1970s, Governor Marvin Mandel was forced into calling out the National Guard to quell anti-war demonstrations at the University of Maryland.

The uniformed police officer, as government's most outwardly visible sign of authority, absorbed most of the anti-establishment sentiment. Encouraged by a small but vocal radical element, many young people viewed the police as authoritarian figures aiding the governmental oppression. Frequently referred to as "pigs" and literally spat upon, the police were often viewed with contempt. "Off with the pigs" became a so-called rallying cry for many revolutionary youths. According to the FBI, 558 police officers were killed between 1974 and 1978. Shockingly, forty-eight of these deaths were classified as ambush-type slayings; in other words, the killer laid in wait and then maliciously killed the officer.

During the 1970s, three Prince George's County policemen and one U. S. park police officer were killed in the line of duty. In Feburary 1977, the county police department became the first major police agency in the metropolitan area to issue bullet-proof vests to its officers. The county police and U. S. park police were not the only law enforcement agencies to suffer tragedy within Prince George's County. One Maryland state trooper was killed in an automobile accident, and two other troopers died when their helicopter crashed near Laurel. The helicopter was returning to the county after transporting an injured county policeman to the Shock Trauma Center in Baltimore.

Concern over an increasing number of alleged excessive force complaints against county police officers surfaced in the 1960s and continued into the 1970s. The issue of police brutality was further complicated by well-publicized allegations that the predominantly white county police department used excessive force when arresting blacks. Several steps, including the formation of a police community relations division, were initiated by the police and county government in an attempt to improve the department's overall image. In 1974, the department entered into a consent decree with the U.S. Department of Justice and agreed to formulate an Affirmative Action Plan to hire minority officers. At the time, only 29 of the department's 802 officers were black.

Chief Sweitzer also implemented some internal changes to improve the police image within the county's growing black community. A Community Relations Unit was formed for the sole purpose of fostering better police/community relations. Several of the department's general orders were amended to lessen the possibility of police/citizen confrontations. A four-day special cultural-awareness training program became a mandatory part of the police academy's yearly in-service training. The goal of this training was to make officers aware that they had to function in a multicultural society, and that they had a responsibility to serve all county residents equally. Although some members of the community maintained that the excessive force problem did not improve, an article in the *Prince George's Journal* of September 29, 1978, reported police brutality complaints had declined by 50 percent. On April 27, 1979, the *Prince George's Journal* published a news story under the caption, "2 Counties Lead P.G. In Brutality Complaints, Fairfax Has 32, Montgomery 25, P.G. 17."

Concern for the mental health of the nation's police officers surfaced in the 1970s. Police work had gained the reputation of being both a physically dangerous and mentally demanding occupation. Many of the nation's police executives became concerned with the high rate of attrition among police officers, the effect stress had on job performance, and the long-term effects that prolonged stress had upon the human body. In 1976, the Prince George's County Police Department hired the metropolitan area's first full-time staff psychologist to head a Psychological Services Unit. The unit offered a counseling service to all police department employees and their families.

During the late 1970s, the county's population peaked and actually started to decline slightly. At the same time, the county's black population, which had been declining for decades, started to increase. In 1970, blacks accounted for less than 15 percent of the county's total population. In 1977, it was estimated that blacks made up nearly one third of the county's population. An article in the *Washington Post* of December 3, 1979, stated that, "Prince George's County, once Washington's fastest-growing suburb, is continuing to lose population as the movement of black families into its neighborhoods is failing to offset sharp losses in white population." A demographer interviewed by the *Washington Post* said that the black families moving into the county were generally smaller than the white families moving out, and that most of the blacks would fall under the category of upwardly mobile households.

The problem of finding funds to adequately support the

Anti-Vietnam War and anti-establishment sentiments reached an all-time high during the 1970s. To show their patriotic support, the VFW Post in Monringside issued American flag pins to the department's 500-plus police officers. The flag pin remained part of the police uniform until 1988 when it was discontinued because the new police badge had an American flag embossed upon it. Pictured here receiving the first issued flag pin is Officer Steve Mayes of the Hyattsville Station. Also pictured, left to right, are Commander Charles Done of VFW Post 9619, County Commission Chairman Francis Aluisi, and Police Chief Vincent Free.
PGPD photo

police department had plagued Prince George's County for many years. In 1976, the need for officers became so critical that the department created a special Telephone Reporting Unit. Assigning officers on a light duty status to this unit allowed the department the option, with complainant approval, of taking minor incident reports over the telephone. The beat patrol car could then remain in service and available to handle the more serious calls for service. As the decade came to a close, Prince George's County was ranked directly behind the District of Columbia in population size and crime rate. Despite the fact that crime and calls for service were on the increase, austerity caused the county government to cut the police budget. The *Washington Star* of September 8, 1977, reports that the county council had cut police funding by $249,173, and that layoffs might occur within the police department.

In 1978 a taxpayer's revolt occurred with the ballot-box adoption of a TRIM Proposition. The proposition, which became law, placed a freeze on the county's current tax rate and accordingly prohibited the county government from expanding its already inadequate services. The *Prince George's Journal* of May 23, 1979, reported that the county executive was tentatively planning to trim thirty police officer positions and that the council might cut an additional $890,000 from the budget. The article goes on to quote Lt. Col. Vincent duCellier, head of the Bureau of Patrol, as saying, "It's going to be tight . . . in Washington they have 4,500 officers and they are concentrated in 25 square miles. We have 480 square miles and only 860 police officers to cover them."

In March 1979, the Prince George's and Montgomery County

Police Departments joined together to form a Regional Automated Fingerprint Identification System (RAFIS). The system, which was partially financed with a $687,000 federal grant, was the second fingerprint system in the world to make use of the latest computer technology. The inked fingerprints of all persons arrested are classified and stored within one shared computer file. Unidentified latent prints found at various crimes scenes are also scanned and classified by the same computer. The computer then searches its entire file of identified inked prints and attempts to match the unidentified prints with those prints found within its ten-finger inked print file.

Prince George's County came of age in the 1970s, taking on all the characteristics of a twentieth-century urban jurisdiction. From Laurel to Oxon Hill, from Seat Pleasant to Eagle Harbor, the county's high-density population all but eradicated the last vestiges of a previously rural and homogeneous county. Not only had the demographic changes been phenomenal, but urban sprawl had changed the county's very landscape. The transition was not without pain. Enduring governmental misjudgments occurred in the 1960s and the 1970s, but it should be noted that there was no one best way to guide the county through a time when its population would increase by more than 85 percent. An equally difficult assignment for the men and women of the police department was the task of maintaining quality police services during some particularly troublesome and austere times. In 1970, the police department responded to 171,501 calls for service. By the end of the 1970s, requests for service had increased by 65 percent, reaching a 1979 high of 282,937 calls.

Police officers have always been deeply appreciative of assistance received from the general public. On May 28, 1970, PFC A. D. Johnson directed a letter to Major Thomas A. Rogato requesting that the department and Fraternal Order of Police recognize the bravery of a citizen who had assisted in the capture of an armed robbery suspect. The letter tells how a cab driver, named Wilbur Newton, observed three suspects in the process of committing an armed robbery at a High's Store in Coral Hills. Mr. Newton located county policeman G. R. Lowther about one block away and returned to the store with him. While driving back to the scene, the three robbery suspects were seen fleeing across the parking lot. Mr. Newton went after one suspect in his cab. Although the suspect escaped, he was forced to touch the cab's hood to avoid being struck. Mr. Newton then jumped from his vehicle and successfully apprehended a second suspect who was armed with a .22 caliber revolver. A good set of latent fingerprints were later removed from the hood of Mr. Newton's cab and it was believed that they could be used to positively identify one of the two suspects who had made good his escape.

On June 20, 1970, Mr. Wilbur Newton of Washington, D.C., was awarded a Certificate of Commendation by the police department and FOP Lodge 89. The certificate stated that Mr. Newton's "willingness to become involved and his personal actions in assisting the police to apprehend two armed robbery suspects required tremendous courage and an unselfish disregard for his own safety." Pictured, left to right, are County Police Chief Vincent Free, Patrol Division Commander, Major Thomas Rogato, and Mr. Wilbur Newton. PGPD photo

Demonstrations became commonplace in the 1970s, and the police department became the central point for several grievance-type demonstrations. In 1970, a group of Central High School students gathered at the Seat Pleasant Station to protest their dissatisfaction with a police policy. PGPD photo

In mid-July 1971, Police Chief Vincent S. Free retired. Lt. Col. Roland B. Sweitzer, a well-known and highly respected thirty-year county policeman, was named as the county's new police chief.
PGPD photo

The department ordered several specially built multi-purpose patrol wagons in 1971. Although designed to transport prisoners, the vehicles were frequently used for routine patrol. Each vehicle carried eight shotguns and a complete tear-gas kit.
PGPD photo

In early 1968, Chief George Panagoulis recognized the need to improve the police department's image and asked retired MPDC Deputy Chief John Winters to formulate a plan for improving the county police department's community image. In August 1971, the department formally assigned Capt. Ralph Kalmus and several other officers to a Community Relations Division. In addition to coordinating and stimulating police-community relations activities, the division also hired a civilian press information officer who assumed the responsibility for, "The development of various programs designed and maintaining good relationships with all news media." Officers assigned to the division are shown here preparing for a public display. Pvt. Samuel Gross wipes down the display car's exterior, while Pvt. Charles Morse cleans the interior. Cpl. John Brooke carries a box of display items from the station while PFC Richard Donato carries a traffic control sign.
PGPD photo

PFC Kenneth Savoid of the Community Relations Division stands in front of a departmental display at Iverson Mall.
PGPD photo

201

Policeman Is Shot By Bandit

By CHARLES A. McALEER
Star Staff Writer

An off-duty U.S. Park Police officer was critically wounded last night while attempting to thwart a $40 holdup at a 7-Eleven food store in Silver Hill, Prince Georges County.

Officer Raymond Leonard Hawkins, 28, a Washington resident assigned to the Park Police substation in Anacostia, was shot once in the back of the head during the holdup about 9:25 p.m. at the store at 3204 Curtis Drive.

He was admitted to Cafritz Hospital a short time later, where he was given about a "1 in 20 chance" of living according to county police. He underwent surgery, then was placed in the hospital's intensive care unit.

For Hawkins, son of a recently retired D.C. fireman, it is the second time in five years that he has been seriously wounded.

In 1961, after only 21 days as a soldier in Vietnam, he was hit by a Viet Cong hand grenade tossed at his combat patrol. Wounded in the chest, neck, hands and arms, he spent more than six months in service hospitals.

Hawkins, a bachelor who lives at 1714 33rd Place SE, walked into the store, just off Branch Avenue near the District line, with his fiancee, Carol Elizabeth McKeever, during the robbery, police reported.

POLICE SAID there were two employes, Chan Chai Vises, 27, and James Henry Bentley, 32, in the store when three holdup men entered.

One bandit, with a blue steel revolver, told Vises to put money in a paper bag and left, leaving his two accomplices.

About this time, police said, Hawkins, out of uniform, came in and saw another holdup man taking money from Bentley.

The policeman pulled his revolver and ordered the bandit to walk to a soft drink cabinet, leaned him against it and began searching him.

As Hawkins did, the bandit spoke: "Friend, come out!"

With this, police said, the third bandit appeared behind the policeman and struck him on the head with a pistol, then shot him at "very close range."

THE TWO BANDITS then ran from the store and were last seen running on Curtis Drive. Police made an intensive search of the area without finding the men.

Police gave this description of the first bandit: Black male, about 20, 5 feet 5 or 6 inches tall, weighing 115-118 pounds, with a small bush haircut, clean shaven, and wearing a black hat with a white ball in the center, a blue waist-length jacket and black trousers.

The second robber, the one Hawkins was frisking, was described as black, about 27 years old, 6 feet tall, weighing 175 pounds, with a small bush hairdo, a Fu Manchu mustache, long sideburns and wearing a yellow jacket.

The third man was said to be black, about 20 years old, 5 feet 8 and 120 pounds, with a small bush hairdo, and wearing a black and white knit hat, a black jacket with white lapels and armed with an unknown type of handgun.

Police said it was the third holdup at the store in the last nine days. Two bandits got $79 in a robbery at 12:57 a.m. Dec. 15 and two others got about $60 in another robbery at 12:20

See SHOOTING, Page -3

SHOOTING
Off-Duty Policeman Wounded by Robber

Continued From Page B-1

a.m. Wednesday. Police said the description of the robbers were different each time. In both those robberies, another employe, Wasun Potipimpanon, 25, was the victim.

Joined May 4, 1969

Hawkins was appointed to the Park Police on May 4, 1969, after working about two years as a mailman. He lives with his parents, all natives of Washington.

Before being drafted into the Army for two years' service, he graduated from Woodward Preparatory School, attended Western Kentucky College for a year, and worked briefly for the District Highway Department.

His father, Clayton R. Hawkins, retired Aug. 1 after 30 years as a fireman. At the time, he was an aide to the fire department's 3rd Battalion chief in Anacostia.

According to his father, Hawkins was assigned to combat duty in Vietnam with the 25th Infantry Division after about six months' basic training in this country and had been there 21 days when he was wounded.

Hospitalized in Japan

At the time, he was an artillery private serving as a forward observer with an infantry unit on patrol. He was hospitalized in Japan for a while, then was flown back to the United States.

His father said Hawkins and his fiancee went to the store last night to buy Christmas wrapping paper.

After the shooting, Miss McKeever, 26, of 2822 31st St. SE, was reported in a state of shock. She was treated at Cafritz Hospital, where she remained most of the night, checking on Hawkins' condition.

It is the second time in eight months that an off-duty U.S. Park Police officer has been severely wounded trying to thwart a holdup in Prince Georges County.

R. L. HAWKINS

Officer Henderson Kea, 29, was wounded in an exchange of gunfire with bandits at a liquor store in the Oxon Run shopping center on April 7.

One robber was slain in that exchange and another died two months later from wounds he received. Officer Kea eventually recovered from three wounds in the abdomen.

On December 23, 1971, U. S. Park Policeman Raymond L. Hawkins was off duty and in civilian clothing when he observed a robbery in progress at a Hillcrest Heights 7-Eleven Store. Officer Hawkins arrested one suspect, but was shot from the rear by another unobserved suspect. Officer Hawkins later died of these wounds.
Evening Star *news article*

On three occasions, between 1970 and 1973, Governor Marvin Mandel was forced to call out the National Guard to quell large anti-war demonstrations at the University of Maryland's College Park campus. Policing the campus was primarily a responsibility of the campus and state police, but violent demonstrations forced the governor to declare a state of emergency and bring in the National Guard. The county police assumed primary responsibility for those areas immediately surrounding the campus.

These three photographs were obtained from the May 1970 edition of a now defunct campus publication titled *Argus*.

Because the county police were frequently removed from the heat of on-campus activity, there were extended periods of seemingly endless boredom. Officers not specifically on assignment were kept at a command post, ready to respond at a moment's notice to a trouble spot. Many of those officers clearly remember the many trouble alarms that were sounded and the often heard command, "Everyone on the bus." In the vast majority of situations, the trouble call turned out to be false. After a long monotonous wait on the bus, the inevitable order came, "Everyone off the bus."

In this photograph, a nonviolent demonstrator walks along a police line as Officer Hugh Chinn counters his boredom by chewing a wad of bubble gum. The police officers directly to the rear of Officer Chinn are from Baltimore City. Governor Mandel had sent in the Baltimore City Police Department's Tactical Squad as back-up for the state and county police.

Photo courtesy of Sandy Chinn and the Washington Post

NOTE: In the early 1970s it became fashionable for many young people to wear military fatigues. Many of these people also donned their fatigues with military-type patches. On December 2, 1971, Chief of Police Roland Sweitzer issued a special order concerning the, "Disposal of Unserviceable Uniform Items." The order said that, "a hippie-type individual was apprehended wearing a Police Department shoulder patch," and that henceforth police personnel disposing of distinctive uniform items would be required to "mutilate and destroy" the items. The order further stated that the wearing of the police patch by unauthorized persons was "undesirable and does nothing to enhance the image of the Department."

204

Maj. Thomas Rogato of the county police swears in a group of Maryland National Capital Park and Planning Commission police to help protect the College Park area. The swearing in was necessary because, at that time, the jurisdiction of the park police was limited to Park Commission property.
PGPD photo

On March 30, 1972, Police Officer Jack E. Greenhill of the Hyattsville Station was honored for his unassisted arrest of three armed robbery suspects. A police department press release states that Officer Greenhill had just begun his 11:00 p.m. to 7:00 a.m. tour of duty on February 15, 1972, when he saw two men robbing the Arby's Restaurant at 6350 New Hampshire Avenue. The suspects ran from the restaurant and jumped into an escape vehicle occupied by a third suspect. As the suspects' vehicle attempted to pull away, Officer Greenhill blocked its path with his police cruiser and apprehended all three suspects. The stolen money, a knife, and one handgun were recovered from the vehicle. Presenting Officer Greenhill with the Officer of the Month Award is Police Chief Roland Sweitzer.
PGPD photo

During the early 1970s, all female civilian employees assigned to station duty and those working in Central Records wore uniforms. Record clerks Gloria MacDonald (left) and Kathy Wilson are shown here at their work stations.
Photo courtesy of Kathy Wilson Barney

On November 11, 1971, the department initiated one of the nation's first personal car programs to increase overall police effectiveness. Officers who made their home in the county were assigned a personal patrol car and allowed to use the car while off duty. Personnel participating in the program agreed to monitor the police radio while driving the vehicle off duty and to handle, or assist in the handling of, nearby emergency situations. A 1974 police department brochure states that officers participating in the program responded to 63,020 calls or incidents resulting in 873 felony arrests, 2,662 misdemeanor criminal arrests, 5,698 traffic arrests, and 17,667 citizen assists.
PGPD photo

Police Chief Sweitzer presents Cpl. Don Kabala with the keys to his newly assigned personal police car. PGPD photo

Officer Larry Garrett tests one of the department's first four-channel portable radios. Previous to the mid-1970s almost all radio communication was limited to the interior confines of a patrol car. PGPD photo

On August 16, 1971, the Washington Post *printed a public interest story titled, "Motorcycle Wedding Fest." The article described a motorcycle gang wedding party, occurring in somebody's back yard, near Indian Head Highway. Obviously, such events inevitably attract police attention. One of several photographs accompanying the article bears the caption, "The ceremony had been delayed because Spider, at right, who was driving the food and drink wagon, was busted by the County Police on an old warrant for non-support."*

Facing the camera is Officer Mike Monahan, the officer with his back toward the camera is Tom Vernon.

Washington Post *photo courtesy of Lt. Mike Monahan*

Police radio dispatcher Bob Spigner works one of the three radio consoles serving the southern, central, and northern portions of the county.
PGPD photo

Police dispatcher Bob Spigner, receives an Award of Merit from Lt. Oral O. Husk. On January 26, 1972, two county policemen observed an automobile wanted by the MPDC in connection with an abduction, rape, and robbery. As the vehicle sped off, one of the two suspects fired at the police car with a double-barreled shotgun. After a short chase, the suspects abandoned their vehicle at a brickyard on Sheriff Road and fled into a wooded area, again firing at the pursuing officers. According to the commendation written by Sgt. Bernard Schwartz, police dispatcher Bob Spigner coordinated and directed the pursuing police units in such a way as to cordon off the immediate area and make escape impossible.
PGPD photo

On June 5, 1972, the department broke with the tradition of hiring female police officers for the sole purpose of working with juveniles. Training Session 44, contained five female officers, who had been hired for the purpose of assuming normal uniformed patrol duties. Chief Roland Sweitzer is quoted in a local newspaper as saying, "The Department will neither favor nor discriminate against the women and will assign them to the same duties as male officers."
PGPD photo

Unidentified newspaper photo of Cpl. Sam Corbin conducting a morning inspection of Session 44.

After a difficult twenty-week training program, forty-six officers graduated from the police academy as members of Training Session 44. From left to right are Officers Mary Henley, Janet Brown, and Brenda Farmer, the three female members of the class who successfully completed the training program.
PGPD photo

On May 15, 1972, Alabama Governor George
Wallace, a presidential candidate, was shot
while attending a campaign rally at the
Laurel Shopping Center. The would-be
assassin, Arthur Bremer, was captured at the
scene of the crime by several county officers
assigned to the Wallace detail.

A widely publicized photo, taken immedi-
ately after Arthur Bremer's arrest, shows
members of the Tactical Squad subduing
Arthur Bremer. Pictured left to right are
Officers Dave McCamley, Tom Kane, Rick
Lohfeld, Mike Landrum (with arm around
Bremer), Larry Jensen, and Terry Evans. The
officer just below Bremer is John Davey.
Copyrighted photo reprinted with permission
from Joseph Kundrat of Laurel

Officer William Corcoran comforts a wounded
bystander while waiting for an ambulance to
arrive.

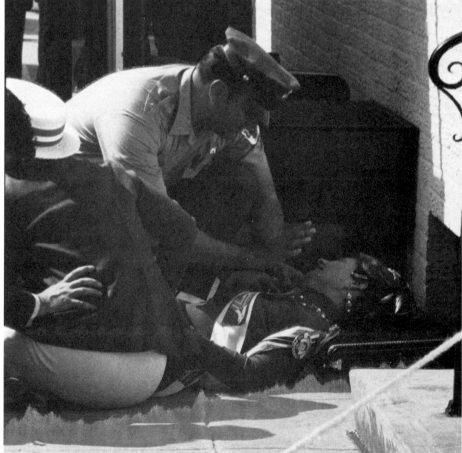

The original badge worn by police department cadets consisted of an unattractive yellow cardboard shield encased in clear plastic. Police Cadet John Harhai, Jr., is shown in this late 1960s photograph wearing the original badge.

In 1972, Chief Sweitzer adopted a newly designed cadet badge. In a formal ceremony, Chief Sweitzer presented each cadet with his or her new badge. Pictured, left to right, in the first row are Edward Burke, Jim Hasty, Lester Bethel, George King, Chief Sweitzer, Dale Anderson, Jim Swan, Pete Quimby, and Sarah Smith. Second row: Dave Dunn, Steve Long, Jim White, Dave Gainer, Jim May, Larry Chicca, Brian Swart, and Bill Ale. Third row: Dave Brown, Gary Amey, unidentified, Smokey Schaffer, Chuck Lanier, Jim Priest, Darryl Kingman, and Rusty Claggett. Fourth row: Rex Foster, James Seabolt, Ray Kane, Bob Murphy, Tom Kane, and Steve Gibson. Photos courtesy of PGPD and Cpl. John Harhai

CARROLL D. GARRISON

Killed in the line of duty
February 20, 1973

Born and raised in the Hyattsville area, Carroll D. Garrison enlisted in the U.S. Navy after graduating from high school. After serving a nine-year enlistment, Bo decided that he would like to follow in his father's footsteps and joined the county police department in 1968. Bo's father, Sgt. Carroll V. Garrison, had recently retired from the department after being shot in a Forestville bank holdup.

On February 20, 1973, at about 8:10 p.m., Officer Carroll D. Garrison responded to a burglary-in-progress call at 6519 Medwick Drive in Chillum. The call was made by a neighbor who had seen flashlight movement from within the home and, believing the residents were out, thought the home was being burglarized. Arriving on the scene, Officer Garrison checked the front of the home and found nothing unusual. As Garrison walked to the rear of the home, Officer Edward Adams arrived as a backup. Garrison found a broken pane of glass in the rear door and approached the house for a closer look. At this point, someone inside the home fired a shotgun. The blast hit Garrison in the chest. Officer Adams, realizing what had occurred, went to call for help and was also fired upon by someone inside the home. Additional officers arrived on the scene and fired into the home to provide protective cover for several other officers who carried the wounded Garrison to a waiting ambulance. Transported to Washington Adventist Hospital, Officer Garrison died on the operating table.

After establishing a perimeter, officers used a bull horn to urge those inside the house to surrender, but received no response. Shortly thereafter, police communications received a telephone call from a woman who said that someone was shooting at her and her husband from outside of their Medwick Drive home. The dispatcher told the woman that police were outside and that her husband should throw out his gun and surrender. Moments later thirty-one-year old James C. Law gave himself up to police. Mr. Law stated that his home had been broken into previously and that he had purchased a shotgun for protection. Shortly after going to bed, he heard noises coming from the back of his home and got his shotgun because he thought the house was being broken into again. Mr. Law said that he entered the kitchen and saw movement at the back door. Presuming that the person on the other side of the door was a burglar, he fired his weapon.

Officer Carroll "Bo" Garrison was thirty-one years old at the time of his death. He was married, but had no children.

Police Clerk, Corinne Hackett, Marlboro Precinct, wrote the following verse as a tribute to Officer Bo Garrison.

"*. . . Greater love than this hath no man*
He heard and obeyed the command
Devotion to duty, full obedience he gave
How many lives his courage saved
Our hearts with grief and love swell
This hero of ours, we knew him well. . . ."

Evening Star *photo*

Cpl. Raymond Donohue .

.1972 THE WASHINGTON POST

He Ran Out of Bullets, Officer Says of Slain Gunman

By Ivan G. Goldman
Washington Post Staff Writer

Prince George's County Police Cpl. Raymond Donohue lay in a hospital bed yesterday, five bullet wounds attesting to his morning's work.

"It was a real Mexican standoff," he said in an even, unhurried voice. "We were never more than 10 feet apart. I remember him lying on the floor when it was over. My gun was empty, and he was pointing his at me and still pulling the trigger. I was sure glad he was out of bullets, too."

Donohue, 29, said in a telephone interview that he entered the Hot Shoppe Jr. Restaurant at 7415 Landover Rd., in Kentland, for a late cup of coffee. It was 1:20 a.m., and he was off-duty, in civilian clothes.

Moments later, he and a would-be robber lay bleeding on the floor. The other man, mortally wounded, died in the emergency room at Prince George's General Hospital an hour and six minutes later.

Donohue, with two bullet holes in his left hand, two in his left ankle, and a fifth in his right shoulder, was in fair condition at the same hospital, receiving visitors, most of them fellow policemen, in his fifth-floor room.

Police identified the gunman as Denly Sonny Patterson, 32, of 453 N St. NW.

According to police, moments after Donohue entered the restaurant through a side door, a man entered behind him, thrusting a gun in his back.

As he told the three employees to "get down," the gunman did not know Donohue, veteran of 5½ years on the force, was a policeman and was armed. (Prince George's police are required to carry pistols when off duty.)

Donohue landed face down on the restaurant floor, the police report said, then rolled over, drew his pistol and shot Patterson five times. Patterson almost simultaneously emptied his gun—five bullets—into Donohue.

County police, under orders from the county prosecutor's office, are not allowed to reveal specific information about guns used in shootings, but sources close to the investigation said the gunman fired a .22-caliber pistol, and Donohue a more powerful .9 millimeter, German-made Luger semi-automatic.

Police said four of Donohue's shots struck Patterson in the chest and abdomen, a fifth hitting him in the right leg.

"I feel like a sieve," Donohue said. "All the bullets passed through me. I was quite fortunate that I was able to come out as well as I did.

"He was a big guy, about 6 foot 3, 260 pounds. I knew I emptied my gun at him, but there he was, still pulling the trigger." Donohue is 5 feet 11, and weighs 173 pounds.

Donohue said the restaurant was closed when he entered, and the employees had begun the nightly cleanup. He was acquainted with the night crew.

Last Nov. 15, Donohue and another policeman foiled an armed robbery in the same restaurant. Donohue was on duty that time, responding to the holdup alarm of a 7-Eleven grocery store next door at 11:01 p.m.

John Weyrich, an off-duty policeman riding in a police cruiser with the radio on, also answered the call. In the grocery they learned a holdup was in progress at the restaurant, that an employee had sneaked out and informed the 7-Eleven manager, who pressed his own holdup alarm.

Donohue and Weyrich arrested two robbers in the store without firing a shot. A third escaped, but was arrested minutes later by other police searching the neighborhood.

This month two of the robbers were convicted of armed robbery and sentenced to 10 years in prison each. The third was held as a juvenile offender.

Sources said that Donohue was heard joking as he was taken to the hospital yesterday that the gunman had ruined his new boots with his shots.

"Well, you have to have a bit of humor when something like this happens to you," Donohue told a reporter. "You have to keep up morale—esprit de corps.

"But it's a shame the world is so violent that a policeman has to carry an off-duty gun to preserve the domestic tranquillity of a neighborhood."

It would be an impossible task to recount every act of police heroism that has occurred over the years. This newspaper article, which appeared in the May 31, 1972 issue of the Washington Post *tells of an incident where off-duty Cpl. Raymond Donohue of the Seat Pleasant Station encountered a suspect robbing the Hot Shoppe Jr. in Kentland. The reporter, in this particular case, vividly recounts not only tense moments of the initial encounter, but the lingering aftermath that the officer must live with for the rest of his life.*
Courtesy of the Washington Post

Sgt. Wayne Beavers conducts a Tactical Squad field roll call at Penn-Mar Shopping Center. A Patrol Division reorganization in early 1973 placed the Tactical Squad, K-9 Corps, and Radar Unit under the command of a newly formed Special Operations Division.
PGPD photo

Sgt. Loren Nelson conducts a similar roll call of personnel assigned to the Seat Pleasant Station.
PGPD photo

On March 14, 1973, Officers Bernie Hinds and Bruce Gentile were assigned to the Seat Pleasant Station's patrol wagon. As part of a daily routine, the officers made a trip to the police academy to pick up station supplies. While in the supply room the officers were told that they could pick up their recently approved Blauer Jackets. The jackets, although authorized, had not yet been issued. Both officers immediately took off their cumbersome blouses and donned the more comfortable jackets.

Later that day, a serious train wreck occurred at Kenilworth Avenue and Route 50. Because there were a number of personal injuries, all available police and fire units responded to the scene. The Seat Pleasant wagon also responded, with Officers Hinds and Gentile standing out like sore thumbs because of their different uniforms. Many years later, Cpl. Hinds recounted his many supervisory encounters, with each supervisor questioning him about the previously unseen uniform.

In this photograph, Officer Hinds walks toward the camera while Officer Gentile is seen in the background. All other police personnel are dressed in their blouses. Until 1973, officers wore the blouse and Sam Browne gear for six to seven months out of the year. Although an extremely impressionable looking uniform, the blouse was uncomfortable and cumbersome to wear.
PGPD photo

The Capital Centre opened on December 2, 1973, with a Washington Bullets basketball game and a huge traffic jam.
Photo courtesy of the Capital Centre

Rock concerts held at the Capital Centre would later present the county and park police with another problem: how to control large and sometimes hostile crowds of young people. The use and sale of drugs at rock concerts also presented a unique problem. The narcotics problem was reduced through the use of undercover officers who pointed out those involved in the sale of drugs to uniformed officers. As an additional deterrent, Capital Centre management implemented a policy of conducting random entrance searches, thereby keeping out most contraband.
Photo courtesy of Sgt. Tim Bowen and Cpl. Harold Ruslander

In addition to training all county police officers, the department's Training and Education Division has provided basic police training to countless other Maryland law enforcement agencies. The forty-eight members of Session 45 shown here completed their training on March 30, 1973. The class consisted of forty-two Prince George's County officers, four Howard County officers, and two Maryland Park Police officers.
PGPD photo

The Tactical Alarm Response Squad (TARS) was formed in 1974. The specially trained and equipped squad had the responsibility of identifying and saturating those business areas experiencing a high rate of armed robberies.

Left to right, in the first row, are William Jones, John Davey, Donald Chamblee, Lt. Thomas Taylor (Officer in Charge), Bradley Garner, Peter Gallaher, and Stephen Grant. Second row: Bernard Hamilton, Roland Sweitzer, Jr., Jack Greenhill, Michael Cepko, Solemon Harris, and Mathew Sawyer. Third row: Allen D. Johnson, Lon McCamey, Ronald Smith, and John Cherba. Rear row: Ron Smith, David Weaver, Alfred Dalseg, Butch Reynolds, John Bond, and Robert Fabey.
PGPD photo

The Tactical Alarm Response Squad has participated in thousands of robbery stake outs without resorting to the use of dealy force. The unit's ability to formulate a strategic response, to deploy its officers in such a way as to cut off escape routes, and the use of electronic surveillance equipment has resulted in numerous arrests of armed suspects. Pictured here, left to right, are John Davey, Jonathan Norris, Thomas Wilson, Stephen Lennon, and William Buie.
Photo courtesy of Sgt. John Davey

In June 1974, County Executive William W. Gullett, Sr., signed the county's first labor contract with the FOP Lodge 89. Present at the ceremony, from left to right, are Police Chief Roland Sweitzer, Labor Negotiator Vincent Malin, President of Lodge 89 Cpl. Jack Cornett, and County Executive William Gullett.
Photo courtesy of the Prince George's government

On January 10, 1975, the Washington Star *reported that Officer Carol J. Murphy had been transferred to the county police department's Crimes Against Persons Division. The division consisted of a Homicide Squad, Sex Squad, and Robbery Squad. Detective Murphy was the first female county officer to be assigned standard criminal investigative duties. Newspaper clipping courtesy of PFC Carol Murphy Landrum*

FIRST IN P.G. AT 22

Detective's a Blonde

By Donald Hirzel
Star-News Staff Writer

Carol J. Murphy is a cute blue-eyed blond. She also is a cop.

In fact, she is the first woman detective in the history of the Prince Georges County Police Department.

Pvt. Murphy, 22, was transferred recently from the uniform divisionto detectives and has been assigned to investigate sex offenses.

POLICE CHIEF Roland B. Sweitzer said the transfer "realizes a long-term goal of providing a female detective to interview sex victims who might feel uncomfortable being interviewed by a man."

The use of a woman in such interviews was recommended by a task force named by the county to study treatment of victims of sexual assaults.

The task force, critical of the treatment of victims, recommended a series of improvements including a special rape crisis center at the county hospital and a woman detective to interview victims.

Working on sex crimes is a far cry from the career the young woman originally intended to pursue.

SHE WANTED to be a singer. She majored in music at the University of Miami in Florida, but quit after 2½ years to join the Continental Singers in a tour of California.

After that brief singing career, she came to Maryland with her parents when her father, a Navy man, was transferred here. The parents now live n Crofton, and the father is retired.

The young woman went to work in a bank in Annapolis "but I didn't stay too long. The job in the bank was not for me."

She then got a job with the Federal Bureau of Narcotics and Dangerous Drugs in Washington, where he worked as a secretary-dispatcher.

That job "was not too exciting, but it got me interested in the work of the agency."

ALTHOUGH SHE had no previous interest in becoming a police-woman, Pvt. Murphy joined the county police department "because it looked like they were opening up opportunities for women."

She went through the regular training at the Police Academy in Forestsville, and is proud that as a woman, "I did everything required of the men."

—Star News Staff

DETECTIVE CAROL MURPHY

After graduation, she was assigned to the Bowie substation, where she served in general police work for 14 months, first with an experienced officer and later on patrols by herself.

"I did the same general duties as the men, took the same reports, gave the same advice and thoroughly enjoyed my duty there," she said.

She obviously is aware that as the county's first woman detective, she will have to do a good job if the door is to be open to other women. At present there are 10 women in the police department of 850

Cpl. A. D. Johnson approaches a traffic violator.

Although the original 1927 county police force was authorized to buy a motorcycle, it seems the vehicle was never purchased. In 1931, the county commissioners specifically prohibited the police force from purchasing motorcycles. Some forty-three years later the motorcycle ban was lifted when the department borrowed two Harley-Davidsons from the U. S. Park Police. Cpls. A. D. Johnson and Mike Landrum were chosen to participate in a six-month evaluation of the motorcycle as a police vehicle. The final report on the evaluation stated that there was a definite need within the department for a motorcycle patrol.
PGPD photos

Cpl. Mike Landrum stands next to his Harley-Davidson motorcycle.

Police Motor Scooter Training Class in 1975. Use of these vehicles was limited to special assignments where the use of a regular patrol car was impractical. Pictured left to right are Lt. Robert Borruso, Chief Roland Sweitzer, and instructors Cpl. Harold Toren, and Cpl. Louis Schmidt. Attending the training were PFCs Thomas Murphy, Stephen McKimmie, Edward Ciesielski, Pvt. William Thorne, Cpl. Harold Ruslander, and PFC John Wyne. PGPD photo

On March 6, 1975, Police Chief Sweitzer announced his intention to end his thirty-four-year police career and retire effective May 1, 1975. County Executive Winfield Kelly immediately nominated Lt. Col. John W. Rhoads as the next chief of police. Chief Rhoads, an eighteen-year police veteran, received his county council confirmation on May 6, 1975, and assumed command of the 830-member police department. PGPD photo

In 1975, the police department functioned within the framework of a $23,338,463 budget; however, the midpoint salary of a county officer was said to be the lowest in the metropolitan area. Members of the FOP, which represented the department's rank-and-file membership, began negotiating their second labor contract with the county in early 1975. In mid-October, the county government said that the FOP demands were unrealistic. The FOP countered by stating that the county was not negotiating in good faith. On October 15, the FOP implemented a work slowdown to express its dissatisfaction with the county. The slowdown included a work-to-the-rule action on routine calls, with the FOP assuring the public that emergency calls would be handled promptly. Part of the FOP action called for officers to turn in all police cars in need of repair. Within a matter of a few days, this action resulted in placing almost one-third of the fleet out of service. As the dispute continued, it became more serious and the county found it necessary to ask the Circuit Court for an injunction to stop the slowdown. With the issuance of an injunction, the job action stopped and police activity quickly returned to normal. The dispute was then placed in the hands of a fact-finder who later ruled that the police should receive a 14.5 percent pay raise over a two-year period.
Photo courtesy of the Prince George's Journal

Eating on the go. Most patrol officers have only two choices, brown-bagging it or eating a quick meal from a fast-food restaurant. The hustle and bustle of responding to one radio call after another does not usually allow an officer the luxury of sitting down and enjoying a quiet meal. A quick hamburger, some fries, a soft drink, and a couple of Tums tablets is about the best that can be expected. In this photograph, police officers Jim Pressagno (left), Don Dement (center), and Chuck Cooke take time out from an assignment to enjoy a quick snack.
Photo courtesy of Mark Reinstein

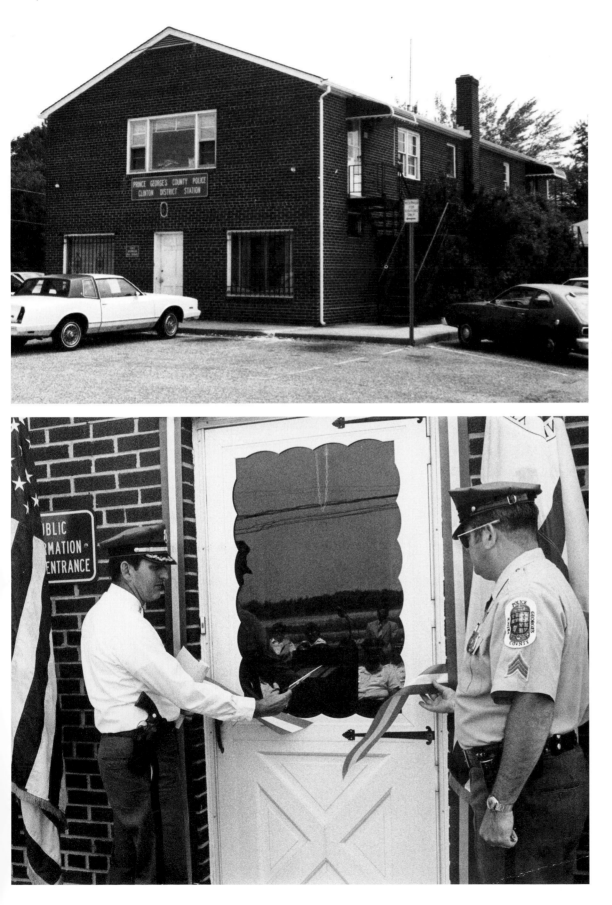

In 1976, the police department opened its Clinton Station in a rented facility at 8804 Woodyard Road. The station remained in this building until a county-owned building was obtained in 1986. Cutting the ribbon at opening day ceremonies are Capt. Daniel Robertson (left) and Sgt. Hugh Chinn.
PGPD photos

In order to celebrate the nation's 200th birthday (1776–1976), the county purchased several red, white, and blue police cruisers. In this photo, Police Officer Bruce Elliot poses with one of the newly purchased bicentennial cars.
Photo courtesy of Sgt. Bruce Elliott

The rapid rate of population growth, occurring between 1950 and 1975, tended to overwhelm every county public service agency. Office space became a critical factor and many agencies were forced to rent business space in widely dispersed locations. In 1976, the county dedicated a new County Administration Building (CAB) in Upper Marlboro. Although satellite facilities were still required, the new CAB allowed many agencies to consolidate their administrative headquarters in Upper Marlboro.
Photo by author

When two Montgomery County police officers were shot to death in early 1976, seven Prince George's County police officers offered to shave their heads if their fellow officers donated a certain amount of money to a fund for the slain officers' families. This photograph clearly illustrates that the department had no trouble raising the money. Pictured, left to right, are PFC Nicholas Valltos, Pvt. Darryl Kingman, PFC Roger Linger, and Pvt. Tony Camp. Not pictured are Sgt. Vincent Raubaugh, Sgt. Corky Snow, and Det. Bruce Hatley.
Photo courtesy of the Prince George's Journal

On August 17, 1976, Police Officers John Decker and Nancy White responded to the call of a burglary at 5708 Chillum Heights Drive. Officer Decker knocked on the door of apartment 301 and identified himself as a police officer. The door opened and a woman ran out holding a baby. Someone inside the apartment then fired a gun, hitting Decker in the chest. Although wounded, Officer Decker drew his service revolver and fired as the door was slammed shut. Going down the apartment steps, the officer reloaded his weapon and used his police radio to call for additional officers and an ambulance. It turned out that the suspect had forced his way into the apartment while the occupant was talking to her sister on the telephone. The sister overheard what was happening and notified the police of the burglary in progress.

In 1976, the department took a number of steps to increase officers' safety. A special two-squad Emergency Services Team was formed and specially trained to handle barricade situations. A study was also initiated to examine the feasibility of issuing bulletproof vests to all police officers. Portable radios were issued so that every officer could immediately contact the dispatcher, even when away from the police car. The Communications Division also began operating a Telephone Reporting Unit (TRU). The unit's main function was to take minor police reports over the telephone, thus freeing patrol officers for the more urgent calls.

Harold Parker was arrested for shooting Officer Decker. Placing the suspect in a police car are Officers Gary Amey (left) and Louis Long.
Photo courtesy of the Prince George's Journal

Original members of the department's 1976 Emergency Services Team. In the front row, left to right are, Officer Rick Thomas, Officer Jerry Smith, PFC Don Chamblee, Cpl. Terry Evans, and Sgt. Paul Tucker. In the back row are, PFC Stan Birckhead, PFC Gary Hutchison, PFC Steve McKimmie, Cpl. Charles Trotter, and Sgt. William Spalding. PGPD photo

Although primarily responsible for the handling of hostage/barricade situations, the Emergency Services Team quickly expanded into other service areas requiring extensive training. Some of the services provided by the unit include emergency rescue and underwater search operations.
PGPD photos

In September 1976, Cpl. Vaughn Worth and his partner, Striker, set a national record while participating in the National Canine Competition in Fort Worth, Texas. Cpl. Worth and Striker obtained 257.1 attack-proficiency points out of a possible 260.
PGPD photo

The department formed its first official Motorcycle Squad in 1976. Left to right are Officer Wayne Dotzenrod, Officer Everett Boswell, Cpl. Robert Fuller, and Cpl. Allan D. Johnson. The motorcycles and uniform pants were borrowed from the U. S. Park Police.
PGPD photo

As the county's population increased so did the need for additional police services. The department entered into the 1970s with 502 officers. It ended the decade with the employment of 864 officers. Session 52, a typical 1970s basic training class, graduated from the police academy on December 9, 1976. Pictured left to right in the first row: Brian Cayer (Anne Arundel Co. P.D.) Steve Folkee, Peter Morgan, Ed Moroney, Chief Rhoads, Wayne Bare, Paul Mazzei, Bill Clelland, and Paul Reese. Second row: Joe Wiggs, Sam Stokes, Wilson Collins, Major Coleman, Carlton Fletcher, Paul Karlsven, and Tony Prestandrea. Third row: Mike Schenning (A.A.Co. P.D.) Barry Beam, Jim Nowlin, Richard Moran, Randy Jaquith, John Moss, and Tom Lawrence. Fourth row: Tony Coley, Ted Sterling, Larry Boggs, Alphonso Hawkins, Larry Bowman, and Charles Montgomery. Fifth row: Mike Wilson (A.A.Co. P.D.), Mike Bernardon, Larry Rash, and Jeffrey Lloyd (A.A.Co. P.D.) Sixth row: Bill Richards, Craig VanLowe, George Swope, Jimmy Stewart, Ed Kollmann, Tony Coleman, Richard Grigsby, and Carl Lewis.
PGPD photo

Officer Carl R. Lewis, a member of Session 52, is inspected by Chief Rhoads just prior to graduation.
PGPD photos

NAACP requests federal investigation of county force
'Police brutality capital of the world'

by Carol Ostrinsky

Numerous complaints of police brutality in Prince George's County have prompted the local chapter of the National Association for the Advancement of Colored People (NAACP) to request a Justice Department investigation of police practices in the county.

Police and county officials, however, deny brutality complaints have increased.

"We've had more than 40 complaints of police brutality in the past six months," said county NAACP president Sylvester J. Vaughins. "These range from simple harrassments to serious use of force."

When the NAACP receives brutality complaints, the usual procedure is to ask the person to file a formal complaint with the county Human Relations Commission (HRC) and the Internal Affairs Section of the county police department.

"We got tired of channelling complaints and waiting for trials because we know people need relief now," explained Vaughins. "That's why we wrote to the Justice Department asking for an investigation into the police brutality complaints we've had."

"We feel police brutality denies people equal protection under the law," he said.

Last week the Justice Department informed the NAACP they are not empowered to investigate broad allegations against police departments, but would investigate any specific allegations NAACP sent them.

Vaughins said he plans to meet with local attorneys this week to prepare several complaints to submit to the Justice Department for investigation.

"Most of the calls we get are from Blacks," said Vaughins. "But of course police brutality doesn't confine itself to Blacks."

"We've dubbed Prince George's County police brutality capital of the world," said Vaughins. "This is because we feel the only way to solve the problem will be to wmbarrass the county government so much with that title that it will become a political decision to resolve the problem in the county," said Vaughins.

William Welch, executive director of the county Human Relations Commission said "We can't say police brutality complaints have increased."

The commission currently lists 77 "open" cases of alleged police misconduct, according to Welch. These fall into three basic categories: demeaning language, harrassment and excessive force.

By comparison, the Montgomery County Human Relations Commission documented only 16 cases of alleged police misconduct in the first six months of 1974, according to Barbara McMillan of Montgomery County's HRC.

The Prince George's HRC deals with many areas of human relations including employment, housing and police. They are presently in the process of completing an annual report that will include a study of police relations in the county.

"We are taking a look at all the cases during the past fiscal year to determine the nature and character of the alleged offenses," said Welch. "We're trying to determine the nature and character of the alleged offenses to see who is affected in terms of race, sex, and age."

One purpose of this study, according to Welch, is to try to uncover trends and possible ways of speeding up resolution of problems."

When the HRC receives a police brutality complaint, the matter is investigated by the staff and is also sent to the internal affairs section of the police department.

"We will recommend action if we can, or in some cases we find the complaint can't be sustained," said Welch.

The police internal affairs section will often conduct a board hearing, according to Capt. Albert Frank of Internal Affairs. "Disciplinary action, if necessary runs the gamut from a verbal reprimand to dismissal from the force.

"Complaints of brutality don't seem to be on the rise from what I can tell," said Frank. "It's not by any means an everyday thing."

"There has been no dramatic increase in police brutality complaints in the county," according to John Hoxie.

In the first six months of 1974 the department investigated 17 police brutality complaints referred by the HRC. Of those cases three were sustained, 10 were dismissed and the remainder may not yet be closed, according to Hoxie.

"By comparison, in the first six months of 1973 we investigated 19 cases, where two were sustained," he said.

"It's hard to tell exactly if the cases of brutality are on the rise, for two reasons," said Hoxie.

"First, we don't know if we get complaints from all those who feel they have been mistreated," he said. "Second, among those we do get, many are unsustained. This means we can't prove the complaint true or false becasue it's one person's word against another's."

A big department like Prince George's County will always encounter some incidents of misconduct, according to Hoxie. "It's an on-going problem, and we're currently trying to find ways to break down the tensions that casue poor police-community relations.

Newspaper clipping from the Diamondback *September 30, 1974*

Police Brutality—Both Sides of the Issue
Adverse publicity concerning the alleged used of excessive force has frequently presented the police department in a less than favorable light. The likelihood of encountering a hostile individual during any one tour of duty remains more than a distinct possibility for the average patrol officer. Unfortunately, the use of physical force in controlling some of these individuals is sometimes a necessity. Because conflict is sometimes unavoidable, a certain number of excessive force complaints should be expected. Many police officers believe that the news media has taken a less than balanced stance in reporting some of these excessive force complaints and that some media presentations have had a decidedly anti-police tone. Particularly frustrating to the police, is the fact that a person can approach the media, make an excessive force complaint, and then reap the rewards of favorable coverage. The police, in turn, are frequently prohibited from releasing exculpatory information because of pending civil or criminal litigation.

Police Brutality:
View From The Street

By John M. O'Connell

P.G. Post
1-8-76

What effect does the recent fury over police brutality have on county police officers? Are the complaints valid? Why so many?

These and other questions were posed to three officers of the Prince George's County Police Force this week in an interview at the Hyattsville station. The officers, Stephen J. Roberts, Thomas G. Singleton and R. H. Webster, were selected by Capt. Rice Turner at the request of The Post.

The officers had mixed opinions on the effect of recent brutality complaints on the morale of men in the department, with Roberts denying that such complaints had any real effect at all. Officer Singleton, however, held an opposite view, noting that bad publicity and complaints did adversely affect the morale of most policemen.

"The officer who is doing his job conscientiously,which is the case for most of us, has to pay the dues for those who mess up," he commented.

Webster, with still another view, noted, "I think officers begin to look at themselves. They begin to ask, 'What is the answer to it; what must we do to earn public confidence and change people's attitudes?'" But Webster added that he believed some problems—as well as reported complaints—amount to little more than "the public jumping on the bandwagon."

As for the legitimacy of many complaints, the officers again held varying views. Roberts said he thought one reason for the increase in complaints was the availability of official forms to the public.

But he added that he believed part of the problem to lie in the attitude of citizens.

"What has a guy got to loose? He can't be sued by the police officer," he said. "The public's attitude is already set. If you tell people to do anything against the way they feel, they will be against you."

This attitude and other behavior by citizens result in changes in police officers, Roberts said. "I thought I was fair-minded when I came on the department, but during the year, my attitude changed. The job makes you change your views. You talk to people who are rude to you and it changes you," said the three-year veteran who graduated from the University of Maryland.

Because of the citizen factor,

Roberts notes that officers have become wary of facing the public, even on routine traffic stops.

"The person may be an average citizen, but what is an average citizen? How do we know? He can be a crazy nut or a docile person," he said.

Officer Singleton has a different view of the recent rash of complaints. Noting personal experience, Singleton said he thought part of the reason citizens complain is in an effort to have charges lowered or dropped altogether.

"Some people seem to think that if you complain, the process of a civil suit and publicity will result in lowering of the charges," he said.

As for the basis of the complaints and their legitimacy, Singleton said, "I don't think I ever locked anyone up who thought he had violated the law."

Webster pointed the blame at the relative youth of the county's force, saying that the lack of experience is a big part of the problem. "The more practical experience you have, the more efficient, better-qualified police officer you will be," he said.

Noting that the force currently has an average of only slightly over one year of experience for its members, he added that the department was attempting to get "more bodies than experience" to cope with the rising population and crime rate.

Webster pointed out what he believed may be another facet of the problem. Referring to current labor negotiations being conducted, Webster noted that the county's force is one of the lowest paid in the metropolitan area.

"The majority of police didn't enter the field to make a whole lot of money, but they do have families to support." He added that problems such as these, combined with "other things, such as oftentimes a patrol officer spends a lot of time alone in a car with only a radio and plenty of time to think," which has an effect on the officer's performance.

Although all of the officers said they thought the procedure of making complaint forms available to the public was a good measure, there were recommendations on solving the problems of both brutality and groundless complaints.

Webster said the police depart-

ment should give officers more training. Singleton, however, thought the officers should have an equal opportunity to defend themselves with court recourse.

Pointing out that policemen only receive a single-page letter after a complaint case has been closed exonerating the officer, Singleton said he thought such officers should be able to benefit from court actions.

"An officer should be entitled to court recourse, if for no other reason but to prove his innocence. He will be able to say, 'I was right and I've shown I was,'" Singleton said.

Newspaper clipping from the Prince George's Post *January 8, 1976*

To a police officer, retirement is considered the equivalent of stepping into another world. This is not only true for the officer, but for the other half of the family (usually referred to as the better half) as well. Anyone who has experienced life in a police home knows about the difficulties, the anxieties, and the hardships that come with a law enforcement career.
Receiving his retirement badge on January 1, 1977, is Lt. John Haas and his wife Peggy. Also pictured is Major Robert Zidek (far left) and Chief of Police John Rhoads (far right).
PGPD photo

Photo courtesy of Lt. Wayne Spencer

A new $965,000 Bowie-Marlboro Station opened on October 22, 1977. This station, the first police facility to be built in twenty-three years, was placed under the command of Capt. Ernest Reiss. The new facility replaced space that had been lent to the police department in 1962 by the city of Bowie.

Photo of Capt. Ernest Reiss courtesy of PGPD

ALBERT M. CLAGGETT IV-JAMES B. SWART

Killed in the line of duty
June 26, 1978

During the early morning hours of June 26, 1978, Police Officers Albert M. Claggett IV and James Brian Swart arrested Terrance and Melvin Johnson for the theft of several laundry room coin boxes. The officers transported both brothers to the Hyattsville Station where eighteen-year-old Melvin Johnson was handcuffed to a bench in the prisoner processing area. Officer Claggett then began to administratively process fifteen-year-old Terrance Johnson as a juvenile offender. During the fingerprinting process, Terrance Johnson tore Officer Claggett's service revolver from its holster and shot the officer in the chest. Officer Swart, who was in an adjoining room, heard the shot and immediately ran into the processing room where the suspect also shot him in the chest. Terrance Johnson then ran into a hallway, where he continued firing Officer Claggett's weapon. Other officers in the station were unable to return Johnson's fire for fear of hitting several citizens who happened to be in the same hallway. Cpl. Paul Low maneuvered himself into a position just behind Johnson and disarmed him without further incident. The two wounded officers were taken to Prince George's Hospital where they were pronounced dead.

Albert M. "Rusty" Claggett was twenty-six-years old at the time of his death. He was married and the father of two young children. The son of retired county police Lt. Albert M. Claggett III, the younger Claggett had joined the department as a cadet in 1972. Appointed as a police officer in late 1972, Rusty was initially assigned to the Seat Pleasant Station, but later transferred to Hyattsville.

James Brian Swart was twenty-five-years old at the time of his death. The son of a retired MPDC detective sergeant, Brian Swart was also the product of a police family. Raised in the Riverdale area of Prince George's County, Brian joined the police department as a cadet in 1972. Entering the police academy in late 1973, Officer Swart graduated on March 4, 1974, and was assigned to the Hyattsville Station.

The police department's anguish in losing two brother officers was made even more tragic when a jury convicted Terrance Johnson of manslaughter and not murder in the death of Officer Claggett. The same jury then returned a verdict of not guilty, by reason of insanity, in the death of Officer Swart.

The never-ending work of a data entry clerk. In 1978, the police department's Central Records Section filed 110,361 reports. Pictured here processing some of those reports are Police Clerks Markeeta Faconer (left) and Ernestine Landrum.
PGPD photo

Number of Crimes In Prince George's In 1978

Homicide	**49**
Murder	36
Manslaughter	13
Rape	**316**
Rape by force	226
Assault to rape-attempts	90
Robbery	**1,999**
Firearm	926
Knife or cutting instrument	121
Other dangerous weapon	68
Strong arm (hands, fists, etc.)	884
Assault	**4,512**
Firearm	419
Knife or cutting instrument	414
Other dangerous weapon	584
Hands, feet, etc.	200
Other assaults, not aggravated	2,895
Breaking or Entering	**10,264**
Forcible entry	8,869
Unlawful entry, no force	242
Attempted forcible entry	1,053
Larceny-Theft	**21,184**
Except motor vehicle theft	21,184
Motor Vehicle Theft	**3,397**
Autos	2,638
Trucks and buses	346
Other vehicles	413
Total for 1978	**41,721**

The increasingly high rate of serious crime continued to be the major public safety concern for the police department. The March 2, 1979 edition of the Prince George's Journal *reported, "There were 6,227 crimes per 100,000 population in the County in 1978. The District of Columbia was the only jurisdiction with a higher rate, 7161."*
Courtesy of the Prince George's Journal

Two typical examples of those holding the line on crime at the district station level.

Uniformed officers at the Seat Pleasant Station, left to right in the front row, are Berkeley Jones, Jim Nowlin, and Nick Valltos. Second row: Darryl Kingman, George Swope, and John Calhoon. Third row are Sgt. Corky Snow, Tony Camp, Lester Bethel, Greg Delia, and Jeff Gray. Photo courtesy of Sgt. Bruce Hatley

Oxon Hill Station Detectives, left to right in the front, are Garland Price, Alan Creveling, and Dave Lutz. Second row: Gene Shook, Melvin Shapiro, and John San Felice. Third row: Sgt. Bob Cross, Pat Morrissette, Russ Knodle, and Richard Reagan. Fourth row: Bill Worden, Lt. Bob Howard, and Bob Padgett. Photo courtesy of Sgt. Bruce Hatley

Police service is a tradition in the Rash family. Sgt. James D. Rash is shown in 1978 with his new retirement badge. The Rashes' departmental lineage remained secure with three sons still serving within the department. Officers Larry Rash (left) and Robert Rash (right) pose with their father after his retirement. Police Officer Allan Rash is not pictured.
PGPD photo

Andre Brown, a twelve-year-old safety patrol officer from Oxon Hill, tries on the chief's hat for size. The youngster served a one-day stint as the department's honorary police chief in recognition of his heroism in pulling a five-year-old from the path of a speeding car.
Copyrighted photo courtesy of the Prince George's Journal

In March 1979, the Prince George's and Montgomery County Police departments entered into a joint venture to operate a Regional Automated Fingerprint Identification System (RAFIS). The system, which uses a computer, classifies and stores the fingerprints of all persons arrested in both counties. The system also stores unidentified prints found at crime scenes and searches its files in an attempt to match those unidentified prints with the known prints of those who have been arrested. As an example, a home is reported to the police as being burglarized. The police have no known suspects, but unidentified fingerprints are found on a pane of window glass. The unidentified prints are routinely forwarded to RAFIS and run through the computer. The computer makes a match between the unidentified crime scene prints and those of a man who had been previously arrested for shoplifting. The RAFIS system, when implemented, was the second such system of its kind in the world.

On June 29, 1979, Chief of Police John Rhoads retired as a result of a job-related disability. County Executive Larry Hogan announced that he would appoint Lt. Col. Joseph Vasco as the department's acting chief of police. After a six-month search, the county executive presented an out-of-town police chief as his nominee for the chief's position. The nomination was rejected after some heated debating between the Republican county executive and the Democratic county council. To stabilize conditions within the police department, the executive appointed his senior public safety assistant, John E. McHale, Jr., as the acting chief of police. Mr. McHale's law enforcement experience included some twenty-seven years as a special agent with the Federal Bureau of Investigation. Chief McHale's appointment was made permanent by the council in early February 1980. PGPD photo

Chief John E. McHale, Jr.

On Wednesday, May 6, 1981, two men on a motorcycle drove by the Oxon Hill Station and fired a handgun. Off-duty Cpl. Fenton Hinson, who lived nearby, heard the shot and saw the men drive by at a high rate of speed. Corporal Hinson pursued the motorcycle in his personal police car, radioing for assistance. Two

CHAPTER VIII

1980–1991
Drugs and Violence/
Technology/
Urban Complexity

arrests were made after the motorcycle rounded a curve and struck a responding police car. In this photograph, Officer Joseph Lomax poses behind the station window struck by the bullet. Copyrighted photo by Lon Slepicka, courtesy of the Prince George's Journal

As far as I'm concerned, death doesn't make them a hero. What makes them a hero is the fact they're walking out of the academy, they're putting on a gun, they're wearing a badge. And in this day and age that takes a lot of courage.
—Vivian Eney,
Wife of a U.S. Capitol Police Officer
accidentally killed during a police training session.

Events occurring in the 1970s had a profound impact on Prince George's County. The county had changed, the last vestiges of old line tradition all but totally disappeared from a now urbanized county. The rate of population growth had leveled off near the 665,000 figure and several noteworthy demographic occurrences had taken place. A January 3, 1980 article from the *Washington Post* reported that "County experts point to two main population trends . . . the flight of white families seeking to avoid school bussing and the major in-migration of black families. These trends have helped change the county from 15 percent non-white in 1970 to 30 percent non-white in 1977."

Important criminal justice issues such as police protection, violent crime, increased drug usage, backlogged courts, and an overcrowded jail continued to concern many residents. Practices within the police department concerning equal employment opportunities, promotional procedures, and internal discipline were now being scrutinized by a number of governmental and private organizations. Allegations concerning the excessive use of force and the general perception that people had of their county police became increasingly more important topic matters to many people from inside and outside the police department.

The development of modern technology also changed the department. A police officer who retired in the mid-1970s would have been awed by the sophisticated electronic equipment that officers now used. Computers, previously unknown to police work, were being used on a daily basis to analyze and predict crime, to assist in dispatching calls for service, to classify fingerprints, and to match those prints with unidentified prints found at crime scenes.

In 1981, the department celebrated its fiftieth anniversary as an independent county agency. In the short span of fifty years, astronomical change had taken place. Chief of Police John McHale, Jr., in hosting a formal golden anniversary dinner, told the department's 831 officers and 292 civilian employees that "The twenty-first century may bring us all sorts of Buck Rogers' inventions, ranging from laser beams and neutron activation units to jet aircraft and increasingly complex computer systems, but if we forget that our primary mission is one of helping people, then we will have fallen back rather than moved forward."

On May 5, 1981, the county government appointed Tom Davis as a deputy chief of police. Mr. Davis, a retired military officer, had worked as a civilian instructor in the police department's Training and Education Division for the previous six years. The need to increase minority representation in the department's upper echelon had led County Executive Lawrence Hogan to enact special legislation which exempted all future deputy chief positions from County Merit Law. Mr. Hogan, in announcing the appointment of Colonel Davis, said that there is a "vital need for minority representation in the upper ranks of the Police Department . . . even though I am convinced we do not have a problem of racism or brutality in the department, this is the culmination of an effort in trying to address the problem, real or imagined."

On July 22, 1981, the *Washington Post* reported that "Violent crime, particularly armed robberies, continues to increase dramatically in the county. For the first three months of 1981, there were 1,700 violent crimes . . . compared to 1,344 in 1980." Various newspapers also reported that the county government was experiencing a severe financial crisis and that every county agency's budget was being restricted. Discontent over the issue of low pay had been festering for years within the police department. The July 23, 1981 edition of the *Washington Post* quoted FOP President Laney Hester as stating, "The present $14,727 starting salary for police, set two years ago, is the lowest in the region."

In September 1981, the county and state police signed a "Memorandum of Understanding." The agreement assigned primary responsibility for the investigation of most criminal activity to the county police; while the state police assumed major traffic enforcement responsibility for all interstate highways and most of the county's heavily traveled state highways. The agreement followed a fourteen-year-old International Association of Chiefs of Police recommendation that the two agencies reach a cooperative agreement "which clearly delineates and fixes responsibilities of their respective agencies for the performance of law enforcement duties within Prince George's County."

Recently developed police procedures, which encouraged community involvement in the reduction of crime, began to pay dividends in the early 1980s. In August 1982, the police department announced that the crime rate had unexpectedly dropped by almost 7 percent. The drop was attributed to several joint police/citizen self-help programs intended to reduce neighborhood crime. In one of the more successful programs police officers responded to the calls of interested citizens and conducted home security surveys. Officers conducting the surveys would make recommendations to better protect the home against theft and burglary. A similar service was also established for the business community. With police assistance several Neighborhood Watch committees were established. Citizens participating in this program received police training on how to identify and report suspicious activity. People were also encouraged to engrave their valuable property with an identification number.

A local Crime Solvers program was also formed in the late 1970s. Crime Solvers, a privately funded program with a civilian board of directors, encourages citizens to anonymously cooperate with the police in solving crime. Reward money, raised by cooperating private sector businesses, is offered for information leading to an arrest and indictment. In the program's first ten years of operation, Prince George's County Crime Solvers tips led to the arrest of more than five hundred people, the recovery of property valued at $928,600, and the seizure of illegal drugs with a street value that exceeded $1,569,000.

On April 3, 1982, two men kidnapped Stephanie Ann Roper after her automobile ran off a rural Prince George's County roadway. The victim, a college student, was taken to St. Mary's County where she was raped, beaten with a chain, shot, doused with gasoline, and then set on fire.

When Miss Roper, a Prince George's County resident, failed to return home, her parents filed a missing person report. County police, fearing foul play, initiated a massive search for Miss Roper after finding her abandoned car. Her body was found one week later. State police in St. Mary's County later arrested two men and charged them with murdering Miss Roper.

Both defendants were convicted in a Baltimore County change-of-venue trial of first-degree murder, rape, and kidnapping. Although receiving life sentences, each would be eligible for parole in twelve years. The sentence, and the possibility of early probation, shocked and outraged many people. The Roper family and their many supporters publicly asked, "Does justice no longer serve the victim? What about the victims and their rights, and what about the rights of the families who must live with grief long beyond twelve or fifteen years or any number of years." Prince George's County State's Attorney Arthur Marshall reported that his office was besieged with angry callers. Outraged by the leniency of the sentence, Mr. Marshall took the unusual step of presenting the Prince George's County kidnapping case to the Grand Jury. Indictments were returned charging the defendants with the kidnapping in Prince George's County.

The Stephanie Roper Committee served as a catalyst, bringing the plight of crime victims and their families into the public spotlight. Miss Roper's parents and their supporters formed Maryland's first victim's rights advocacy group and actively lobby for the passage of laws which protect the human dignity of crime victims. The Stephanie Roper Foundation also offers support to crime victims who are in the process of offering criminal trial testimony.

In November 1982, Parris N. Glendening, a former county council member defeated his opponent in the race for the county executive's seat. During the campaign, Mr. Glendening supported a ballot referendum to lift some of the tax imposed restrictions imposed by the TRIM amendment. The referendum was defeated and the taxing restrictions imposed by TRIM remained in effect. Within one week of his election, Mr. Glendening announced that he expected the county to have a deficit of $32 to $38 million. Mr. Glendening indicated that the shortfall was directly attributed to TRIM and could result in the layoff of some county employees.

The police department opened a new station in the Beltsville area on November 14, 1982. Housed in the old Chestnut Hills Elementary School, the police share the renovated building with a branch library. Officers assigned to the station provide a service to 70,000 people residing in the heavily populated Laurel-Beltsville area. The area had previously been patrolled by personnel assigned to the Hyattsville Station.

Although operating within an austere budget, the county continued to go forth with projects that had already been financed. On November 25, 1982, the County Combined Communications Facility officially opened in the old Randolph Village Elementary School. Costing $2.5 million for renovation and equipment, the new facility gave the police and fire departments one of the nation's most up-to-date radio communications facilities.

In September 1983, County Executive Glendening appointed Maj. Michael J. Flaherty as his new chief of police. Major Flaherty joined the police department in 1966 and quickly rose through the rank structure. Promoted to major in 1980, he assumed command of the 700-member Bureau of Patrol. In March 1983, Major Flaherty was appointed to the acting director's position of the overcrowded and trouble-plagued County Detention Center. The county executive stated that he was conducting a national search for a new corrections administrator, but needed someone with strong administrative experience to temporarily fill the vacancy. Major Flaherty remained at the detention center until his September 27, 1983 appointment as chief of police.

Controversy surrounding the TRIM amendment continued to cause budgetary havoc and hamper the expansion of governmental services. The increasing unpopularity of TRIM caused many individuals and private organizations to speak out against the amendment and again ask for a ballot repudiation of the budgetary restrictions which the amendment imposed. Two outspoken opponents of the amendment were Chief Flaherty and the Fraternal Order of Police. TRIM advocates, powerless to attack the FOP lobbying, were sharply critical of Chief Flaherty's outspoken stance on the need to amend TRIM. In November 1984, the voters chose to lift the amendment's property tax freeze, thus allowing the county to generate additional tax revenue.

An early priority of Mr. Glendening's administration was that of modernizing many of the police department's antiquated facilities. These efforts culminated in 1984, when Mr. Glendening announced an ambitious building schedule. In making his announcement the executive said that the police occupied several buildings that were "an absolute disgrace," and that "the improvements, financed by bonds already approved will transform inadequate police quarters into modern adequate facilities." Planned projects included a new Criminal Justice Center in Hyattsville, a central area Police Services Complex in Palmer Park, a new Clinton Station, and replacement quarters for the Records Division.

Crime statistics began spiraling upward in 1985 with 42,854 serious crimes being reported. Drug usage was increasing and many law enforcement officials believed that there was a direct connection between the increasing rate of serious crime and drug abuse. The hallucinogenic, mind-altering, and highly dangerous drug PCP was causing law enforcement a serious problem. Easily manufactured, the drug was a particularly troublesome problem because of its tendency "to turn mild-mannered people into violent, super-powerful maniacs." Some police officials also indicated that they saw a trend toward the increased use of cocaine within every class of society. Drug experts predicted that cocaine's increasing popularity could become epidemic and present society with massive health, social, and enforcement problems.

Increased drug usage also led to a dramatic rise in the number of narcotic-related arrests. In 1984, the State Police Drug Laboratory indicated that Prince George's County accounted for 25 percent of the state's drug analysis work. In response to this problem the County Council authorized the construction of a drug laboratory in the proposed Palmer Park Police Complex.

County officials authorized the police department to create a Master Patrol Officers program in July 1985. Substantially altering the department's promotional system, this program allowed younger officers to become eligible for advancement into the supervisory ranks at a more rapid pace. The first promotional cycle under the new program allowed for the promotion of 377 officers, mostly at the rank of police officer first class and corporal. The police department's budget for the year 1985 rose to $49.3 million.

National statistics accumulated in the early 1980s revealed that the nation was experiencing an across the board increase in its crime rate. A public hue and cry for more and improved police protection caused many local, state, and federal governmental agencies to increase the amount of money being allocated for law enforcement purposes. The need to attract well-qualified applicants and retain those officers who were already on board led to the creation of a more competitive salary in the mid 1980s. Faced with the challenge of hiring a racially and sexually diverse group of new employees, the department was able to hire 387 officers between November 22, 1982, and July 27, 1989.

Prince George's County was tragically thrown into the national limelight on June 19, 1986. University of Maryland basketball star Len Bias, an all-American college athlete, died from a cocaine overdose. The tragic death occurred on the College Park Campus, just two days after the young man signed a multi-million dollar contract with the Boston Celtics. The circumstances surrounding Len Bias' death and the highly publicized Grand Jury inquiry that followed vividly illustrated the detrimental effect that drug usage was having on some of the nation's most promising young people.

The nationwide tendency toward increased violent crime, the easy availability of guns, contempt for authority, and a diminishing value on human life all served to make law enforcement a highly dangerous career field. Prince George's County was not spared from its share of tragedy. Between 1978 and 1983, six county police officers were shot to death. Another officer died from injuries received when a man, under the influence of drugs, drove off the roadway and struck the officer. A sergeant, at the scene of a barricade situation, fell from a ladder and suffered a paralyzing injury. A deranged shoplifter stabbed an officer in the chest, severing an artery and causing the officer to go into a coma. The officer never regained consciousness; he died three years later. Another officer was accidentally killed while executing a drug-related search warrant.

The Prince George's County Police Department is composed of individuals who feel a sacred obligation to their oath of office. In addition to the physical dangers normally associated with police work, every officer faces an awesome array of moral, mental, and legal responsibilities. Officers are frequently called upon to make irrevocable split-second decisions of momentous importance. Decisions that may, under certain circumstances, take away a person's liberty or life itself.

The Prince George's County Police Department is a quasi-military organization with in-depth regulations that govern the behavior of all employees. Departmental policy requires that all allegations of misconduct be investigated. If an allegation is sustained, some form of disciplinary action is initiated against the affected employee. Investigations which reveal the possibility of criminal misconduct are automatically forwarded to the State's Attorney's Office for review.

Opened on October 1, 1987, the Drug Analysis Laboratory was the first unit to occupy the new Police Services Complex. Costing nearly $600,000 for construction and equipment, the laboratory increased the county's ability to wage war on illicit drug trafficking. During the calendar year 1988, county officers made 3,395 drug-related arrests and submitted 2,347 suspected drug samples for chemical analysis.

The police department has been continually overwhelmed by an ever-increasing number of calls for service. In 1988, the county police responded to 387,092 calls for service. The average day of a police officer frequently began and ended on a hectic pace. Dispatchers found it necessary to prioritize calls, holding back on those requests for service that appeared to be of a less severe nature. During particularly busy time periods it is not unusual to find an entire patrol sector with only one or two in-service patrol cars. Preventive patrol, that time when an officer simply patrolled his assigned beat as a deterrent to crime, frequently became impossible. The 387,092 calls for service responded to in 1988 included 94 murders, 383 rapes, 2,545 robberies, 2,994 aggravated assaults, 8,653 burglaries, 18,108 thefts, and 8,822 motor vehicle thefts. County officers also made 15,329 criminal arrests and issued 64,892 traffic citations.

On March 29, 1989, the police department officially closed its Seat Pleasant Station (District III) and moved to the Police Services Complex in Palmer Park. The Criminal Investigation and Narcotics Enforcement divisions moved into the complex a short time later. The complex was fully occupied in the spring of 1991 when Headquarters and the Training Division moved into the building.

In May 1989, a black man by the name of Gregory Habib died of injuries suffered while resisting arrest. The incident received a tremendous amount of news media attention and developed into a full-fledged controversy over the alleged use of excessive police force. The Habib case was further complicated when State's Attorney Alex Williams held a press conference to announce that the grand jury had returned misdemeanor indictments against one of the four policemen involved in the incident. The state's attorney also expressed his disappointment with the grand jury's failure to return additional indictments. He then indicated that certain information had come to his attention which led him to believe that the grand jury inquiry had been tainted. Accordingly, he was requesting the attorney general's office to conduct a special investigation into Mr. Habib's death and the possible obstruction of justice by certain police officers and possibly members of his own staff.

In mid-July inflammatory rhetoric concerning the Habib case had reached a boiling point. County Executive Parris Glendening attempted to calm escalating emotions over the Habib case by meeting with various community leaders and forming a Blue Ribbon Commission on Public Safety and Community Relations to recommend methods for improving police/community relations. In January 1990, the commission submitted a lengthy report outlining eight critical problem areas confronting the police department. The commission additionally made fifty recommendations concerning improved police-community relations. Most of these recommendations were immediately implemented. Others were scheduled for adoption as time and money permitted.

A final state prosecutor's report, submitted in late 1989, ruled that Mr. Habib's death was an unusual accident. The investigation and medical evidence revealed that the death had been caused when two officers fell on Mr. Habib during the process of a struggle. The state prosecutor also revealed that no evidence had been uncovered to indicate that the grand jury investigation had been tainted. In submitting his report the special prosecutor recommended that the three misdemeanor indictments against the policeman be dismissed.

Interest in the police department's minority employment policies has substantially increased over the years. In the early 1970s the county government entered into a voluntary minority employment consent decree with the U.S. Department of Justice. Successive county administrations have continued to place emphasis upon the recruitment and retention of minority officers. In March 1983, a group of black officers formed a Black Police Officers Association. The association's primary purpose is that of encouraging minority recruitment, retention, and promotion. Increasing its membership over the years the association has expanded its activities to include community affairs and county politics. On July 27, 1989, the department promoted two black lieutenants to the rank of captain. Edward E. Adams and John E. Moss, were the first black officers to work their way up through the ranks and assume the merit rank of captain.

The county executive's proposed budget for 1990 came to $905 million. The budget allocated $71,981,278 to the police department. As approved, the budget authorized the department to increase its strength to twelve hundred officers. The executive also revealed a new master staffing plan that called for the employment of fourteen hundred officers. The newly allocated positions would allow the police department, for the first time in its history, to reach the national average of two officers for every one thousand residents.

In late December 1989, Chief of Police Michael J. Flaherty submitted his request for retirement. In making the announcement Chief Flaherty stated that he had been contemplating retirement for several years, but had remained in office to accomplish several lingering goals. The chief further stated that controversy surrounding the Habib death had delayed his retirement, in that he did not want to leave the agency when it was embroiled in controversy.

On January 2, 1990, Lt. Col. David B. Mitchell, was appointed by the county executive as the acting chief of police. On January 23, 1990, the council unanimously confirmed the appointment of Colonel Mitchell as the department's eleventh chief of police. The new chief indicated that a top priority of his administration would be that of strengthening police/community bonds. Chief Mitchell said that he intended to implement a Community-Oriented Policing Program. Officers providing this service would act as community activists, working to improve the overall quality of neighborhood life.

A major organizational restructuring took place as a result of the commission's recommendations concerning the need for increased supervision and management oversight. On January 24, 1990, Chief Mitchell made fifty-six management/supervisory promotions. On October 7, 1990, the chief further strengthened

the department's ability to improve its performance accountability by promoting another fifty-seven officers. The two 1990 promotion cycles resulted in the promotion of one lieutenant colonel, six majors, eighteen captains, thirty-eight lieutenants, and fifty sergeants.

An early indicator that the department's efforts to improve its image were beginning to pay dividends surfaced in September 1990. A *Washington Post* public opinion survey showed that three out of every four residents interviewed rated the department as doing an excellent or good job, but that some suspicion remained as to the unfair police treatment of minorities. This indicator was bolstered when the state chapter of the NAACP issued a report lauding the county police for their aggressive affirmative action hiring program and their efforts in combating the problem of "police brutality." Chief Mitchell indicated that the department was now composed of 40 percent protected class employees and that a multifaceted attack on the problem of perceived excessive force had reduced the number of complaints for the past three consecutive years. Records reveal that the county police had made more than 422,000 public contacts in 1990 and that a total of forty-nine complaints of excessive force had been received.

A blue Ribbon Committee recommendation concerning the

In February 1980, the police department adopted a Conflict Management Team approach for the handling of high risk hostage/barricade situations. The team consisted of specially trained command officers, communications specialists, hostage negotiators, and the Emergency Services Team. Since its conception in 1980, the Conflict Management Team has responded to and successfully resolved over three hundred life-threatening incidents.

The twenty-four original hostage negotiators are picture here after receiving their initial eighty hours of training. Sitting, left to right, are Robert Sheehan, William Hogewood, Corky Snow, Edward Ciesielski, Elizabeth Mints, John San Felice, Jeffrey Krauss, John Montgomery, John Blaney, Raymond Daniels, Henry Anderson, and Jerry Leighty. Standing are Stephen Mayes, Richard Welch, Samuel Corbin, Michael Betts, Roy Gilmore, Richard Hobbs, Lester Morris, Michael Morrissette, James Wiseman, Donald Studds, Tony Camp, and Samuel Hicks. PGPD photo

fair resolution of citizen complaints against police officers led to the enactment of legislation creating a Citizens Complaint Oversight Panel. A panel, composed of seven citizens appointed by the county executive, reviews all investigative reports relating to allegations of excessive force, abusive language, or harassment by county police officers. The panel, after reviewing the police department's internal investigation, then issues a report to the chief of police as to the completeness and objectivity of the police reports. The panel can agree or disagree with the police findings, or recommend that the case be remanded for further investigation.

In an attempt to gain a true measure of excellence the police department applied for national accreditation with the Commission of Accreditation for Law Enforcement Agencies in the spring of 1987. The department had to illustrate its compliance with nearly nine hundred rigorous professional standards that embrace every facet of police operations. The department successfully passed its on-site examination in January 1991, and received its full and unconditional accreditation in March 1991.

In January 1991, the county executive announced that he was expecting a $72.3 million revenue shortfall and that every county agency would probably experience layoffs. In an attempt to avoid the layoffs of police officers, the executive asked the FOP to consider deferring a 7 percent pay raise and to make several other monetary concessions. On March 14, 1991, the FOP voted to alter its contract in exchange for a no-layoff pledge. In speaking of the membership, FOP President Darryl

Jones, Sr., said, "I'm pretty proud of them. Not because they agreed to defer the pay raise, but because they voted to save jobs."

Progress made during the 1980s far outdistanced that of any previous decade. Gigantic strides were made to professionalize the department, staffing deficiencies were decreased, equipment purchases kept pace with growth, and many of the department's dilapidated facilities were replaced. But the early 1990s economic recession brought an abrupt end to departmental expansion.

No rational person can dispute the fact that law enforcement has experienced some dramatic changes over the years. Some people have said that the changes are inadequate and have come too late. Others will charge that we have gone too far; implementing changes that have weakened law enforcement and caused it to be less effective. One aspect of law enforcement that remains constant is that the work generally attracts people who have a sincere commitment to protecting and serving the public, dedicated people who thrive on performing a public service that is designed to assist people in need.

History has shown us that the job of being a Prince George's County police officer has never been a simple task. Population growth spurred on the hue and cry for the creation of a county police force in 1927. Continually out-distanced, first by prolonged population growth and later by crime, the department has found itself in a continuing struggle to keep pace with society's demand for improved police services.

ANTONIO M. KELSEY

Killed in the line of duty
February 2, 1980

Antonio M. Kelsey was born, raised, and educated in Washington, D.C. The son of a former MPDC officer, he had wanted to become a policeman since grammar school. Graduating from high school, Tony successfully applied to become a Prince George's County police cadet. Cadet Kelsey served the department for two years before receiving his appointment as a police officer on December 5, 1978. Upon graduating from the police academy, he was assigned to the Seat Pleasant Station.

Known as a dedicated and compassionate police officer, Tony Kelsey was the type of person who would not hesitate to help a stranger in need. Like many other officers, Tony worked part time to make ends meet. On the evening of February 2, 1980, Officer Kelsey reported to a part-time security job at Cox's Liquor Store on George Palmer Highway in Landover. A man entered the store at about 9:00 p.m. and pulled out a bag of marijuana. The man then walked over to Tony, who was not in uniform, and said, "What are you going to do about it." When Officer Kelsey came out from behind the counter with his police radio, the suspect fled through the front door and ran toward some homes located behind the store. Officer Kelsey, using his portable radio, advised the dispatcher that he was in pursuit of a suspect. A few minutes later, responding police units found Officer Kelsey in front of 7112 Columbia Park Road. He had been shot in the head. An ensuing investigation revealed that Officer Kelsey and the suspect became involved in a struggle, the suspect gained control of the officer's weapon and fatally shot the off-duty officer. The suspect, later identified as Steven Baines, was arrested and convicted of second-degree murder.

Officer Tony Kelsey was the first black officer to be killed in the line of duty. He was twenty-two years old at the time of his death. Although he had only been a police officer for fourteen months, Tony Kelsey was well known and liked by his fellow officers. He was described as a true professional who had the admiration of his fellow workers and the community he served. Officer William Stott, a close friend and co-worker, eulogized Tony Kelsey by saying, "Some dream of material professions, some dream of fame and glory, but few dream of protecting and serving the community. That was Tony's dream."

In 1981, the police department held a
series of events to celebrate its golden
anniversary as an independent agency. A
formal dinner/dance, attracting more than
eight hundred people, was held on the
evening of September 18, 1981. Attending
and pictured here, left to right, are retired
Police Chief Roland Sweitzer, current
Chief of Police John McHale, retired
Chief John Rhoads, and retired Chief
George Panagoulis.
PGPD photo

RAYMOND HUBBARD

Killed in the line of duty
February 8, 1982

Raymond Hubbard was born and raised in Warner Robins, Georgia. As a child, Ray Hubbard dreamed of someday becoming a fireman or policeman. He came to Washington, D.C., in 1972, and went to work for the FBI as a fingerprint examiner. Enlisting in the U.S. Air Force he attended firefighters school and was later assigned to Bolling Air Force Base. Promoted to the rank of staff sergeant, Airman Hubbard continued to retain his interest in becoming a police officer. Receiving an honorable discharge in January 1979, Raymond Hubbard began his law enforcement career with the Alexandria Police Department in Virginia. He served with that agency until April 7, 1980, when he accepted employment with the Prince George's County Police Department. A member of County Police Lateral Transfer Class No. 4, Officer Hubbard graduated from the police academy on June 13, 1980, and was assigned to the Oxon Hill Station.

Officer Hubbard was off duty on February 8, 1982. He left his apartment shortly before 6:00 p.m. and went to nearby Iverson Mall to buy a gift. Simultaneously, three armed men entered the mall and donned ski masks as they walked into Kay's Jewelry Store. Announcing a holdup, the men ordered everyone to lie on the floor. Vaulting a counter, the suspects ransacked a cash register and took some jewelry. A customer was able to slip out of the store and warned others of the robbery in progress.

Officer Hubbard probably became aware of the robbery through other shoppers in the mall. A witness stated that the officer drew his weapon and ran toward the jewelry store as two suspects came out onto the crowded concourse. A fusillade of shots suddenly rang out. When the shooting was over, Ray Hubbard was found lying on the concourse floor, mortally wounded. According to witnesses, the officer never had a chance, having been caught in a cross fire by two of the three holdup men.

Raymond Hubbard was twenty-eight years old at the time of his death. A Fraternal Order of Police eulogy praised his courage in the performance of duty. "He was a special breed of person with a deep sense of duty who believed that someone must stand up to those who would victimize their weaker neighbors." Although the suspects escaped, four men were later arrested and convicted of murdering Officer Hubbard.

A new home for the Special Operations Division. SOD personnel moved into their new home in 1982 after personally completing much of the renovation work. Located in a former elementary school the building is shared with the Maryland Park Police.
Copyrighted photo, courtesy of the Prince George's Journal

Police firearms training took place at any number of borrowed make-shift ranges over the years. In 1982, the police department entered into a joint project with the Park and Planning Commission to construct a permanent firearms range in the Cheltenham area. The range, built by the Park and Planning Commission, is a shared facility with the Maryland Park Police.
PGPD photo

We work our detectives to the bone. Detectives have been traditionally known as hard workers who don't mind the long hours required to successfully close a serious crime. Sgt. Bill Johnson of the Evidence Unit came to work after a short vacation to find that his desk had been taken over by a hardworking detective who was in the process of enjoying a cigar and cup of coffee when the sergeant showed up. Sergeant Johnson jokingly demanded his desk be vacated.
Photo courtesy of retired Sgt. William Johnson

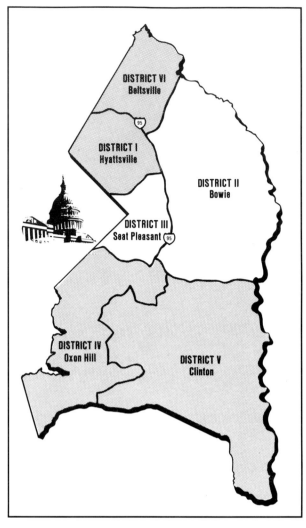

The police department opened its sixth patrol district when the new Beltsville Station was dedicated on November 14, 1982. The fifty-six officers assigned to the station provide a service to approximately seventy thousand residents residing in the county's most northern region.
PGPD photo

ALLAN D. JOHNSON

Died of injuries sustained in the line of duty
December 6, 1982

On December 6, 1982, Cpl. Allan D. Johnson, a Prince George's County motorcycle officer, stopped a traffic violator on Interstate 95. After obtaining a driver's license and registration, Corporal Johnson walked to a location just to the rear of the violator's vehicle. At this point, another vehicle left the travelled portion of the highway and struck the officer. The operator of that vehicle was later charged with manslaughter by automobile and driving under the influence of PCP.

Cpl. Allan D. Johnson, known to his friends as "A. D.," was taken to Prince George's Hospital suffering from massive injuries. After a long surgical procedure the doctors announced that A. D. had less than an hour to live. For the next forty-seven hours this courageous, strong-willed police officer fought for his life, amazing the doctors with his stubborn tenacity. A. D.'s injuries were extensive and eventually sapped every ounce of his stamina. He died on the morning of December 8, 1982.

The legacy Corporal Johnson left behind can be found, not in his death, but in his nineteen years of service to the people of Prince George's County. Born and raised in Renovo, Pennsylvania, A. D. Johnson came to Prince George's County after a hitch with the Army's 101st Airborne Division. Hired by the police department in August 1962, A. D. served tours of duty at Seat Pleasant, Oxon Hill and the Special Operations Division. Known and respected by his fellow officers and supervisors, Corporal Johnson had received ten Awards of Merit and thirty-two Letters of Commendation.

Corporal Johnson was also an avid motorcycle enthusiast. In 1973, he participated in a year-long experimental program to evaluate the use of full-sized motorcycles for traffic enforcement duties. In 1976, A. D. saw his dream come true with the formation of a permanent police motorcycle unit. Corporal Johnson was assigned the radio call sign of "Motor No. 1," and placed in charge of the unit because he was everyone's personification of what a motorcycle officer should be. During the next six years, Corporal Johnson led that unit to four championships in police motorcycle competitions. As the Motorcycle Show and Drill Team leader, A. D. Johnson led by example. Nothing short of perfection was acceptable.

As a tribute of their respect for Corporal Johnson, the Special Operations Division permanently retired the designated call number of "Motor No. 1." Corporal Johnson is survived by his wife, a grown daughter, and a young son.

CARLTON X. FLETCHER

Killed in the line of duty
June 11, 1983

Carlton Xavier Fletcher was the product of a large family. His parents, who raised six sons and one daughter, moved to Prince George's County in 1953. As a teenager, Carlton Fletcher attended Fairmount Heights High School, graduating in June 1969. After graduation he went to work at Goddard Flight Center in Greenbelt. He also enlisted in the Air National Guard at Andrews Air Force Base, obtaining the rank of staff sergeant just prior to his honorable discharge in 1975.

Carlton Fletcher became a Prince George's County police officer on July 18, 1976. Graduating from the police academy on December 9, 1976, he was assigned to the Hyattsville Station. On November 14, 1982, Officer Fletcher and his entire squad moved to the newly opened Beltsville Station. Like many other officers attempting to raise a family, Carlton Fletcher found it necessary to supplement his police income with part-time work.

On the evening of June 11, 1983, Officer Fletcher reported to an off-duty security job at a Greenbelt Road convenience store. Dressed in civilian clothes, the officer had taken his marked police car to the job as a deterrent to crime. Sitting in the car at about 11:45 p.m., Officer Fletcher intended to accompany a store clerk on a night deposit. While he was waiting for the clerk, two men approached the vehicle and fired a shotgun blast through the car window. The men then went into the store and shot the clerk. Both men made a successful escape from the crime scene, taking a large amount of money.

Carlton Fletcher and the store clerk, a Vietnamese college student at the University of Maryland, died from their wounds. An extensive investigation into the "ambush execution" of Officer Fletcher and the wanton murder of the store clerk led to the arrest of a former store employee and his roommate. Both were later convicted of first-degree murder and given life sentences. At the time of his death, Officer Fletcher had been a county policeman for seven years. He is survived by his wife, who was six months pregnant, and a three-year-old daughter.

Michael J. Flaherty was confirmed as the police department's new chief of police on September 17, 1983. Appointed to the police department in March 1967, the seventeen-year veteran police officer received his bachelor of science degree from American University in 1975 and a master's degree in management and supervision from Central Michigan University in 1977. Progressing through the department's rank structure, Michael Flaherty was promoted the rank of major in 1980 and assuming command of the 700-member Bureau of Patrol. In March 1983, the county executive asked the police department for assistance in managing the trouble-plagued Department of Corrections. Major Flaherty was selected to fill the acting director's position at the Department of Corrections and remained assigned to the detention center until his appointment as police chief.
PGPD photo

Emergency Service Team members leave the scene of a barricade situation that was resolved without resorting to the use of force. Team members contributed to successfully resolved more than three hundred hostage/barricade situation through the use of negotiation and tactics. *Copyrighted photo, courtesy of the* Prince George's Journal

The old wood-frame home that had been part of the Oxon Hill Station since 1963 was torn down in August 1982. A $95,000 renovation project called for the erection of a new brick structure to blend in with an extension that was added on in 1966. Copyrighted construction photo, courtesy of the Prince George's Journal
Rear addition photo by author

RICHARD J. BEAVERS

Killed in the line of duty
November 29, 1983

apt. Richard J. Beavers was thirty-seven years old at the time of his death. Raised in the Lewisdale section of Prince George's County, he attended Northwestern High School, graduating in 1966. He enlisted in the U.S. Air Force shortly after graduation, but the young airman was forced into a hardship discharge with the 1967 death of his father. Returning home to help support his mother, Dick Beavers made application to become a Prince George's County police officer. Appointed to the department on October 16, 1967, Officer Beavers completed his academy training on February 19, 1968, and was assigned to the Hyattsville Station. He was promoted to the rank of detective in 1970 and assigned to the Vice Control Section as a narcotics detective. Assimilating himself into the drug scene, Dick Beavers gained the reputation of a well-liked, extremely dedicated, and professional narcotics investigator.

A likeable and intelligent officer, Dick Beavers rose through the ranks with little difficulty. Promoted to the rank of captain in 1979, he was assigned as an Operations Duty Commander. Within one year, Captain Beavers was given command of the Clinton Station, and remained there until his transfer to the larger Oxon Hill Station in January 1982. Besides assuming responsibility for the operation of a much more active station, Captain Beavers oversaw a $95,000 renovation to the station house.

On November 28, 1983, Captain Beavers drove his unmarked police car onto the parking lot of 3513 St. Barnabus Road. While sitting in the car the captain observed two men approaching his vehicle, one was armed with a handgun. Realizing that he was about to be the victim of a robbery, the captain drew his service revolver. During the ensuing shootout Captain Beavers received a fatal gunshot wound. The two men responsible for his death were apprehended and convicted of first-degree murder.

At the time of his death, Captain Beavers was one of five contenders for promotion to the rank of major. Chief of Police Michael Flaherty posthumously promoted him to that rank on November 30, 1983. Major Beavers is survived by his wife, son, and daughter.

Lt. Robert A. Luther, the assistant district commander at Oxon Hill, was a close personal friend of Captain Beavers. Bob Luther went to the Beavers' home after being notified of the captain's death and spent the next two frantic days making funeral arrangements and consoling the family. Returning home late on evening of December 1, 1983, Lieutenant Luther complained of not feeling well. Shortly thereafter, he died of a massive heart attack. Bob Luther's sudden and unexpected passing devastated the entire police department. The deaths of two highly respected commissioned officers stunned and saddened a department that had seen more than its fair share of death over the past few years.
Photo courtesy of the Luther family

A group of police department school crossing guards celebrate thirty years of dedicated service to the children of Prince George's County.
PGPD photo

The idea for a County Police Bagpipe Band came with the death of retired Sgt. Yorke Flynn. Yorke loved bagpipe music and his wife requested that arrangements be made to have a piper play at the gravesite. After the graveside ceremonies, the piper suggested to Cpl. Pat Grogan that the department consider forming a band. The rest is history.
Photo courtesy of the Prince George's County Police Bagpipe Band

In a series of thirteen drug raids police culminated a year long investigation with the seizure of three homes valued at $410,000, ten cars worth $110,000, drugs valued at $280,000, and $22,000 in cash. Chief Flaherty and Major James Ross of the Criminal Investigations Division look over some of the material seized.
Copyrighted photo by Ron Ceasar, courtesy of the Prince George's Journal

Cpl. Rafael Hylton hands out balloons to deserving children at the department's annual Christmas Party.
Copyrighted photo by Ron Ceasar, courtesy of the Prince George's Journal

261

On June 20, 1985, Sgt. Paul Tucker, of the Emergency Services Team, sustained a spinal cord injury when he fell from a ladder at the scene of a barricade situation. Sergeant Tucker, a nineteen-year police veteran and original member of the Emergency Services Team, was paralyzed as a result of this injury and confined to a wheelchair.
PGPD photo

In 1986, President Ronald Reagan took time out of his busy schedule to meet with Sergeant Tucker and his family. The president thanked Sergeant Tucker for the many occasions when the Emergency Services Team had assisted the U.S. Secret Service with VIP security at Andrews Air Force Base. Forced to retire as a result of his injuries, Sgt. Tucker now works for the department as a civilian armorer and firearms instructor.
Official White House photo, courtesy of Terry Arthur

A group of detectives pose after the arduous task of counting $1,000,000 in drug money. The money, which a court later forfeited to the county, was found at the scene of a double homicide. Pictured left to right are: Danny Morris, Pam Oertly, Mickey Ferriter, Tom Bruciak, Al Chertok, Terry Eaton, Art Kowalski, and Bernie Hines
PGPD photo

263

On June 11, 1986, more than sixty county police officers helped raise $2,600 by participating in a "Law Enforcement Torch Run." Police officers from across the nation join together on an annual basis to raise funds for the Special Olympics. In this photograph, Cpl. Steve Grimes carries the "Torch of Hope." Also shown are PFC Jeffery Henderson (rear left) and Cpl. James Rozar (left foreground). Cpl. Paul Reese of the Motorcycle Unit serves as an escort.
PGPD photo

More than 250 citizens and dignitaries gathered on August 23, 1986, to attend grand opening ceremonies at the new Clinton Station. Formerly the Crestview Elementary School, more than $800,000 was spent in renovating the 14,000-square-foot station.
Photo courtesy of Capt. Jack San Felice

The Prince George's County Retired Police Association was formed in 1979 to renew old friendships and further the cause of those police officers who had retired. In September 1986, the association held its annual crab feast at the home of retired Lt. Pete Perrygo. At the outing, Chief of Police Michael Flaherty presented retired Capt. Edwin (Easy Ed) Thompson (1938–1964) and retired Lt. Charles (Pete) Perrygo (1943–1965) with retirement plagues bearing the department's newly designed badge.
Photo by author

Pete Perrygo 1946

Easy Ed Thompson 1938

265

HARRY L. KINIKIN

Died of injuries sustained in the line of duty
January 13, 1990

On October 17, 1986, Cpl. Harry L. Kinikin, Jr., drove onto the parking lot of a 7-Eleven Store in Landover to make a telephone call. While on the lot, he was approached by the store's manager who pointed out a female shoplifting suspect. Corporal Kinikin stopped the suspect on the parking lot of an adjacent gas station. The suspect, without provocation or warning, turned and stabbed the officer twice, once in the chest and once in the side. Corporal Kiniken then drew his weapon and fired two shots, wounding the suspect. He then advised the radio dispatcher that he had been stabbed and needed an ambulance for himself and the suspect. Police and fire department paramedics responding to the scene saw that Corporal Kinikin was not breathing and immediately administered CPR. Transported to Prince George's Hospital, it was determined that the knife had pierced the left ventricle to the heart and that insufficient blood circulation had caused partial brain death. Corporal Kinikin never regained full consciousness.

The suspect who stabbed Corporal Kinikin was found to be mentally incompetent and, therefore, unable to stand trial. She remains confined to a state mental institution.

Corporal Kinikin, a thirteen-year police veteran, remained hospitalized for an extended period of time. Retired as a result of his injuries, Harry Kinikin spent the next three years of his life in convalescence homes. Periodically opening his eyes and sometimes appearing to follow sound, Harry's condition steadily deteriorated. He died on January 13, 1990.

Harry Kinikin was raised in the Marlow Heights/Temple Hills area of Prince George's County and graduated from Potomac High School. After graduation he went to work in a bank, but found the work unsatisfying. On December 29, 1972, Harry filled out a job application with the Prince George's County Police Department indicating that, "I enjoy community relations. Working with the public, in showing them that the police are working for the benefit of all people. This, I feel, is extremely important." Receiving his appointment to the police academy, Harry Kinikin began his career as a law enforcement officer on June 25, 1973. Quickly realizing the importance of a good education, Officer Kinikin began the arduous task of attending night classes at Prince George's County Community College. Graduating from the community college, he started classes at the University of Maryland and obtained a Bachelor of Science Degree.

Known as a devoted family man, Corporal Kinikin is survived by his wife, a thirteen-year-old son, and a nine-year-old daughter.

On January 16, 1990, more than four hundred police officers gathered to pay their final respects to Cpl. Harry Kinikin. After the services, a two-mile-long cortege accompanied Corporal Kinikin to his final resting place at Cedar Hill Cemetery in Suitland.
PGPD photo

A new Police Records Center was formally dedicated October 23, 1986. The center is staffed by sixty employees and remains operational twenty-four hours a day, seven days a week. In 1985, Police Records processed and disseminated 991,000 reports. PGPD photo

The Fraternal Order of Police, Lodge 89 Auxiliary, was formed in 1958. Known for many years as the Ladies Auxiliary, the organization recently opened its membership to the mothers, fathers, and male spouses of female officers. The auxiliaries primary function is that of a support group that promotes the police family. In addition to sponsoring several family-type social events, the auxiliary is available to assist those police families who have special needs. The auxiliary is also responsible for the creation of a annual police memorial day service to honor those officers who have lost their lives in the line of duty.
Photo courtesy of the FOP Ladies Auxiliary

Lt. William Mathews, and his son Cpl. Scott Matthews, pose together after the lieutenant received his thirty-year silver service plate. Hired on January 3, 1956, Lieutenant Mathews retired on December 30, 1989. Photo from The Open Mike *(departmental newsletter) of April 1987*

Utilizing the department's mobile command post, hostage negotiators William Hogewood (standing), Elizabeth Mints, and Milton Michaelis ponder their next move. Hostage negotiation teams, backed by police telephone technicians, have been instrumental in allowing the department to talk its way out of hundreds of potentially dangerous hostage/barricade situations. The department's training program for negotiators has been nationally recognized, with numerous outside law enforcement agencies requesting that their negotiators be trained by the county police.
Photo courtesy of the Prince George's Journal

The hazards of all-weather driving are known to every police officer. The officer in this January 1986 accident was not seriously injured.
Courtesy of Carl Bower and the Prince George's Journal

In August 1987, Sgt. Gary Hutchison, a seventeen-year police officer, outscored over six-hundred officers in the National Rifle Association's (NRA) National Revolver Competition. Sergeant Hutchison, a left-handed shooter, won the championship round in a driving rain by scoring 1,492 out of a possible 1,500 points, with 91 shots in the X ring.

Six other Prince George's County police officers competed in the national championships. Cpl. Jack Magruder won first place in the High Masters Class-County Division, and second place in the Three-Gun Service Revolver Championship. Corporal Magruder and Sergeant Hutchison also won third place in the Two-Man Team Competition. Cpl. Mark Murphy won third place in the Master Class-County Division. Cpls. Jack Magruder and Randy Jaquith placed seventh and eleventh respectively in the shotgun competition, an event with more than six-hundred shooters.

Pistol Team members competing in the NRA National Championship included (left to right) Cpl. Mark Murphy, Cpl. Jeffrey Henderson, Cpl. Jack Magruder, Sgt. Gary Hutchison, Cpl. Randy Jaquith, and Cpl. James Priest.
PGPG photo

In October 1988, Corporal Magruder (left) and Sergeant Hutchison met with thirty-five hundred competitors from twenty-three countries at the international Olympic Police Games in Sydney, Australia. Cpl. Magruder's shooting skills earned him five gold and one bronze medals. Sgt. Hutchison's expertise netted him one gold, two silver, and two bronze medals.
PGPD photo

Lt. Col. Elmer H. Tippett, retired from the Prince George's County Police Department on November 20, 1987. Colonel Tippett ended his twenty-one-year career with the county police to accept an appointment as the superintendent of the Maryland State Police.
Photos courtesy of the Maryland State and Prince George's County Police Departments

In the fall of 1987, the Survey Research Center at the University of Maryland conducted a survey to gauge public opinion about police performance. Ninety percent of the 505 randomly selected persons contacted gave the police a fair to excellent rating. Chart from The Open Mike *(departmental newsletter) of September 1987*

Police performance

How do county residents feel about the Prince George's County police force?

Agree	Disagree	Neutral

I rate the County Police as fair to excellent

90%	6%	4%

The county police use excessive force

35%	42%	23%

The county police are a credit to the community

82%	10%	8%

The county police are not effective

15%	77%	8%

The county police should get more recognition

71%	17%	12%

On November 13, 1987, Majors David B. Mitchell (left) and Robert A. Phillips posed with Chief Flaherty after receiving their promotions to the rank of lieutenant colonel. PGPD photo

The police department, in addition to its sworn police officers, has another large group of dedicated employees who play a low key, but vitally important support role in the delivery of police services. One of those employees is Sandra Willhide, a twenty-two-year-veteran clerk who works at the Hyattsville Station.

In 1987, Sandy's fellow employees nominated her for a special civilian employee award. These employees described Sandy by saying that "She is always willing to lend a helping hand . . . any officer assigned to her shift has loved her for all the torn uniforms she has sewn, listening to their problems and getting them through the daily routine of the job. In all the years she has dealt with the public, her attitude toward her job and life has never changed. She has always listened patiently to people's problems, regardless if they were police related or not. And if she was capable of helping in any way, she would." The Open Mike, the police department's official newsletter, published an article paying tribute to Sandy's achievements. The story said that Sandy had done it all, "She's located a person who escaped from Spring Grove Hospital; assisted with a hostage situation; and helped an elderly woman in trouble with a telephone billing office. She's found employment and housing for a homeless couple expecting a child; helped a woman whose apartment flooded; and notified families of the death of a loved one. She even received a commendation from an officer assigned to her shift who just wanted to thank her for her never-ending help and kindness." Sandra Willhide is just one of the many dedicated police civilian employees who perform those arduous behind-the-scene tasks that all too often go unrecognized.

Pictured left to right, are William and Jude Willhide (Sandy's son and daughter); Sandra Willhide, 1987 Police Civilian Employee's Association's Employee of the Year, Chief Michael Flaherty, Councilman Anthony Cicoria, and Police Clerk Jean Barton (Sandy's sister). PGPD photo

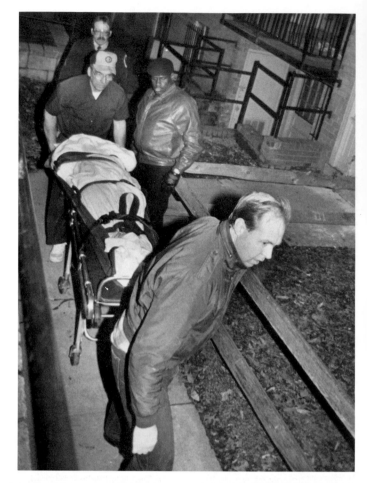

Cpl. John Harhai of the Evidence Unit (foreground) assists an attendant from the Coroner's Office in removing one of five murder victims from a Landover apartment house. Cpl. Wayne Dotzenrod (uniformed officer in rear) and PFC Wayne Heatley (in leather jacket) look on. The January 22, 1988, execution-style slayings were believed to have been ordered by Jamaican drug dealers operating between here and New York City. The county recorded a record 102 homicides in 1988, 65 percent of them drug related. Photo courtesy of Tom Carter

On February 22, 1988, County Executive Parris Glendening and Chief Michael Flaherty announced that a nationwide trend towards the criminal use of automatic and semi-automatic weapons had caused the department to break with its long tradition of arming officers with six-shot revolvers. Henceforth, the department would arm its officers with the more modern and powerful Beretta, sixteen-shot, semi-automatic handgun. The phase-out of the old revolvers is expected to take place over several years. Photo courtesy of Capt. Jack San Felice

After many agonizing years of attempting to raise construction funds, FOP Lodge 89 formally dedicated a new lodge hall in March 1988. The old lodge hall, pictured in the background, was converted to office space in 1989.
Photo by author

On April 3, 1988, the county broke ground for a new Hyattsville Justice Center. Located on Rhode Island Avenue, just south of the County Service Building, the nineteen million dollar building will house the Hyattsville Station and a Department of Corrections work-release facility. Fifteen years in planning, the 50,000-square-foot center was touted as the "crown jewel" of a revitalized older Hyattsville. Additional phases of the county's efforts to revitalize Hyattsville include a $5 million renovation of the County Service Building and the construction of a new District Court Building. The building was formally dedicated in the summer of 1990.
Photo courtesy of Capt. Jack San Felice

MARK K. MURPHY

Died in the line of duty
September 1, 1988

Mark Kevin Murphy was born and raised in Tacoma, Washington. Arriving in the Washington, D.C., area, he began work as an FBI fingerprint technician. Desiring to become a police officer, Mark Murphy sought employment with the Prince George's County Police Department. He was appointed to the department on March 10, 1974, and completed his academy training in August. Assigned to the Seat Pleasant Station, Mark Murphy's superior performance was quickly noted. Officer Murphy transferred to the Special Operations Division in 1976.

Officer Murphy was accepted into the division's elite Emergency Services Team in 1978. As a member of this unit, he responded to approximately 250 hostage/barricade situations and participated in more than six-hundred vice raids. Officer Murphy obtained a certified instructor status as a counter sniper, sub machine gunner, revolver, and CPR instructor. He was also a certified scuba diver and hostage negotiator. Known as an excellent marksman, Mark Murphy also won a position on the department's nationally recognized pistol team. Despite his busy schedule, Officer Murphy was able to obtain a Bachelor of Arts Degree from the University of Maryland and be promoted to the rank of corporal.

On the evening of August 31, 1988, the Emergency Services Team and members of the Narcotics Enforcement Division held a preraid briefing prior to the execution of a narcotic search warrant at a Riverdale apartment house. Officers attending the meeting were told that information had been obtained to indicate that there might be automatic weapons in the apartment. As his team's point man, Corporal Murphy approached the front door to the apartment, got down on his hands and knees, and placed a hydraulic jack into the apartment's door jambs. The purpose of the jack was to aid in a quick entry. As the jack expanded a loud crack was heard, the noise apparently sounded similar to a gunshot. Two members of the team directly behind Murphy believed that the team was being fired upon and discharged their weapons. It appears that Corporal Murphy was also surprised by the sharp noise and reacted by raising his body. He was struck and fatally wounded by the police gunfire.

Cpl. Mark Murphy was thirty-five years old at the time of his death, and recently remarried. He is survived by his wife Rose, a daughter, and a step-daughter. A eulogy for Mark contained these words: "... When the Mark Murphys of this world leave us, we lose their bodies, their souls. But what is left behind is something indescribable, ineffable. Something of which they would want every one of us to share. Have some ... it will make you stronger."

As a symbol of respect, Police Chief Flaherty posthumously promoted Mark Murphy to the rank of sergeant.

Sgt. "Buzz" Sawyer, President, Fraternal Order of Police, Lodge 89, made the following remarks at the church services for Sergeant Murphy. "Mark Murphy, husband, father, and son; Mark Murphy, police officer and friend. Mark is my brother! Not of blood—but profession. Both Mark and I chose a career in law enforcement and in doing so we joined a very special family. A proud family, an elite family, a family bonded together out of necessity—bonded out of compassion, out of love for our nation and the citizens we serve, and bonded together to see the good in our nation preserved. . . ." Cpl. Darryl Jones and Sgt. Mark Murphy at the scene of a 1987 barricade.
Copyrighted photo by Phil Masturzo, courtesy of the Prince George's Journal

Sergeant Murphy is carried from the Riverdale Baptist Church by his fellow team members. Photo courtesy of Tom Carter

In May 1988, the Prince George's County Chamber of Commerce honored nine police officers and nine firefighters at the Eleventh Annual Fire/Police Awards Ceremony. Each year this program recognizes those public safety employees who performed exceptional acts involving outstanding displays of courage, initiative, and judgement. Shown with Chief Flaherty are the 1987 Valor Award recipients. From left to right, in the front row, are Cpl. Herman Johnson, Cpl. William Buie, Jr., PFC William Cotton, Cpl. Walter Anderson, and Cpl. Lawrence Gordon. From left to right in the back row are PFC Robert Edwards, Cpl. Eric Olsen, Cpl. Howard "Gene" Shook, and Cpl. Wayne McBride. PGPD photo

In March 1988, Prince George's County Community College President Robert I. Bickford and Police Chief Michael Flaherty signed an articulation agreement. The agreement grants twelve college credits to every officer graduating from the police academy's 24-week basic training course. Photo courtesy of the Community College

In 1988, the police department formed a Drug Task Force to stem the frequent occurrence of street drug sales. The force, assisted by law enforcement personnel from the Park Police and Sheriff's Office, concentrated on the arrests of both the drug pusher and user.

This Prince George's Journal photograph depicts the drug arrest of a twenty-one-year-old woman who had attempted to buy drugs while accompanied by an infant and small child. Copyrighted photo by Lon Slepicka, courtesy of the Prince George's Journal

Undercover officers assigned to task force duties first identify and then move into an open-air drug market. The officers, after observing a drug purchase, arrest the dealer and immediately transport him from the scene. An undercover officer then poses as the drug dealer. If approached and solicited to sell drugs, the officer consummates the sale with an exchange of money. At this point other members of the team move in to arrest the buyer.
Photo courtesy of the Street Narcotics Unit

Neighborhood groups and children join the fight on drugs, making it known that drug pushers are not welcomed in their neighborhood. Photo courtesy of Tom Carter

Sgt. Mark Wright of the Public Information Office briefs the news media at the scene of a 1988 incident. Previous to 1970, all press releases were handled by supervisory personnel or the detective assigned to investigate a particular crime. Increased crime and news media complaints about the slow and inadequate release of information caused the department to rethink its policy on the release of news media information. In 1971, the department formed a special Public Information Office to deal with and expedite the flow of information to news media organizations. Photo courtesy of Tom Carter

On the morning of December 6, 1988, Cpl. McKenzie Perritt responded to a radio call for a residential robbery. Arriving at the home, the officer was met by a seventy-seven-year-old female victim. The woman stated that a man had broken into her home, wrapped an extension cord around her neck, choked her, and then threw her to the floor. The man fled after taking the victim's purse which contained her monthly social security check.

Realizing that the victim was destitute, Corporal Perritt asked some of his fellow officers for help. Kicking off a plea for donations, Corporal Perritt made a personal contribution of $25. Personnel assigned to the Seat Pleasant Station responded to the plea by donating more than $200. Arrangements were also made to have a Christmas food basket delivery. Corporal Perritt's compassionate and humanitarian actions represent a picture of law enforcement that is all too frequently hidden from public view.

Capt. Daniel Brown, Commander of the Seat Pleasant Station, joins Mary Jane Cook of the Stephanie Roper Committee in presenting Cpl. McKenzie Perritt with the Governor's Victim Assistance Award. PGPD photo

Patrol duty at a glance.
Photos courtesy of Tom Carter

Report writing.

Traffic control.

282

Accident investigation.

Shooting scene.

This photo, from the Prince George's Journal, *bears the title "Crossin' through a grape line." School Crossing Guard Blondell Long is assisted in her duties by an Ice Capades California Raisin. The department's 157 crossing guards work 480 separate daily assignments, insuring the safety of 18,500 children who must cross the county's busiest and most dangerous streets. Copyrighted photo by Lon Slepicka, courtesy of the* Prince George's Journal

District III photo by author

Phase II of the police department's new Police Services Complex was completed on March 29, 1989, when the District III Station, Criminal Investigations Division, and Narcotics Enforcement Division moved into their new office space. Phase III of the complex's construction was completed on July 11, 1990. With the Grand Opening of a new Police Headquarters and Training Academy, the county had expended more than $25 million renovating the 47,000-square-foot former Kent Middle School.

Cutting the ribbon to officially open the District III Station are, left to right, Vivian Dodson, Mayor of Capitol Heights; Congressman Steny Hoyer; Council Chairwoman Jo Ann Bell; County Executive Parris Glendening; Council members Frank Casula, Hilda Pemberton; and Chief of Police Michael Flaherty.
Dedication photo by Tom Carter

Criminal Investigations Division photo by author

The county government, wanting to rid the neighborhood of an eyesore, wasted no time in calling in a demolition crew. More than a few old-time Seat Pleasant officers, upon hearing that the bulldozers were at work, made one last trip to 410 Addison Road to pick up a red-brick memento.

Those employees, both sworn and civilian, who survived Seat Pleasant know that there will never again be anything to compare with the experience and unexplainable pride of having worked in that now infamous station house. At least we hope not! *PGPD photos*

SEAT PLEASANT—THE LEGACY

Only those officers who have experienced the joy, camaraderie, sorrow, and discomfort of having worked out of the Seat Pleasant Station can truly appreciate that station's true worth. Time will inevitably lessen the impact that Seat Pleasant had upon the people who worked there, but that special feeling of having shared in an incredibly awesome experience can never be totally erased. Those employees who worked at Seat Pleasant, both sworn and civilian, will probably look back upon their experiences with fond memories and say to themselves with pride, "I survived."

Unbelievable, but true, stories will be passed down to future generations of police officers. The worst that our society has to offer: the habitual drunk, the spaced-out LSD and PCP junkies, the remorseless criminal, and the obnoxiously profane were never far away. In sharp contrast stood the unfortunate senior citizen who was beaten up and robbed of his or her monthly social security check, the rape victim, the neighborhood child who has to cross the street to avoid the drug pushers, and the honest hardworking couple who returned home from work to find that a burglar had walked away with everything they owned.

The physical condition of the thirty-five-year-old station is another sordid story of remembrance. Tales of a terribly overcrowded and busy station will abound. Stories of plumbing that continually overflowed, of exposed electrical wiring, overloaded circuits, and a continually leaking roof are indelibly etched upon the memories of those employees who were assigned to this station. Long-time station clerks working on the top floor can readily recall how it was necessary to place trash cans on certain desks in order to catch the rain water that leaked through the roof during rain and snow storms. Conversely, who can forget those unbearably hot humid summer days when the numerous window air conditioners failed to work, or those cold winter nights when the hot water heating system failed to function because of rust-clogged pipes?

The legend of Seat Pleasant will forever abound with unusual anecdotes such as the encounter that a certain no nonsense police lieutenant had with a pugnacious janitor who refused to clean up the station's squad room, or the sergeant who accidentally discharged a shotgun into the ceiling directly under Chief Panagoulis' office. Many officers also have a vivid recollection of the war that Lt. Ted Peters waged against the Seat Pleasant Air Force. The air force was composed of gnats that seemed to flourish near the first-floor men's room. Or the time a local thug got drunk and climbed the station's radio tower. After an hour-long tirade of shouting obscenities at some officers, the man threatened to jump from the tower. He was talked out of the suicide attempt by one of the Seat Pleasant officers he had been so vehemently insulting.

The faces of police officers John Leatherbury, Bob Yeszerski, Bill Gullett, Tony Kelsey, and Harry Kinikin are forever imbedded into the minds of their fellow Seat Pleasant officers. The shedding of a graveside tear did not lessen the impact of their deaths, but served as an etching acid, indelibly imprinting their memories into the deepest recesses of the soul. The memories of those who lost their lives in the line of duty can never be forgotten by those who share in the common experience of wearing the badge and uniform.

The ability to function under less-than-desirable working conditions, the fast pace of police services, the unique camaraderie, and the need to depend upon one another acted as an emotional catalyst, binding together the men and women of the Seat Pleasant Station. The experience of having working at Seat Pleasant gave many newly appointed officers a firm foundation upon which to begin their law enforcement careers. Nobody wanted to spend an entire career at Seat Pleasant, but the experience gained in working at this station could prove to be invaluable.

Taking office in 1980, County Executive Parris Glendening recognized that inadequate facilities detracted from the department's professional image and embarked on a campaign to improve many of the buildings that housed the police department. In March 1989, the police department closed its Seat Pleasant Station and moved into a new Police Services Complex in Palmer Park. Speaking at the complex's dedication ceremonies, Mr. Glendening stated, "We are celebrating County employees who are finally being provided with surroundings that are conducive to professional work; and, we are celebrating a community that will be better served because of our new adequate facilities."

The police department has provided twenty-eight foreign countries with specialized antiterrorism training. The training, which is sponsored by the State Department's Bureau of Diplomatic Security, is provided under a contract with the federal government. In this photograph, a group of police officers from Poland poses with several State Department agents. Also pictured are their Police Department instructors Sergeant William Spalding (kneeling far right), Sergeant Gary Sommers (kneeling far left), Chief Mitchell, and Captain John San Felice of Training Services. PGPD photo

On July 13, 1989, WRC Radio sponsored a "town meeting" at the Glenarden Municipal Center to discuss allegations of excessive police force. Titled, "Police Brutality in Prince George's County: Real or Perceived?" The program drew an audience of more than seven hundred people, about four hundred of them police officers. Cpl. Darryl Jones, a member of the Special Operations Division, was one of many persons to express their views during the talk show. Corporal Jones was elected as FOP president in the November 1989 elections.
Photo courtesy of Tom Carter

Recruit Class 2-69 graduated from the police academy on October 3, 1969. Twenty years later the class held a reunion celebration at FOP Lodge 89. Only nineteen of the original forty-two members remained on active duty and many of those anticipated retirement in the near future.
Class 2-69 and Chief of Police Vincent S. Free as they appeared on May 3, 1969.
PGPD photo

Class 2-69 as they appeared twenty years later. In posing for the photograph, one member remarked that the fifteen remaining members took up as much space as the original forty-two member class. In the first row, left to right, are Lt. John Calhoon, Sgt. John Davey, retired Cpl. Mike Betts, Sgt. Tim Bowen, and Cpl. Steve Holton. In the rear are Sgt. Richard Reinoehl, Cpl. George Van Duzer, Cpl. Dave Hatfield, Capt. Allen MacDonald, Lt. Merle Miller, Cpl. Tom Bruciak, Sgt. Bill Hogewood, Cpl. Art Kowalski, and Cpl. Bob Ivison. Not pictured, but still employed were: Lt. Mike Monahan, Lt. Ted Cox, Sgt. John Dorman, Cpl. Wayne Watson, and Cpl. Wayne Johnson.
Reunion photo courtesy of retired Cpl. Mike Betts

Stoney's Restaurant is a well-known neighbor-hood establishment located on Old Branch Avenue in Clinton. A senseless coldblooded tragedy occurred at the restaurant during the early morning hours of October 12, 1989. The establishment had closed before midnight with the owner and several employees remaining inside to clean up and prepare for the next day's business. Cpl. Robert McDaniel of the police department's Criminal Investigations Division had gone to the restaurant to make arrangements for a reunion of his high school class. Corporal McDaniel, a personal friend of the owner, was off-duty at the time and remained inside after closing. At 12:15 a.m., when an employee unlocked the front door to let a co-worker out, two armed men forced their way into the restaurant and ordered everyone to lie on the floor. After obtaining the night's receipts, the suspects began to shoot the still prone victims. Kevin Shelly, the restaurant's manager, and Arnold Baston, a

cook, were shot to death before they could move. Corporal McDaniel and the restaurant's owner, Allen Stone, realized that they were about to be executed. Moving away from the gunmen McDaniel received a serious gunshot wound to the face. Allen Stone received a less serious elbow wound. Ironically, Kevin Shelly, one of the murder victims, was an active member of the Prince George's County Crime Solvers program. Two weeks prior to the shooting he had received a Chief's Award for his efforts in raising $45,000 for Crime Solvers.

In late November, several suspects were arrested for a series of armed robberies occurring in both Prince George's and Charles counties. Follow up investigation revealed information which allowed the police to charge the suspects with the robbery and murders occurring at Stoney's Restaurant.

Sgt. John Wyne oversees the removal of a victim from Stoney's Restaurant.
Photo courtesy of Tom Carter

Timothy Silk is one of many police dispatchers to receive an award for saving a life. Answering a 911 emergency call from a hysterical woman, Silk was told that her three-month old baby had drowned in a bathtub. Relying upon his training and eleven years experience, dispatcher Silk calmed the woman and instructed her on how to administer CPR. Within seconds the child started to cry. Tim Silk, later said that "it (the cry) was the most beautiful sound I've ever heard."
Photo by Ron Ceasar, courtesy of the Prince George's Journal

On November 17, 1989, County Executive Parris Glendening announced that Fire Chief M. H. "Jim" Estepp was retiring to accept a position as the county's new deputy chief administrative officer for public safety. Mr. Estepp, with over thirty years of fire service, would assume responsibility for coordinating all police, fire, corrections, and emergency preparedness activities.

*Strongly held convictions associated with the issue of abortion led to pro-
and anti-abortion demonstrations at clinics in Suitland and Greenbelt.
Cpls. Buckey Mills and Jim Rozar arrest and carry off a demonstrator at
a Greenbelt clinic.*
Photo courtesy of Tom Carter

*Fire Lt. William Goddard and Police Cpl. Robert Tapscott discuss a plan
of action prior to the fire department's examination of a suspected
briefcase bomb. Cooperation between the two public safety agencies has
been a longstanding tradition. Also pictured are fire department
investigative personnel Major Daniel Jarboe (far left) and Captain
Timothy Augustine (far right).*
Photo courtesy of Tom Carter

The county government's need to adequately staff its police department surfaced during budget discussions for fiscal year 1991. The executive and council, spurred on by the Fraternal Order of Police, acknowledged that there was a real need to substantially increase the size of the police department. The ever-increasing number of calls for service (430,000 in 1989), the spiralling rate of serious crime, and the county's "war on drugs" gave county government little choice but to approve the increase in size of its police department. To the credit of both the county executive and council a plan was submitted which would allow for the employment of fourteen hundred police officers by the end of fiscal year 1991.

Normal attrition, plus the four hundred new officers that the county executive and council were expected to authorize would require the police department to hire and train almost five hundred police officers between July 1989, and December 1991.
Photo courtesy of Tom Carter

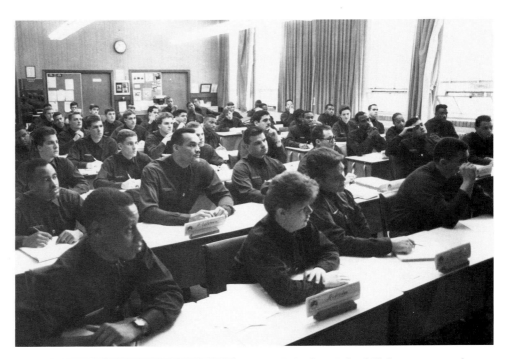

Chief of Police Michael Flaherty announced his retirement effective December 29, 1989. At a press conference the chief indicated that he was leaving the department in good hands with the nomination of Lt. Col. David B. Mitchell as the next chief of police. Chief Flaherty also said that he felt a great weight had been lifted from his shoulders. This cartoon makes light of the fact that another portion of the chief's anatomy would feel some degree of relief.
Copyrighted cartoon by Mike Jenkins, courtesy of the Prince George's Journal

A caption in the February 1990 issue of The Open Mike reads, "NEW YEAR BRINGS POLICE DEPARTMENT NEW COMMAND." The article accompanying this caption begins by saying, "The first working day of the last decade of the 20th century brought with it a change at the helm of the Prince George's County Police Department when Michael J. Flaherty handed over the agency's reins to David B. Mitchell."

Chief David B. Mitchell, flanked by County Executive Parris N. Glendening and former Chief Michael J. Flaherty, appears at a press conference announcing the new chief's nomination. Chief Mitchell indicated that one of his first priorities would be that of developing a bank account of good will between the police and community.

David B. Mitchell was appointed to the police department on November 8, 1971. After graduating from the police academy he was assigned to the Hyattsville Station. Fourteen of his eighteen years with the department have been spent at either the Hyattsville Station or the Special Operations Division. Promoted to the rank of lieutenant colonel in 1987, he has served in the respective positions of chief, Bureau of Support Services, and chief, Bureau of Patrol. Chief Mitchell received his associate's degree from the Community College in 1979, a bachelor of science from the University of Maryland in 1981, and a master of public policy in financial management from the University of Maryland in 1986. Enrolled in the University of Maryland Law School at the time of his appointment, the chief requested a leave of absence from his studies. The chief is also a 1988 graduate of the FBI's National Academy and a 1991 graduate of the National Executive Institute.

In April 1990, the department experienced a first when Police Officer Anthony Mills (center) graduated from the Police Academy to join his mother Cpl. Ann Mills and his father Sgt. Michael Mills in pursuing a law enforcement career.
Copyrighted photo courtesy of the Prince George's Journal

A Table of Organization defines responsibility by dividing the police department into three bureaus. Each bureau being commanded by a chief.

Lt. Col. Robert A. Phillips, a twenty-three year police officer, commands the Bureau of Patrol. The bureau provides all uniformed services and those investigative duties that are performed at the district level. The Special Operations Division is also under Colonel Phillips command.

Lt. Col. Leo J. Rossiter, a twenty-two year police officer, commands the Bureau of Support Services. The bureau provides all specialized investigative services, radio communications, and police record keeping services. Several management support units are also under Colonel Rossiter's command.

Lt. Col. Theodore R. Carr, Jr. , is a twenty-seven year veteran of the Metropolitan Police Department. Colonel Carr retired as a deputy chief and accepted a command appointment with the county police in 1985. He presently commands the Bureau of Administration and is responsible for all training, personnel matters, school crossing guards, and community relations.

PRINCE GEORGE'S
THE Journal

Prince George's County's daily newspaper

VOL.17 NO.51   6 sections
© 1991 Journal Newspapers Inc.   **March 15, 1991**   **WEEKEND EDITION**   The Audit Bureau   50 cents

FOP votes to 'save jobs,' not raises

By MEREDITH JORDAN
Journal staff writer

In a record turnout yesterday, members of the Fraternal Order of Police voted overwhelmingly to postpone scheduled raises in exchange for a no-layoff pledge from the county executive.

The 725 to 230 vote, deferring a 7-percent raise from July 1 until April 1, 1992, settles "one of the most difficult and divisive issues to hit the FOP in at least a decade," said FOP President Darryl A. Jones Sr.

"I'm pretty proud of them. Not because they agreed to defer the pay raise, but because they voted to save jobs," Jones said.

"A lot of people are still upset about it, but when it came down to it, they did the right thing." Young officers most vulnerable to layoffs turned out heavily, but so did everyone else, he said.

The vote means the police have joined with the county's firefighters in accepting the proposal of County Executive Parris Glendening, who is trying to avert an anticipated deficit of at least $70 million for the fiscal year beginning July 1.

Nearly 80 percent of the county's police officers voted, Jones said, beating the turnout for all previous contract ratifications. The heavy vote — at district stations and five other locations — was even more significant, he said, because contract votes are usually scheduled on paydays. Yesterday was not a payday.

Six-year veteran Cpl. Crista Tubb expressed the feelings of many officers. "I'd like to have my pay, but I'd rather have my backup," she said, referring to the reinforcements called to crime scenes.

Jones said many officers resented having to choose between layoffs and a raise promised in their contract and blamed Glendening for misrepresenting the county's financial situation during contract negotiations.

"I'm not going to suggest there aren't some hard feelings out there, but it isn't directed at other FOP members," Jones said. "[It is] directed against the county executive."

Cpl. George Munkelwitz, a 16-year veteran of the department, who voted at the Bowie precinct, said he wanted to "congratulate" Glendening for his "skillful manipulation of the troops."

"He managed to spend the money he promised us in good faith and has come out of it smelling like a rose."

During the vote at the Hyattsville precinct, most officers were confident the measure would pass. "We're not going to let 200 guys go," said Sgt. David Crawford. "It took too long to get them."

Lt. Stephen Spindler agreed. "I'm sure we're going to vote to keep our brother officers," he said.

"It's terrible we have to make this decision," said officer Mark Elie, who has been with the department for three years.

Police also approved a 50 percent cut in their annual clothing allowance, from $825 to $412.50. In exchange, the county has improved police retirement benefits, agreed to maintain the department with a strength of 1,232 officers, and promised to restore raises if the economy improves.

Sixth-graders protest cuts

By W. CHRISTOPHER CASON
Journal staff writer

His feet were soaked, and big,

Attack at high school

Two students injured at Northwestern

A severe national recession, occurring in early 1991, placed the county in a precarious financial situation. Faced with a $72.3 million deficit, the county executive cancelled plans to increase the police department's strength to 1,400 officers. The 44 recruit officers then in training received formal notification that they might be laid off immediately after graduating from the police academy. In an attempt to avoid lay-offs the county executive asked the police and fire unions to accept a postponement in their scheduled pay raises.

On March 14, 1991, the FOP membership voted to defer a 7 percent pay raise and accept the county executive's pledge of no lay-off. The 725 to 230 vote potentially saved the jobs of approximately 200 probationary officers. Authorized departmental strength now stood at 1,232 officers.

From the Prince George's Journal

After three years of strenuous preparation the police department achieved its goal of receiving national accreditation on March 20, 1991. Meeting more than 870 law enforcement standards, the department is one of only 172 agencies in the country to gain national accreditation from the Commission on Accreditation for Law Enforcement Agencies (CALEA).

Pictured, left to right, receiving the department's certificate of accreditation are Public Safety Director Jim Estepp, Chief David Mitchell, Major Roy Gilmore, CALEA Executive Director Ken Medeiros, County Executive Parris Glendening, Capt. Tony Narr, and CALEA Commissioner Mike Muth.
Photo courtesy of Allan Hare

Police Training Session 76, the class that almost wasn't, graduated from the police academy on April 5, 1991. Their youthful aspirations, devotion, and vigor will serve to heighten and refresh the time wearied experience of their more seasoned counterparts. Photos courtesy of Cpl. Keith Evans

INDEX

ABOUT THE AUTHOR

Dennis Campbell, a twenty-six-year county police officer, came to the Washington, D.C. area after being discharged from the Army in 1961. Employed with the Metropolitan Police Department in Washington, D.C., he was assigned to the old Fifth Precinct. He resigned in July 1964, to take an appointment with the Prince George's County Police Department. Transferred to the Detective Bureau in 1966, he remained assigned to investigative duties until his promotion to the rank of lieutenant in 1972. Successive duty assignments included: Bowie Station, Special Operations Division, Vice Squad, Headquarters, Oxon Hill, and the Seat Pleasant Station's Investigative Section. This was followed by a seven-year assignment with the department's Training and Education Division. Night classes at the University of Maryland led to a 1978 bachelor's degree in the administration of justice. Presently assigned to the Audits and Inspections Division, he has also worked in the department's Public Information Office.

A longtime local history buff, Lieutenant Campbell volunteered to research and write a history for the department's fiftieth anniversary. Published in April 1981, the brief history only served to stimulate an interest in the department's history. People called in with questions, others contributed memorabilia, photographs, and old newspaper clippings. A long and frequently difficult odyssey had begun. This book, this journey through time, is the end result of that odyssey.